Financial Literacy

WALL STREET AND HOW IT WORKS

DR. DENISE R. AMES

Published in 2013 by Global Awareness Publishing, LLC

ISBN-13: 978-0-9822180-4-4

Book and cover design by Daryl S. Fuller

The princpal text of this book was composed in Adobe Caslon Pro.

The Center for Global Awareness
Albuquerque, New Mexico, USA
www.global-awareness.org

Acknowledgments

This book, *Financial Literacy: Wall Street and How it Works*, has emerged out of my interest and research into the global economy. My interest in the global economy had been evolving for many years prior to when I started to actually sit down and write about it. I would first like to thank Frank Beurksens for introducing me to the topic back in the 1970s. He patiently described options and futures trading to me until I finally grasped a semblance of the topic. I found during a trip to the Soviet Union in 1989 with a group of agricultural economists that the global economy was not an exact science, and I could hold my own in a discussion of the topic with them.

I continued my exploration of the global economy in the 1990s as part of my research and teaching in world history. I discovered that the economy changed through time, like other cultural elements. Our current organization of the global economy is not at all etched in stone and is certainly subject to continuous change. Special thanks to my thesis and dissertation advisor and friend, Professor Joseph Grabill, for helping to guide and mentor me through this exploration.

My teaching, research and interest in the global economy continued through the 2000s as I conducted workshops, lectures, and classes for the lay public and educators on the subject. I extend a thank you to all those who listened to my ramblings and insights on the global economy and to those who offered suggestions for improvement.

I started to write this book on the financial sector as a component within the global economy in 2010. It was a formidable journey that I was, nonetheless, happy to embark upon. In this process I especially want to thank my partner in the Center for Global Awareness, Nancy Harmon, for her encouragement, remarks, and crisp editing. Without her unfailing support this book would not have been completed. I would also like to thank Margaret Govoni for her editing and input. Thanks to several readers who provided helpful comments, feedback, and editing: Cliff Wilke, Bob Riley, Sally Jacobsen, and Phil Fisk. Thanks to Daryl Fuller for his creative graphic design of the book and cover. And thanks to our program director Sarah Wilkinson for helping to navigate the logistics of making this book available to the educational community and the general public.

I would like to extend appreciation to my two children, Dennis and Mia, their spouses, Kim and Alex, my cousin, Paula, my friend, Joye, and my granddaughter, Lilly. And finally, a special thank you to my husband, Jim, for his encouragement and support through the years.

Contents

Chapter Four
Ten Fatal Flaws in the Financial Sector: Part II 95

Chapter Five
The Financial Crisis of 2007-2008. 119

Chapter Six
The Aftermath of the 2008 Financial Crisis. 143

Preface

This book, *Financial Literacy: Wall Street and How it Works*, has emerged out of my interest and research into the global economy. This interest had been evolving for many years prior to when I started to actually sit down and write about it. When I was conducting the research and thinking of writing about the global economy, I thought it was important to expand upon the financial sector of the global economy, since it has emerged as such a significant component. Thus, I have expanded the last two chapters in my book *The Global Economy: Connecting the Roots of a Holistic System* into this six chapter book.

My first immersion into examining different economic systems took place on a trip to the Soviet Union in 1989 with a group of agricultural economists. I accompanied my husband who was in the grain marketing business at the time and had a good grasp of economics. I was perplexed by the site of an immaculate modern subway system, complete with chandeliers, in Moscow, while in the countryside, horse-drawn wagons of elderly women with hoes in hand went out to work the fields, and tractors sat idly by in a state of disrepair in the rickety sheds. The vibrant black market also stunned me, where anything, even the coveted caviar, could be bought and sold at a reasonable price, while the state-owned grocers showcased empty shelves, displaying a prized cow-tongue when available. The beautiful production of the classical ballet Swan Lake showed the system worked in some ways, but in others, such as the shabby tractors, it failed miserably. The American economists were unable to explain this discrepancy very well, except for the standard statement about the virtues of the capitalist system.

I continued my fascination with the global economy in the 1990s when I was teaching undergraduate U.S. and world history and working towards my doctoral degree at Illinois State University in Normal, Illinois. Since my students overwhelmingly liked current issues, I wanted to include more up-to-date information about both the world and the U.S. Globalization was the buzzword of the day and frequently in the news, so it was a topic that I investigated with gusto. At first glance, most of what the media wrote about globalization referred to it in glowing terms. The increasing integration of economies and people around the world promised a rosy future of increased prosperity, not only for Americans but for those around the world who embraced innovation, an entrepreneurial spirit, and the desire to make a better life. The media proclaimed that if globalization connected people more through transportation and communication networks, it stood to reason that the world would be a more peaceful place. Communism had collapsed in the Soviet Union and Eastern Europe in the early 1990s and, therefore, the capitalistic economic system and democratic political system appeared to be victorious over their communist Cold War rivals. It all sounded great! After all, the newscasts of the day portrayed the newly-democratic Russians clamoring for American-style blue jeans and the rising middle class youth of China lining up for hours at McDonald's just to get a Big Mac. The media equated globalization with the spreading of American style values and consumption habits. They exclaimed the closed system of communism had given way to open markets, free expression, and democratic ways.

Many in America thought that globalization meant that the rest of the world, especially the former communist countries, had discovered the wonders of the American way of life and were eager to embrace it. Newscasts showed exuberant formerly communist youth dancing to western music in newly-formed night clubs, complete with strobe lights and pulsating rhythms. Others thought that the youth of China were willing to risk their lives for American-style democracy and freedom, as witnessed on cable television when a lone student demonstrator bravely faced a formidable Chinese military tank ready to crush him at any moment in the June 4, 1989, demonstration at Tiananmen Square in Beijing. The business section of any American book store in the 1990s portrayed globalization as a "win-win" proposition with untold profits for entrepreneurs to easily earn with some initiative and little risk. New internet start-up companies, such as Netscape and Amazon, popped up almost daily and promised riches for the founders, as well as for those who invested in their companies. Bill Gates, who founded Microsoft in 1975, was the hero of the 1990s. He was the richest person in the world, and his entrepreneurial spirit and work ethic were the envy of all those who aspired to follow his path to fame and fortune. The media exhorted us to get on the globalization train, since it was an inevitable process that those fearful of change could not hold back. It was an optimistic time.

As often happens with dazzling new trends, the globalization craze of the 1990s turned out to be too good to be true. I realized that some people were able to make a good living and even fortunes from high-tech start-ups and more expanded business opportunities. I acknowledged that the appeal of the "American way of life" is a dream many people around the world aspire to. But I knew that globalization meant more than that. To understand globalization, I needed to dig a little deeper than a CNN newscast or an article written in the pro-business *Fortune* magazine. After the initial euphoria melted away, another side to globalization that the media hadn't told began to emerge. Although some people were profiting from globalization, on the other hand it was adversely affecting other people's lives. Many manufacturing workers in the U.S. were losing their well-paid, secure jobs that companies were outsourcing to Mexico or China. Small farmers in the rural heartland of America, where I lived at the time, were being swallowed up by large corporate farming operations that had better political connections and enormous economies of scale and were able to fatten their bottom profit line with agricultural subsidies funded by American taxpayers. There were also dire effects on the environment that were a direct result (and some indirect) from economic globalization. Tax cuts and new economic rules made it easier for the wealthy to profit from the system, while stagnant wages and higher living costs were squeezing the middle and working classes. As I dug a little deeper into the topic of globalization, I found that it was much more complex than what was simply communicated in the media.

Another viewpoint about globalization burst into public consciousness in November 1999, when 40,000 "anti-globalization" activists converged in Seattle, Washington to protest against the World Trade Organization (WTO) Ministerial Conference, in what became known as the "Battle in Seattle." The protesters ranged from labor unionists to students to religious-based groups to anarchists who wanted to overthrow the government. The media lumped the groups together under the umbrella of anti-globalization protesters, although what they were protesting and the tactics they used varied considerably. Unfortunately, a small percentage of the protesters turned violent, and the police responded with force to quell the disturbances. Many Americans were glued to their TV as angry young protesters randomly smashed store windows, damaged cars, and taunted police. The public linked all those who questioned globalization with violent acts. The media helped to create this distorted message by continuously showing the violent acts committed by angry young protesters; the peaceful protesters, some sporting gray hair and sensible shoes, were of secondary importance. But the protests, despite their violent component, had the effect of raising awareness about the other side of globalization, and I and others became interested in finding out more.

My research into the global economy in the 1990s helped me refine my model for teaching world history. What became apparent was that at the turn of the millennium, a new force was emerging on the world stage that was a noticeable break from the past. In my book *Waves of Global Change: A Holistic World History*, I identify this evident break as the Global Wave. According to my holistic world history model, there have been four other waves or major transformations in our human history, and the Global Wave represents a fifth wave. The other four waves – Communal, Agricultural, Urban and Modern – all represent major discontinuities in our human story. The Global Wave is such a significant transformation as to warrant the distinction of representing a fifth significant change. Thus, the global economy that was changing in the 1990s was morphing into a momentous force shaping many aspects of world society and defining the Global Wave. Therefore, the phenomenon widely known as globalization was more than just a mere business craze or a way to sell more hamburgers around the world; it was a multi-faceted process that continues to be in the making.

Many of you have possibly observed the changes that are presently occurring or have actually experienced the changes yourself. Perhaps you or someone in your family has lost a job as a result of the latest downturn in the economy, or perhaps your company outsourced your job to India or China. If you are a student, perhaps your teachers have admonished you to study harder, since millions of well-educated Chinese students are your global competitors for future jobs. Or perhaps you realize that almost all the clothing you buy is made in China, Indonesia, India, or other places besides the U.S. Or your house has declined in value to the point that you owe more than it is worth, a phenomenon known as being "underwater." Or you realize that our dependence on oil to fuel the economy contributed to British Petroleum's (BP) horrendous oil spill in the Gulf of Mexico in 2010. Or perhaps you are a member of the global elite, and you have made a fortune by expanding your national business into a global business that has tripled its profits. These events are signs of major and disruptive changes that are occurring today.

A study of the financial sector within the global economy will not be an easy task. Many of the concepts and terms may be new to you. But I have designed this book to be an examination of the financial sector today as it really works. Most of us know very little about the financial sector. I certainly didn't until I started to research more about the global economy and the financial sector. Even then, it was hard to uncover the real workings of the financial sector. It always seemed to be covered in a veneer of mistaken assumptions or by an intractable worldview that everyone seemed to accept as reality. But once I started to peel away the layers of veneer covering the real financial sector, I was surprised to find that the reality was quite different from the commonly held assumptions. For example, it was hard for me to understand that the financial sector is not intent on creating value or adding to the betterment of the economy; instead, it is intent on making a profit, which is quite different than adding economic value. I had some rethinking to do as I learned more about the financial sector and uncovered some of the deep-seated assumptions that turned out to be untrue.

As I contemplated writing a book about the global economy and the financial sector as part of the Global Awareness Program series (GAPs), I struggled with how to organize this massive topic. I wanted to simplify the information and put it into an order that readers could grasp.

It seemed to me that when discussing the financial sector, the general public uses many vague terms and makes false assumptions without basis. I thought people's perception of the financial sector is like a wad of hard-as-a rock taffy, all stuck together and difficult to pull apart. So my goal in this book is to pull apart the taffy-like financial sector so that we can see and identify some of the sticky strands. When I did this myself in order to write this book, I found that the financial sector was one of three dimensions of the global economy; each dimension is distinct but interconnected, as well. By organizing the global economy into these three dimensions – neoliberalism, economic globalization, and financialization – we can pull apart the wad of taffy.

I have found in my research that there are very few books that give a general, holistic overview of the financial sector. They may concentrate on what is wrong with the system or the disastrous financial crisis of 2008, but they fail to give us a firm grasp of why this turmoil all started in the first place. Blaming it all on greedy bankers or clueless homeowners doesn't seem to get to the roots of the issue. This book attempts to give an overview of the financial sector today. Once we have a better idea of how the financial sector is organized and who benefits from this organization, then we are better equipped to critique it, see the fault lines, and propose solutions.

I like to think that I am a fitting person to write and teach about the financial sector. What gives me this confidence? My illustrious career as an investment banker on Wall Street? My PhD in global finance from Harvard College? My career in the Treasury Department advising the Secretary of the Treasury during times of economic crisis? Well, none of these remotely apply. Compared to many who are writing about the financial sector, such as Nobel Laureate Paul Krugman, my credentials are modest. But, before you slam this book shut or turn off your Kindle, I do have unique reasons for writing about the financial sector. I do have the degreed credentials, I have taught in the classroom for many years, I have conducted ample research about the topic, I have personally experienced many of the wrenching economic changes that have taken place since the end of World War II, and I am able to place the financial sector into an understandable framework.

Since I have witnessed many of the changes that have taken place over the years, I will chronicle some of my experiences and reflections in this book to give you a personal account of change over time. I encourage you to do the same. Ask others you know about what they experienced during the high unemployment era of the 1970s or the economic changes they witnessed during the Reagan era of the 1980s or the difficulty of finding a well-paying job in the 2010s. You are bound to get interesting insights and a wide reaction to the events. Everyone has his or her own story.

I searched to find an apt title for this book. Since the crisis of 2008, there has been a push by educators to help students become financially literate. Although they often mean giving students information about balancing their checkbook, I think students need to know about the whole financial sector. Otherwise, they won't have enough money in their checkbooks to calculate a balance. The financial sector directly affects students' lives and their future, and it be-hooves us to attempt to provide information that can help them sort out and learn more about this extremely important topic. Therefore, I wanted students to be financially literate and know how the whole financial system works. Since Wall Street is an apt metaphor for the financial sector, I put the two ideas together into the title: *Financial Literacy: Wall Street and How it Works.*

So please join with me in the adventure of examining the financial sector. I hope you will find this holistic approach to the financial sector a journey that is both challenging and worthwhile.

Features of *Financial Literacy: Wall Street and How it Works*

1. Chapter 1: *The Financial Sector: An Overview.* This chapter opens with a description of the financial sector today. It then gives an overview of the global economic systems: capitalism – and its two versions managed and neoliberalism – socialism and communism, and state capitalism. It also describes the five sectors of the global economy. The book highlights the three responses to the crisis of the 1970s, with the rise of the financial sector as one of the responses and the other two neoliberalism and economic globalization. Next the chapter explains the economic philosophy of the financial sector, and how short-term thinking and recklessness are the master narratives shaping finance today.

2. Chapter 2: *Financial Crises.* This chapter first describes patterns found in financial crises. Next it looks at crises before 1980, such as Tulip Mania, the South Sea Bubble, a few panics of the 1800s, the crisis in 1907, the Florida Land Boom of the 1920s, the Stock Market Crash of 1929 and the following regulations. Next, the chapter examines several financial crises from the 1970s onward, including the Dot.com Bubble, Japan's Asset Bubble, the East Asian Financial Crisis, and the financial crisis in Argentina.

3. Chapter 3: *Flaws in the Financial Sector: Part I.* This chapter and the next get to the heart of the financial sector by uncovering its 10 flaws. This chapter investigates the first five flaws that include too big to fail banks (TBTF), unchecked deregulation, a "markets know best" Federal Reserve, a real estate bubble and out of control lending, and mountains of debt.

4. Chapter 4: *Ten Fatal Flaws in the Financial Sector: Part II.* This chapter continues with an analysis of the last five of the 10 fatal flaws: dicey financial products, financial speculative mania, moral hazard and lack of transparency, deceptive rating agencies, and bloated CEO compensation plans.

5. Chapter 5: *The Financial Crisis of 2007-2008.* This chapter starts with the fall of the Lehman Brothers investment bank. It next sets the stage of the financial crisis of 2008 and describes its events such as the trouble in money market funds, the commercial paper market, the actions of the Federal Reserve, and the Troubled Asset Relief Program (TARP). It includes an analysis of the Obama administration's handling of the crisis and the Federal Reserve's role in the financial crisis.

6. Chapter 6: *The Aftermath of the 2008 Financial Crisis.* This chapter opens with a description of the five responses to the financial crisis: revolt, restore, react, reform, and rebuild. Within the rebuild category, the chapter examines five ways to rebuild a more sustainable and equitable global economy: emphasizing small and local, challenging the consumer growth model, renewing public ownership, healing our planet, and changing

to different values. The chapter concludes with insights into the aftermath of the 2008 financial crisis

Accompanying the book are carefully designed supplemental resources for educators and students, for those using the book in a study group, or for whoever wishes to examine this topic more closely. Please visit the Center for Global Awareness website at www.global-awareness. org or email us at info@global-awareness.org for more information.

Kind regards,
Dr. Denise R. Ames
Center for Global Awareness
Albuquerque, New Mexico USA

CHAPTER ONE

The Financial Sector: An Overview

"I see in the near future a crisis approaching that unnerves me and causes me to tremble for the safety of my country... Corporations have been enthroned and an era of corruption in high places will follow, and the money power of the country will endeavor to prolong its reign by working upon the prejudices of the people until all wealth is aggregated in a few hands and the Republic is destroyed."

U.S. President Abraham Lincoln, November 21, 1864

Charles Ponzi, a dapper, five-foot-two-inch rogue, emigrated from Italy to the United States in 1903. Born in 1882, in Lugo, Italy, he allegedly came from a well-to-do family. He was a postal worker in his early years and later attended the University of Rome, which he considered to be a four-year vacation, enjoying the nightlife and opera rather than academic studies. He decided to try his luck in America. According to his own story, Ponzi had $2.50 in his pocket, having gambled away the rest of his life savings during the voyage. "I landed in this country with $2.50 in cash and $1 million in hopes, and those hopes never left me," he later told *The New York Times*.[1] He quickly learned English and spent the next few years doing odd jobs along the east coast, eventually taking a job as a dishwasher in a restaurant, where he slept on the floor at night. He managed to work his way up to the position of waiter, but was fired for theft and shortchanging the customers. Next, Ponzi suckered naïve investors into a supposedly lucrative scheme to buy international postal-reply coupons. Money poured in, until an investigation by the Boston Police revealed that his business was a fake, and the company collapsed owing $4 million to gullible investors.[2] His next big scheme was nothing more than the age-old game: "borrow from Peter to pay Paul." But it would lure gullible investors with visions of easy riches.

CHARLES PONZI CIRCA 1920

Ponzi devised a scam that would bear his name for decades: the Ponzi scheme. For their money Ponzi's investors received 50 percent interest in 90 days and later promised 50 percent interest in 45 days. The money rolled in. Ponzi trained sales agents, who received 10 percent commissions for investments that they brought in to him. Many of these sales agents recruited subagents who received 5 percent commissions for new investors. Word of the financial "wizard" on School Street in Boston spread like wildfire when Ponzi paid off his first round of investors. Many people simply reinvested their profits with Ponzi, thereby relieving him of actually having to make good on his promise of paying out interest. At its height around 40,000 people joined the feeding frenzy operated out of offices from Maine to New Jersey.

The Ponzi scheme's rules were and still are simple: the schemer uses the money taken from today's investors to pay off debts to yesterday's investors. Typically, these investors are lured by the prospect of exorbitant profits – 50, even 100 percent. Often, the schemers coach new investors to recruit more investors to enrich themselves further. The problem is that there is no actual investment going on; the only activity is the shuffling of money from new investors to old ones. Everything runs smoothly until the scheme runs out of new investors and the whole house of cards comes tumbling down.[3] Today, the lesson learned from the Ponzi scheme is that investors need the price of assets to keep rising, so that they can sell at a profit and pay off the interest and the principal. When the market stops rising or does not rise fast enough, then the investors are forced to default and the bubble bursts.[4]

The Ponzi scam needed a constant supply of new investors to provide cash to pay returns to existing investors. The smooth-talking con-man raked in an estimated $15 million in eight months by persuading tens of thousands of trusting Bostonians that he had unlocked the secret to easy wealth. They believed him, at least for awhile. Ponzi's meteoric success at swindling was so remarkable that his name became attached to his simple but devious method.

Questions to Consider

1. What lessons can we learn from the Ponzi scheme?

WHAT IS THE FINANCIAL SECTOR?

You may think it is odd for me to start out this book – *Financial Literacy: Wall Street and How it Works* – describing a scam. I seem to imply that the financial sector is a scam! In fact, I am making a point that indeed parts of the financial sector are scams and that we need to be aware of them. With that said, there are many parts of the financial sector that are legitimate and run by reputable people. But when the scam part of the financial sector gets out of hand, as it did with the culmination of the financial crisis of 2008, it can have a devastating effect on millions of people.

The financial sector of the economy isn't just banks; it encompasses a broad range of businesses and institutions that deal with the management of money. Among these organizations are banks (commercial and investment), the credit card business, insurance companies, consumer finance firms, stock brokerages, investment funds, foreign exchange services, real estate firms, bank holding companies, and some government sponsored enterprises (GSEs). One of the global epicenters of the financial sector is Wall Street, located in lower Manhattan, New York City, New York, in the United States. As a physical place, Wall Street houses some of the biggest powerhouses in the financial industry, including the New York Stock Exchange and numerous multi-billion dollar firms. We sometimes discuss Wall Street as an entity, and a metaphor for the financial sector as a whole.

WALL STREET

This book will look at the scam part of the financial sector as well as its legitimate undertakings. I have organized the book to examine the financial sector, especially since the 1980s when neoliberals implemented economic policies that ultimately changed the global economy. Neoliberalism, which favors minimal government regulation of the economy, ushered in governmental policies that supported the rise and dominance of the financial sector over other economic sectors, such as manufacturing and farming. My argument is that the rise of and concentration of wealth in a virtually unregulated financial sector has contributed to the instability and inequality found in the U.S. today, as well as the entire world. After introducing the basics of the financial sector, we will examine various financial crises from Tulip Mania in 17th century Netherlands to the world-wide 2008 financial crises and its global impact. I contend that the 2008 financial crisis wasn't an aberration. Such crises have repeatedly happened in history, following many of the same patterns as in 2008. I will make the case that the crisis was a result of neoliberal policies that have been in place since the 1980s, the globalization of finance and technological breakthroughs. As you can imagine, the financial sector isn't the only sector of the economy. But first let's step back to look at an overview of the global economy to see how the financial sector fits in.

AN OVERVIEW OF ECONOMIC SYSTEMS

The rules governing the global economy are diverse. Generally speaking, much of the world operates according to capitalist principles. But capitalism is not the only economic system in the world today. In fact, I would argue that it would be hard to find any two nations that have identical economic systems. There is great economic diversity. When you factor in the nations around the world that are at different economic stages of development, then you have increasing variability. But we cannot describe each individual nation's economic system. Therefore, for simplicity's sake I have organized the economic systems of the world into two divisions: capitalism and socialism. Within these two divisions I differentiate neoliberal capitalism from managed capitalism, and within socialism I also describe its branch – communism. A fifth economic system has emerged in the first decade of the 21st century that combines elements of socialism and capitalism with authoritarian rule – state capitalism.

To explain the relationship of the five economic systems, I have placed them on a continuum. At one end are capitalist societies and at the other end of the continuum are communist or command economies and in the middle is state capitalism. In today's global economy, on the right end of the spectrum, are neoliberal economies, often called free trade or **laissez-faire capitalism**. Basically, these economies remove tariffs from imports and exports, and limit government regulation of the economy. Located somewhere in the middle right of the continuum are managed capitalism societies in which there is more government regulation of the economy, home industries are protected by tariffs, and a social safety net protects individuals who have fallen on hard times. Socialist societies, in which the government plays an active role in the economy and which have more of a social safety net to help individuals, would be located on the center left of the continuum. Communist societies would be on the left end of the continuum, where governments run the economies and there is no private enterprise or private property. In the middle are state capitalist societies that have part of their economy following capitalist principles, but the state governs the overall economy. Thinking of these types of economic systems on a continuum helps to recognize that diversity is the norm in the way that each nation creates and changes its economy.

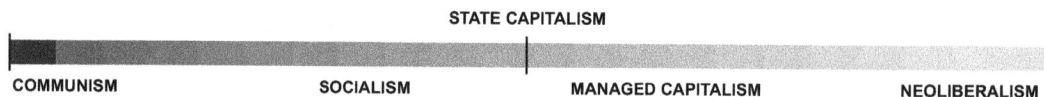

STATE CAPITALISM

| COMMUNISM | SOCIALISM | MANAGED CAPITALISM | NEOLIBERALISM |

In Eastern Europe during the Cold War, this humorous popular graffiti plastered the walls of Communist capitals: "Capitalism is the exploitation of man by man. Communism is the opposite: the exploitation of man by man." This simple riddle, although stressing the negative aspects of both systems, echoes the common roots of the economic systems that operate in nations around the world today. Aside from the small, isolated, local, domestic economies that still dot the landscape in remote areas of the world, the vast majority of the world has an economic system rooted in the modern ideologies of the past 200 years. Paradoxically, communism and capitalism have the same ideological underpinnings.[5]

Capitalism and communism emerged out of the same 19th century modern worldview. The political ideologies of the era – liberalism, communism, and fascism – were also products of the modern worldview. Liberalism evolved during the 17th and 18th centuries in Britain and the Netherlands in response to the absolute rule of monarchs. The state acted as protector of an individual's basic rights of life, liberty, and property; at the same time, an independent parliamentary branch controlled and limited the monarchs' powers. Communism and socialism grew out of the 19th century writings of Karl Marx. He wrote of a system of social organization in which a single and self-perpetuating political party controls all economic and social activity. Fascism is a political philosophy that views the nation above the individual and stands for a centralized despotic government headed by a dictatorial leader who imposes severe economic and social regimentation and forcible suppression of dissent. Generally, the political ideologies of liberalism and fascism embraced a capitalist economic system, and communism embraced a command economy.

Both capitalism and communism believe in the inevitability of continuous progress and continuous change, the ideology of modernism. Both elevated rights for interest groups, such as the corporation or the politburo (communist rulers), above freedom and responsibility for individuals and communities. Both favored the material over the spiritual – for example the former Soviet Union outlawed religion. Both believed in *homo economicus*, economic man, in which the individual is subject to economic forces outside of his/her control. They both highly regarded the implementation of their economic principles by a rational bureaucratic structure – by the command economy or by rational corporate actors. In varying degrees, they scorned traditions and enduring values, disregarded the stability of the family, friendships and relationships, and derided or ignored spiritual aspirations. They both exalted constant change and ridiculed those hostile to change. They both disregard the environment as an externality, but instrumental to material progress.[6] In the name of progress, both economies have exploited the environment. Both economic practices sought to derail the domestic and local economy and bring it into either the communist or capitalist orb. They both embraced industrialization in the 19th and 20th centuries as the preferred method for production of goods and services, but they advocated different systems of ownership and distribution.

Questions to Consider

1. What is your reaction to the list of similarities of the communist and capitalist economic systems? Are you surprised that there are so many similarities?

Capitalism

Before going further with a description of capitalism, let me first offer a definition of it.

Capitalism is defined here as an economic system in which private parties make their goods and services available on a free market and seek to make a profit on their activities. Private parties, either individuals or companies, own the means of production – land, machinery, tools, equipment, buildings, workshops, and raw materials. Private parties decide what to produce. The centerpiece of the system is the market in which individuals or corporations compete, and the forces of supply and demand, not the government, determine the prices received for goods and services. Businesses may realize profits from their endeavors, reinvest the profits gained, or suffer losses.

The people use wages and profits earned from the capitalist system to buy goods and services from the market place with prices determined by supply and demand. The capitalist system rewards those who capture productivity, efficiency, initiative, and creativity, while the marketplace leaves those unable or unwilling to participate to their own means. Although capitalism is sometimes referred to as a market economy, I distinguish between the two. The market economy operates according to capitalist principles but is smaller in scale and mostly locally based.

Capitalism is a multi-dimensional system that has diverse ways of functioning; there is no one standard way in which it operates. When we hear people talk about capitalism or hear about it in the media, it seems as if there is just one type of capitalism, but in reality there are different types.

Capitalism as an economic system can operate with minimal government regulation or with government taking an active role in guiding and regulating the process. Under capitalism, the elites can devise laws and regulations that favor them in their accumulation of wealth or, on the other hand, the government can pass laws and regulations that allocate wealth to greater numbers of people in a more equitable way.

A capitalist economy is not just associated with liberal forms of democracies such as in the U.S., but it can also operate in association with fascism, such as Adolph Hitler's Nazi Germany in the 1930s-40s. Even today, China is politically a communist country, but a portion of its economy operates according to the rules of global capitalism, while another part follows a command economy. Where the dividing line is between the two is anyone's guess. Some Europeans are socialist countries, but in reality they connect their economies to global capitalism and operate according to capitalist principles. Parts of India are tied to the global economy, while parts of the rural areas continue with local methods of exchange or barter. There is no clear cut line drawn between the economic systems of different countries, and even within countries each one operates an economic system compatible with its particular interests. Thus, capitalism takes on different forms. Next, we will discuss neoliberalism and managed capitalism.

1. Neoliberalism

Neoliberalism has prevailed in the U.S. since the early 1980s. Other terms describe the same concept: free market capitalism, free trade capitalism, market capitalism, supply-side economics, laissez-faire capitalism, classical capitalism, or Anglo-American version of capitalism (the UK and U.S.). Sometimes commentators will say capitalism but in reality mean neoliberalism and not make the distinction between the different versions. But it is of utmost importance to distinguish between the different types of capitalism since they vary considerably. I found it difficult to select a term to use consistently throughout the book. However, with some reservation I will use the term neoliberalism because it is more commonly used around the world and in academic circles, yet is not as familiar in everyday usage.

The neo in neoliberalism means new, since it is a newer version of the type of economic system found in the 19th and early 20th century which Great Britain promoted. **Neoliberalism** is the modern politico-economic theory favoring free trade, privatization, minimal government intervention in business and reduced public expenditures on social services.[7] Americans probably use the term free market capitalism more than neoliberalism, but I have problems with the term "free market" capitalism. It implies that there is a free market. We will find out that, indeed, the market is not free. In the U.S. in particular we toss around the word free too freely (pun intended). If we want something to sound good, we just put a "free" in front of it: free choice, free elections, land of the free, or free trade. My favorite use of the word free is food that is calorie free, a dieter's dream! Therefore, I think the term free-market is misleading and prefer to use it sparingly. However, if you prefer to use it in discussions with others about the global economy, since it is more commonly used, then please go ahead; it is the concept that is more important than the particular term.

Neoliberal supporters maintain that it is the best economic system around, especially since the world discredited communism and sent it to the dustbin of history. Neoliberals give several reasons why they consider it the best economic system.

Neoliberalism as an economic philosophy became popular in the early 1980s when two world leaders were enthusiastic cheerleaders of the neoliberal agenda: Margaret Thatcher, prime minister of the United Kingdom (UK) and Ronald Reagan, president of the U.S. They were convinced the principles of neoliberalism were best for their countries and these principles would help reinstate their nations' pre-eminence on the world economic stage. They favored ten principles of neoliberalism.

2. Managed Capitalism

Pushed by Great Britain, the economic powerhouse of the time, neoliberal capitalism generally prevailed in the West in the late 19th and early 20th centuries. World War I (1914-1918) interrupted neoliberalism, but it falteringly resumed during the 1920s. The future of neoliberal capitalism was in doubt with the start of the Great Depression that dominated the whole decade of the 1930s. With the crippling effects of the Great Depression affecting Western nations, many economists advocated for governments to take a more active and responsible role in planning national economies. To these economists, government intervention would soften the "boom and bust" cycles of unfettered, laissez-faire capitalism characteristic of the 19th century. These boom and bust cycles wreaked havoc on workers laid off from jobs during the bust cycles and had to fend for themselves. Business owners would also have to weather the bust cycles when demand for their business products collapsed.

The British economist **John Maynard Keynes** (1883-1946) argued that the government must accept more responsibility for regulating capitalist economies. He advocated regulation through a number of controls: running government surpluses or deficits when necessary; creating public works projects for

Reasons for the Advancement of Neoliberalism[8]

1. Self-interest motivates humans, which they express best through the pursuit of financial gains.

2. The actions that result in financial gains benefit society.

3. Competitive behavior is more rational than cooperation; hence, this motive should structure societies.

4. Economic growth is the measure of progress.

5. Consumerism is the fuel for economic growth.

6. Free markets without government intervention allow for the most efficient allocation of resources.

7. Governments should primarily protect property rights and contracts, and apportion money for defense.

8. Globalization and growth lead to reducing global poverty.

Ten Principles of Neoliberalism[9]

1. Free trade (remove protective tariffs).

2. Deregulate industries (remove government oversight).

3. Cut taxes for the wealthy who will invest in business.

4. Wealth will "trickle down" from the wealthy to the poor.

5. Government support for some infrastructure.

6. Privatize publicly held industries and services.

7. Continued economic growth is the way to prosperity.

8. Rapid commodification of every remaining aspect of life.

9. Tie wages to supply and demand, eliminate the minimum wage and unions.

10. Economic globalization benefits everyone.

the unemployed during economic downturns; adjusting the flow of money and credit; and raising or lowering interest rates. The purpose of these interventions was to make capitalism work better through government planning. The U.S. implemented and accepted Keynes' ideas during the Depression, but Western nations more fully adopted his ideas after World War II. For example, during the Depression President Franklin Roosevelt initiated the New Deal to help stimulate the U.S. economy. Although these programs eased the situation for many working people, the New Deal did not officially end the Depression. An even larger government program, World War II, with its tremendous government spending and astronomically high tax rates on the wealthy, brought an end to the Great Depression.

The ideas of John Maynard Keynes helped to usher in a new version of capitalism: **managed capitalism**. In this type of capitalism the government closely regulates the financial sector to prevent wild financial speculation and insure transparency of the system. Tariffs protect manufacturing jobs in the home country; therefore, wages and prices are set according to supply and demand at the national level rather than the global level. For the most part services such as education, health care, the military, and prisons are government run and paid for through taxes. The state sometimes owns large service providers such as utilities, airlines and transportation networks or closely regulates them. Private enterprise exists but the state carefully regulates it with high tax brackets for the wealthiest individuals, for example hovering as high as 90 percent during World War II and the 1950s. Corporations also pay a substantial share of their profits in taxes with fewer tax loopholes than in the neoliberal model. Labor unions have a powerful say in wages and benefits, as long as their wages keep up with productivity and don't spark inflation. There is a more equal circulation of wealth with managed capitalism than with neoliberal capitalism, resulting in a vital middle and working class and less concentration of wealth in the hands of the elite and corporations.

The "Golden Age" of capitalism, as it is often referred to, was during the period 1947-1973 in the U.S. and later in other Western countries as well. During this heyday of managed capitalism, the U.S., in particular, experienced high growth, low unemployment, and low inflation; the real wages of the middle and working classes rose and prosperity was more widespread than ever before or since. However, the continuance of racial segregation and discrimination excluded many African Americans from this abundance and pockets of rural poverty, such as in Appalachia, were severe. The golden era ended in the mid-1970s. The U.S. and other nations, such as the UK, switched from managed capitalism to neoliberalism in the 1980s. Economic globalization accompanied this shift.

Socialism and Communism

Economic alternatives to the prevailing private, laissez-faire capitalist system arose in 19th century Europe in response to labor's egregious working conditions in the newly industrialized factories. Wages and working conditions for workers in the early years of industrial capitalism were abysmal. Alternatives to capitalism – communism and socialism – arose during this time to remedy the suffering of industrial workers. Therefore, it is not surprising that the key supporters of socialism/communism were/are industrial workers. One of the leading critics of capitalism was **Karl Marx** (1818-1883), who, along with co-author Frederich Engels, proposed a socialist/communist alternative to capitalism in their short book, the *Communist Manifesto* in 1848.

Socialists advocate for collective or governmental ownership and administration of the means of production and distribution of goods and services. Socialism, ideally, is a way of organizing an economy in which the central tenets are that the society owns the means of production or they are placed into collective or common ownership. As far as possible, other forms of distribution based on social needs replaces market exchange. The fundamental feature of a socialist economy is that publicly owned, state or worker-run institutions produce goods and services in key segments of the economy. There is more emphasis on government planning by state officials than in capitalist societies, and less response to supply and demand pressures. Workers in state enterprises have little risk of unemployment and labor unions have more influence than in capitalist societies. As a political ideology, communism, a branch of socialism, is a system of social organization in which the state holds property in common and it ascribes actual ownership of property to the community as a whole or to itself.

The ostensible purpose of a socialist or communist system is to eradicate abject poverty, reduce the degree of economic inequality, both inherent in neoliberal societies, and provide a comfortable safety net for those unable to participate in the workplace. Like capitalism, socialism encompasses a broad range of economic systems, from the former centralized Soviet-style command economy to participatory planning via workplace democracy. Market socialism refers to various economic systems that involve either public ownership or management or worker cooperative ownership over the means of production, or a combination of both, while the market influences production.

With the collapse of the Soviet Union in 1991, there are few "pure" communist countries, if there ever were any. Arguably, North Korea and Cuba are the only hold-outs. In many countries today, the economies are a combination of some large state owned enterprises (socialism) with private capitalism. For example, today Canada has socialized its medical system in order to provide health care for all of its citizens at no charge to individuals. The government pays for this medical care through taxes collected from all citizens. There is no profit derived from this system, since the purpose is to provide good medical care, not enrich individual businesses or shareholders in private insurance companies. About half of the medical care in the U.S. is socialized: Medicare for its senior

KARL MARX, 1875

citizens (65 years and over), veterans, Medicaid for the very poor, and some programs for children not covered by private insurance. Private medical insurance is available for purchase at a substantial cost by those unable to receive government medical programs. Some workplaces offer medical insurance to their employees, who most often must share in the cost. This leaves a vast number, approximately 52 million people in 2010, who "fall through the cracks" and do not have either type of insurance. The marketplace leaves them to their own means to find whatever medical care, if any, they can. [10] The U.S. has found that private insurance companies will not provide affordable insurance for

23

these groups either because of high costs or the inability of the members of these groups to pay for the medical insurance.

State Capitalism

The neoliberal version of capitalism prevailed in the 1990s, but that changed in the 2000s. The power of the state is back in the form of state capitalism. This economic system is not merely the reemergence of socialist central planning in a 21st century package, but it is a form of state engineered capitalism particular to each government that practices it. Writer Ian Bremmer offers a good definition of **state capitalism**: "It is a system in which the state plays the role of leading economic actor and uses markets primarily for political gain."[11] The nations that support a state-capitalist system believe that public wealth, public investment and public enterprise offer the surest path toward politically sustainable economic development. These governments will micromanage entire sectors of their economies to promote national interests and to protect their domestic political standing.[12]

Over the past decade, the governments of several developing countries have worked to ensure that valuable national assets remain in state hands and governments maintain enough influence within their domestic economies to preserve their survival. In some cases, they have used state-owned energy companies to accumulate wealth or to secure access to the long-term supplies of oil and gas needed to fuel further growth. They have created **sovereign wealth funds** – a state-owned investment fund composed of financial assets such as stocks, bonds, property, precious metals or other financial instruments – that invest globally using pools of excess capital. Among the world's leading state capitalist countries are China, Russia, and Saudi Arabia, where there are close ties with institutions like the Chinese Communist Party, the Saudi royal family, or individuals associated with the powerful Russian President Vladimir Putin.[13]

Over the past several years, lists of the world's largest companies published by business magazines such as *Forbes* and *Fortune* have begun to feature state-owned companies. Between 2004 and the start of 2008, 117 state-owned and public companies from Brazil, Russia, India, and China (BRIC countries) appeared for the first time on the *Forbes* Global 2000 list of the world's largest companies, measured by sales, profits, assets, and market value. A total of 239 U.S., Japanese, British, and German companies fell off the list; their market value dropped from 70 percent to 50 percent over those four years. The market value of the BRIC-based companies rose from 4 per-

cent to 16 percent. The corporate failures and government bailouts of 2008-2009 accelerated the trend. *Bloomberg News*, a business news agency, reported in early 2009 that three of the world's four largest banks according to market capitalization were state-owned Chinese firms – Industrial and Commercial Bank of China (ICBC), China Construction, and Bank of China. The 2009 *Forbes* Global 2000 listed ICBC, China Mobile, and Petro China among the world's five largest companies in the world by market value. Energy giants like China

BANK OF CHINA HEADQUARTERS IN BEIJING, CHINA. FOUNDED IN 1927, IN 2010 IT HAD 389,827 EMPLOYEES AND $1.723 TRILLION IN ASSETS. ONCE 100% OWNED BY THE CHINESE STATE, IN 2010 IT WAS 26% PRIVATELY OWNED

National Petroleum Corporation, Petro China, Sinopec, Brazil's Petrobras, Mexico's Pemex, and Russia's Rosneft and Gazprom are among the world's richest companies.[14] State capitalism is a powerful economic system.

Questions to Consider

1. From the brief descriptions of the five global economic systems, which one do you prefer? Explain.

FIVE SECTORS OF THE GLOBAL ECONOMY

Next, let's look at the five different sectors of the economy and see how the financial sector fits in. An easy way to classify different economic activities is to use a three-sector hypothesis developed by Colin Clark and Jean Fourastié. In this economic theory there are three sectors of economic activity and two extensions of the service sector. The following is a brief description of each one.

Five Sectors of the Global Economy

1. Primary Sector
2. Secondary Industry Sector
3. Service (Tertiary) Sector
4. Information (Quaternary) Sector
5. Nonprofit (Quinary) Sector

1. The Primary Sector

The **primary sector** involves changing natural resources into primary products. Most products from this sector are raw materials for other industries associated with the primary sector, including commercial agriculture, mining, forestry, farming, grazing, hunting, gathering, fishing, and quarrying. The packaging and processing of raw materials close to the primary producers is also part of this sector, especially if the raw material is unsuitable for sale or difficult to transport long distances in its raw state.[15] For example, in the past slaves boiled raw sugar cane in huge cast iron pots and processed it into raw sugar adjacent to the plantations where it was grown.

The primary sector is a larger sector in less-developed or periphery countries than in developed or core countries. In core countries, primary industries become more developed and use sophisticated technology. For example, farmers mechanize production with farm machinery, as opposed to hand picking and planting with animal labor. Technological advances and investments in machinery require fewer farm workers, which channels these "surplus" workers to the secondary and tertiary sectors for employment. For example, about 3 percent of the U.S. labor force is engaged in primary sector activity today, while in the mid-19th century more than two-thirds of the labor force worked in the primary sector.[16]

AGRICULTURE, PART OF THE PRIMARY SECTOR. FARMER PLOWING AN ALFALFA FIELD (1921).

2. The Secondary Industrial Sector

The **secondary sector** of the economy manufactures finished goods. Manufacturing, processing, and construction are in the secondary sector. Generally, this sector of industry takes the raw material output from the primary sector and transforms these raw materials into manufactured finished goods using machinery and labor to complete the process. Some activities associated with the secondary sector include metal working, smelting, automobile production, textile production, chemical industries, engineering expertise, aerospace manufacturing, energy utilities, breweries and bottlers, construction, shipbuilding, and so on. This sector is divided into light industry and heavy industry. Many of these industries consume large quantities of energy and require factories, machinery and a large labor force to convert the raw materials into goods and products. If large enough, such as the automobile industry, they use large economies of scale to mass produce goods as efficiently and cheaply as possible. They also produce waste materials that may pose environmental problems or cause pollution. Some economists contrast wealth producing sectors in an economy, such as manufacturing, with the service sector, which tends to be wealth consuming. Manufacturing is an important activity to promote economic growth and development. Nations which export manufactured products tend to generate high GDP (Gross Domestic Product) growth, which supports higher incomes and tax revenue needed to fund quality of life initiatives such as health care and the building of strategic infrastructure. Among core countries this sector is an important source of high paying jobs and it facilitates greater social mobility for workers to achieve middle class status. It also contributes to greater wealth in the economy for successive generations.[17]

3. The Service (Tertiary) Sector

The **tertiary sector** of the economy is the service industry. This sector provides services to the general population and to businesses. **Services** are intangible goods which entrepreneurs transform into commodities. Activities associated with this sector include retail and wholesale sales, transportation and distribution, entertainment (movies, television, radio, music, theater, YouTube), restaurants, clerical services, media, tourism, insurance, finance, banking, healthcare, and law. The focus is making a commodity out of people interacting with people and serving the customer rather than transforming physical goods into commodities. In most core and middle countries, the tertiary sector employs a growing proportion of workers. Tertiary workers comprise more than 80 percent of the labor force in the U.S.

4. The Information (Quaternary) Sector

The **quaternary sector** of the economy consists of informational and intellectual activities. Services associated with this sector include government, culture, libraries, scientific research and development, education, consultation, and information technology. Although some economists incorporate these services into the tertiary sector, other economists argue that informational and intellectual services are significant enough to warrant a separate sector. In core countries, this sector is highly evolved and requires an educated workforce with advanced degrees. The government and companies invest money in the quaternary sector in order to ensure further expansion and profits. For example, service workers direct their efforts into cutting costs, tapping into new markets, producing innovative ideas, creating new production methods, and

MANUFACTURING, PART OF THE INDUSTRIAL SECTOR, A BOEING 787 DREAMLINER, IN SEATTLE, WASHINGTON, USA.

devising new manufacturing strategies, and others. For example, the tertiary and quaternary sectors are the largest part of the United Kingdom (UK) economy, employing 76 percent of the workforce.

5. The Nonprofit (Quinary) Sector

Some economists argue that there is another sector of the economy called the quinary or non-profit sector. A **nonprofit** is an organization that uses surplus revenues to achieve its goals rather than distributing them as profit or dividends. While the government allows not-for-profit organizations to generate surplus revenues, the organization must retain them for its self-preservation, expansion, or future plans.[18] This sector includes education, culture, research, science, healthcare, media, police, fire service, and some government organizations not intended to make a profit. I like this category, since our organization, the Center for Global Awareness, is a nonprofit!

> **Questions to Consider**
> 1. What sector of the economy do you think is the most vital in generating wealth? Explain.

THE RISE OF THE FINANCIAL SECTOR

The financial sector is part of the tertiary or service sector. Yet, there are other sectors that contribute to the national and global economy as well. For example, the structure of the U.S. economy has changed, as it has moved from manufacturing (20 percent of the economy in 1980, to 11.5 percent today) to services.[19] But since the 1980s the financial sector has grown to outsized proportions. One marker of the super-profitability of the financial sector is the fact that it accounts for 40 percent of the total profits of U.S. financial and nonfinancial corporations, up from 10 percent during the golden age of capitalism (1948-1973). Today, 7.7 percent of U.S. gross domestic product consists of the financial sector, which has soared from 2.5 percent in 1947 to 4.4 percent in 1977 to 7.7 percent in 2005. By 2007, this inordinate rise in the financial sector wealth indicated something was out of balance.[20]

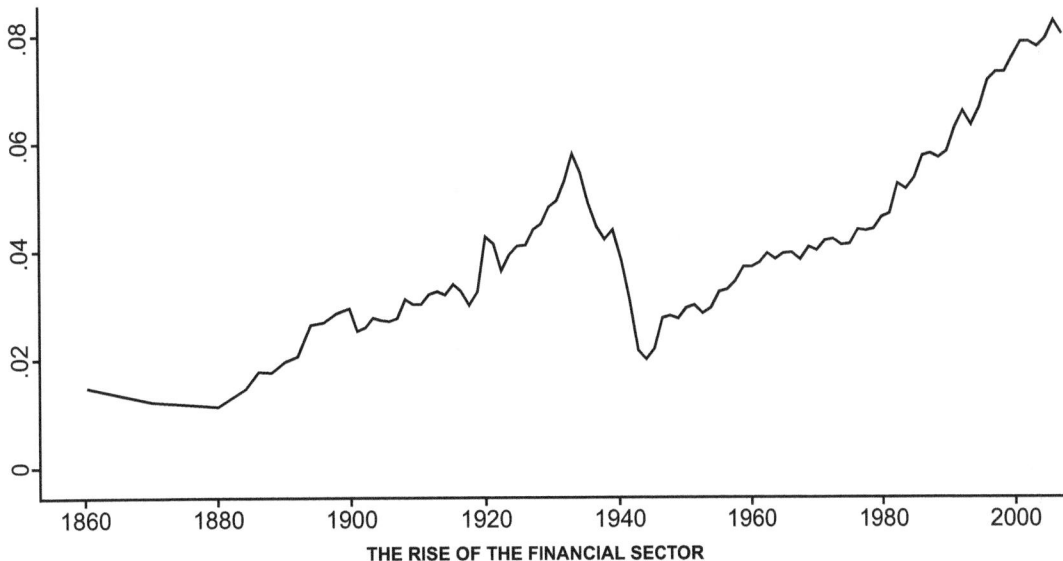

GDP Share of U.S. Financial Industry

THE RISE OF THE FINANCIAL SECTOR

The U.S. has experienced a massive exodus of investment funds from manufacturing into the financial sector. According to economist John Perkins, "Because returns on stocks declined while those from loans skyrocketed, the economy flip-flopped from production to paper shuffling. The business of mergers, acquisitions, derivatives, and hedge funds rose, while the auto, steel, and other industries collapsed."[21]

The problem with many of the financial sector operations is that they are equivalent to squeezing value out of already created value. These operations may create profit, yes, but they do not create new value – only industry, agriculture, trade, and services create new value. Because most financial sector profit is not based on value that is created, investment operations become very volatile and prices of stocks, bonds, and other forms of investment can depart very radically from their real value. For example, stock, land, or other assets can keep on rising, driven mainly by upwardly spiraling financial valuations, then suddenly crash. Thus, profits depend on taking advantage of upward price departures from the value of the asset – selling before reality enforces a correction, which is a crash back to real values. A bubble is the radical rise of prices of an asset far beyond real values.[22] In other words, this process is mere speculation and does not create any real value for the economy.

The outsized and excessive growth of the financial system did little to create any "added value" for investors. High flying asset managers often got higher returns, but investors saw little of it, because the managers charged higher fees for their supposedly indispensable services. Even more startling, the combined income of the nation's top 25 hedge fund (a form of investment) managers in 2005 exceeded the combined income of the Chief Executive Officers (CEO) of all companies listed in the S&P 500 (Standard & Poors). In 2008 no less than one in every $13 in compensation in the U.S. went to people working in finance. By contrast, after World War II a mere $1in $40 in compensation went to finance workers.[23] A noticeable increase.

If America needed evidence of the influence of the financial markets, the contrast between the treatment of banks and the auto industry in the 2008 financial crisis provided it. According to economist Joseph Stiglitz, "The Obama administration articulated a clear double standard: contracts for AIG (American International Group) executives were sacrosanct, but wage contracts for workers in the firms receiving help had to be renegotiated. Obama forced the two companies into bankruptcy."[24] Needless to say, mediators renegotiated the workers' wage contracts at a lower wage rate than previously, while the contracts for AIG executives were not.

The growth of finance has had significant social costs, too, as innovative and creative workers flee from manufacturing and other old-fashioned industries to Wall Street. Finance has attracted an ever-growing number of intelligent, highly educated workers. Among Harvard seniors surveyed in 2007, a whopping 58 percent of the men joining the workforce were bound for jobs, not in medicine or public service, but in finance or consulting.[25]

It is important in a stable economy to maintain a balance between the different economic sectors so that one does not come to dominate the other, because a downturn or collapse of one sector can trigger adverse reactions in the other sectors. For example, the financial crisis of 2008 triggered a near collapse of the automobile industry in the U.S. Without government intervention and loans to the industry there would be no more General Motors, Ford, or Chrysler. Another example is that at the time of the crisis approximately 34 percent of all the assets of major banks in the U.S. were real-estate related; the figure for smaller banks was even higher, roughly 44 percent.[26] This proportion was too heavily laden in just one economic sector: real estate. A problem has arisen in the last 30 years in which the financial sector has come to exert undue influence and power in not only the U.S. economy, but the global economy as well. You may wonder at this point how the financial sec-

tor mushroomed into such a powerhouse that it was able to trigger a global economic recession. In order to more clearly understand how the financial sector has grown, it is helpful to back track a few years to the 1970s.

Questions to Consider

1. What do you think are some of the problems associated with a heavily-favored financial sector?

THE CRISIS OF THE 1970S AND THREE RESPONSES

I lived through the 1970s, so I can attest to the fact that it was an uncertain decade. My husband and I graduated college in 1972 but found that jobs were very scarce in our home state of Illinois. To escape the brutal northern Illinois winters, my parents had packed up their construction company and moved to Jackson, Mississippi, where my father was the superintendent of a large grocery/retail construction project. My husband got a job working in the construction industry with my father (not an ideal situation). I was able to land my first teaching job at Blackburn Junior High School teaching 7th and 8th grade social studies. After two years we followed the construction job to Milledgeville, Georgia, where developers planned to build a Sheraton Hotel in 1975. I found another teaching position in 8th and 9th grade social studies. The recession was so severe that Sheraton Hotel delayed the construction project, so we had to resort to odd jobs to get by. One job I will always remember was during Christmas break when we put together all the parts for 300 school lockers, and then installed them along the walls at the school where I was teaching. There must have been a million screws! During that time, we experienced long lines for gasoline because of the oil embargo imposed by OPEC (Oil Producing and Exporting Countries). After 2 years of delays, the Sheraton Hotel construction job never materialized, so we finally decided to make our way back to Illinois. We packed up the pick-up truck and U-Haul trailer and headed north. Luckily, we found some suitable work and our financial woes eased. However, inflation and interest rates were skyrocketing by the late 1970s. It was at this inopportune time that we decided to build our own house, despite having to pay an interest rate of 17 percent for the construction loan! This chaotic atmosphere of the 1970s not only had a negative impact on my life, but millions of other Americans.

The 1970s proved to be a pivotal era in the world's economic history. The post-war, golden era (1948-1973) operated according to a version of capitalism called managed capitalism that I introduced earlier. The smooth-sailing of the golden age of the post-war economy came to an abrupt end in the 1970s when a series of events rocked the existing order. The position of the United States as the unchallenged superpower of the capitalist world was suddenly bombarded from multiple directions: rising international competition, productive overcapacity, spiking energy prices, declining productivity and profitability, the end of the fixed-rated convertibility of the dollar for gold, soaring inflation, and high unemployment.[27] All these factors were significant, and it is hard to pin point the most important one. They all combined to expose serious defects in the managed form of capitalism of the post-war era. The way forward in the 1970s was not clear.

In the late 1970s and early 1980s, different interest groups fought over their preferred path to structure national and global economies. There were the nationalists and globalists, free market advocates and those who pushed for managed capitalism, those on the political right and those on the left, there were leftists who pushed socialism and rightists who pushed for less government and more corporate power. Their political positions polarized and compromise appeared unattainable. When the dust settled, it was the political right, the free-market advocates, who emerged as the group who had garnered political and popular support. It wasn't an over-night victory, they had been working on their agenda throughout the 1970s and even before, but the victory was decisive and has shaped the economic and political landscape to the present day.

The crisis of the 1970s had been resolved in favor of a different version of capitalism than the managed form that had preceded it. A neoliberal version of capitalism was not a spontaneous creation of nature but a well-orchestrated plan to change the trajectory of U.S. capitalism to a system that benefitted specific groups of people. During the 1970s, these different groups of people clashed with each other over who could grab the ear of government and structure policies and laws to benefit them. Beginning in the 1980s there was a significant shift in groups who had the ear of government. With managed capitalism there was a balancing act between government, labor, the middle class, and business interests. Although not perfect, all generally appeared to profit from the cooperation. Yet, because of unions, regulations, and high taxes, many business interests felt they were limited in their capacity to make more profits. Although neoliberalism was still in the embryo stage during the 1970s crisis, business forces, intent on creating a system that favored their interests, were more organized and better funded to take the lead in shaping the economic system of the future. For them, their hard work and investments were beginning to pay off handsomely.

The Crisis of the 1970s

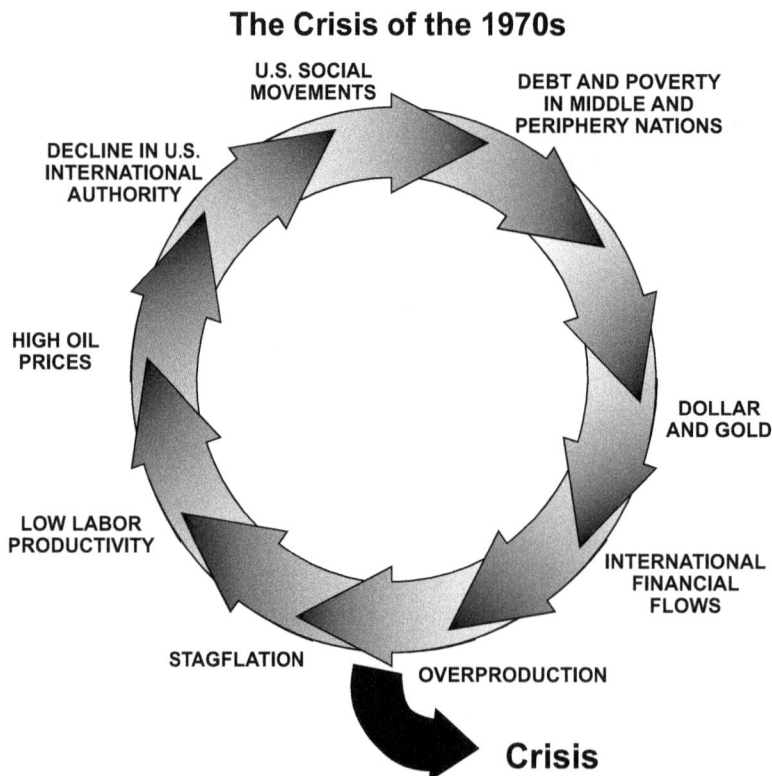

U.S. SOCIAL MOVEMENTS

DEBT AND POVERTY IN MIDDLE AND PERIPHERY NATIONS

DECLINE IN U.S. INTERNATIONAL AUTHORITY

HIGH OIL PRICES

DOLLAR AND GOLD

LOW LABOR PRODUCTIVITY

INTERNATIONAL FINANCIAL FLOWS

STAGFLATION

OVERPRODUCTION

Crisis

The U.S. was not the only country to experience wrenching economic turmoil during the 1970s, but as the world's leading economy, the U.S. had a far more significant role in shaping the global economy during the crisis than other countries. Three dimensions to the global economy formulated and emerged out of the bedlam of the 1970s – neoliberalism, economic globalization, and financialization – all three are interrelated and intricately connected.

Let me first briefly describe these three dimensions of the global economy before we go any further. Neoliberalism is the version of capitalism that has dominated the economic landscape since 1980 in the U.S. (I will use 1980 as the starting date) and to a lesser extent in the UK. As the leading economic power of the time, the U.S. promoted the neoliberal version of capitalism as the one in which it urged all other countries to follow. As mentioned above, there are different versions of capitalism which guide the way an economy is structured – what policies it promotes, what laws it passes, and what jobs it offers. Neoliberalism is just one of the versions of capitalism.

Globalization is a complex, dominant, multi-dimensional phenomenon that interconnects worldwide economic, political, cultural, social, environmental, and technological forces that transcended national boundaries. Greatly intensifying since the 1980s, it reflects the many ways in which people are drawn together not only by their own movements but also through the flow of goods, services, capital, labor, technology, ideas, and information. Globalization refers to the worldwide compression of space and time and reduction of the state in importance. In globalization the world becomes a single place that serves as a frame of reference for everyone, and it influences the way billions of people around the world conduct their everyday lives.

Simply put, globalization is the integration of the world into an interconnected process. When the integration is economic, this process is called economic globalization. Globalization brings areas throughout the world that were not connected before 1980 into the global economy. **Economic globalization** refers to the increasing integration and expansion of the capitalist economy around the world. In this economic system, trade, investment, business, capital, financial flows, production, management, markets, movement of labor (although somewhat restricted), information, competition, and technology are carried out across local and national boundaries on a world stage, subsuming many national and local economies into one integrated economic system. There is also a growing concentration of wealth and influence of multi-national corporations, huge financial institutions, and state-run enterprises. The biggest capitalist "catch," that is the most important country to be brought into the capitalist network, is China with India an important second.

Financialization is a sector of the economy that specializes in commodifying financial products that have a certain value and financiers trade them in the market place. Some financial instruments are insurance, lending money, real estate sales, stocks, bonds, derivatives, and many others. Since the 1980s in the U.S., the government has shifted its taxation and political policies from supporting the manufacturing sector, small businesses and farms to policies that support large corporations and the financial sector. The government directs resources to these two sectors of the economy as the engines for creating wealth and growth in the economy.

The global economic order pulls together these three interrelated dimensions: neoliberalism, economic globalization, and financialization. In the last three decades, there has been a decline in the profitability derived from agriculture and industry as a result of over-capacity and competition. Since money in a capitalist system seeks the highest return on investment, there has been a shift from industries where profits were largely stagnant or low-yielding to the financial sector that channels capital towards investments that have a higher degree of risk but also have higher returns. Often these higher returns in the financial sector come from speculation rather than ordinary investment in companies.[28] Thus, the financial sector has come to be a dominate part of the U.S. economy. My book, *The Global Economy: Connecting the Roots of a Holistic System*, explains neoliberalism, economic globalization, and financialization, while this book explains financialization in more depth. This third dimension – financialization – will be the subject of rest of the book.

Financialization took off after the crisis of the 1970s because of governmental policies, as already mentioned, and also because of technological advancements that made it easier and more efficient to devise financial products. The take-off was also dependent upon the proliferation of novel, sophisticated speculative instruments like derivatives that escaped monitoring and regulation. Instability in the financial sector ultimately derived from the fact that speculative finance boiled down to an effort to squeeze more "value" out of already created value instead of creating new value, since the latter option was precluded by the problem of overproduction in the real economy.

By the late 1990s, the indicators of overproduction in the real economy were stark. For example, the U.S. computer industry's capacity was rising at 40 percent annually, far above projected increases in demand. The world auto industry was selling just 74 percent of the 70.1 million cars it built each year. So much investment took place in global telecommunications infrastructure that traffic carried over fiber-optic networks was only 2.5 percent of capacity. Retailers suffered as well, with giants like K-Mart and Walmart hit with a tremendous surfeit of floor capacity. There was an oversupply of nearly everything. Profits waned in the U.S. corporate sector after 1997, leading firms to a wave of mergers, some motivated by the elimination of competition, others by the hope to extract renewed profitability.[29]

The result of these changes is an increased split between a hyperactive financial economy and a sluggish real economy. A disconnect exists between the real economy collectively known as **Main Street** and the financial economy known as **Wall Street**; they are operating on two different premises. Wall Street is operating according to what economist David Korten calls a "phantom economy," and Main Street operates according to the rules of a "real economy." This is not an accidental development; the financial economy exploded to make up for the stagnation owing to overproduction of the real economy.[30]

Questions to Consider

1. How did financialization get such a stranglehold on the U.S. and world economy?

2. Do you think financialization has helped the U.S. and world economy?

NEW YORK STOCK EXCHANGE IN LOWER MANHATTAN, NEW YORK CITY, NEW YORK, USA

THE ECONOMIC PHILOSOPHY OF THE FINANCIAL SECTOR

Much of our framing and understanding of the worst financial crisis in generations derives from a set of assumptions or a philosophy that the market knows best and that if government interferes in the economy it will always cause problems. Known as the **Efficient Market Theory**, this theory grounds these assumptions in a deep skepticism about the government. Since this philosophy is germane to our understanding of the financial sector and to the recent crisis, it will behoove us to look at its historical roots.

In economics, the Austrian School originated in the late 19th and early 20th centuries with a loosely affiliated group of Austrian economists, among them Frederich Hayek (1899-1992) and Joseph Schumpeter (1883-1950). A pillar of Austrian School economic thought is its promoters hold a deep skepticism of government intervention in the economy. They point to government economic actions such as regulation as interfering with the workings of the free market. The skepticism toward government intervention goes hand in hand with another hallmark of the Austrian school: a focus on individual entrepreneurialism. Schumpeter distilled a theory of entrepreneurship down to a pair of powerful words: creative destruction. In Schumpeter's view, capitalism consists of waves of innovation in prosperous times, followed by a brutal winnowing in times of depression. Society should not avoid this winnowing process: it is a painful but constructive adjustment in which the "fittest" survivors, in Darwinian fashion, will emerge to create a new economic order.[31]

According to the historical philosophy of the Austrian School, the economic policy response to the 2008 financial crisis gave us the worst of all worlds. Economist Nouriel Roubini explains how the Austrian School would have handled the crisis, "Instead of letting the weak, overleveraged banks, corporations, and even households perish in a burst of creative destruction, thereby allowing the strong to survive and thrive, governments around the world have meddled, creating an economy of the living dead: zombie banks that cling to life with endless lines of credit from central banks; and zombie households across the U.S., kept alive by legislation that keeps creditors at bay and that spares them from losing homes they could not afford in the first place." Economists of the Austrian school persuasion are deeply skeptical of the rush to regulate that often occurs in the wake of a crisis. In their view, too much regulation was the cause of the crisis in the first place, and adding more will only make future crises worse.[32]

After World War II, academic departments of economics and finance breathed new life into the old Austrian school fallacy that markets are rational and efficient. The academics had developed a new branch of economics now known as "modern finance." The economics department

FREDERICH HAYEK OF THE AUSTRIAN SCHOOL OF ECONOMIC THOUGHT.

at the University of Chicago – sympathetic to neoliberalism – led the way. Professors began to construct elaborate mathematical models aimed at proving that markets are utterly rational and efficient. They studied financial risk, and how to manage it better, by using complex mathematical models to describe and predict how markets behave. Scores of economists embraced the efficient market theory. For example, according to efficient market theory the price of goods and services correctly reflect all the available information determining those prices. In an efficient market, they believe, the sort of mispricing that is at the heart of a bubble is logically impossible. By the 1970s, the Efficient Market Hypothesis had become conventional wisdom, preached from academic pulpits at the University of Chicago and elsewhere. It remains a truism in many business schools and economics departments to this day.[33]

With the deregulation of the financial sector, which began in the late 1970s and continued in the 1980s, the opportunity to turn the ideas from the university classroom into practical application was readily available. A golden age of financial maneuverings dawned as economists and mathematicians turned abstract theory into real financial products. Such was the complexity of this new business that soon Wall Street was hiring physicists to concoct new and sophisticated financial products such as derivatives.[34]

Finance was elevated to new heights beginning in the 1980s. Many financiers thought they knew what was best for the economy, and accordingly, by paying heed to financial markets, nations would increase growth and prosperity. Among the heroes of the 1990s were the leaders of finance, who themselves became the most passionate missionaries for neoliberal economics and the invisible hand of the market place. They also made lots of money. Wall Street financiers made money on mergers and they made money as they took apart the mergers. They made money as capital flowed into the emerging markets and they made money with the restructuring of debt that followed the economic chaos resulting from pulling money out. They made money as they gave advice, whether that advice was good or bad, or whether the advice was followed or not.[35]

Another assumption neoliberals consider gospel since the 1980s is that economic problems arise from big governments – forcing high taxes upon its citizens, and regulating businesses to the point of strangulation. The public hears this refrain over and over again from politicians to media commentators. To neoliberals, the solution is clear: downsize government, lower taxes, and deregulate. Among those who propagated the myth that government is too large were those who were simultaneously benefiting from the lax regulations. For example, neoliberal supporters gladly accepted government subsidies that helped them in promoting their businesses abroad and from the government's investments in research and development. Much of the "new economy" which gave rise to financial booms rested on the Internet, which government research had created; on the myriad of other innovations derived from basic research; and on biotechnology, which was based on government-funded advances in medicine and biology. Studies have not proven the myth that lower taxes would unleash huge increases in savings and work effort. Reagan lowered taxes markedly, but neither savings nor work effort increased, and indeed, productivity growth hardly budged. Clinton raised taxes on the wealthy, and dire consequences did not emerge. Deregulation did not always unleash powerful forces that led to robust long-term growth; rather, it often unleashed new sources of conflicts of interest and new ways of manipulating markets. Ordinary taxpayers have had to pick up part of the tab for the financial sector excesses – in California, for example, as a result of the Enron debacle of electricity deregulation, and in the looming defaults of corporate pension schemes which investors unwisely put in Wall Street's obscure financial products.[36]

Modern economics has shown the limitations of the invisible hand and unfettered markets, yet no idea has had more power since the 1980s than that of Adam Smith's writing on the invisible hand of the market. The idea is that unfettered markets lead, as if by an invisible hand, to efficient outcomes; that each individual, in pursuing his or her own interest, advances the general interests. The aftermath of financial excesses has proven that the CEOs, in pursuing their own interests, did not strengthen the American economy – and even as they benefited themselves, others paid the price. Since the 1980s events have shown that CEOs did not necessarily work to enhance total share value for their shareholders.[37] The financial crisis showed just the reverse of Adam Smith's invisible hand theory: financial markets do not automatically work well for the interests of the general public and markets are not self-correcting. We have seen that there is an important role for rule-enforcing government after all.[38]

Many of the political policies of the 1990s helped financial markets make more money. Deregulation gave Wall Street many new financial opportunities, which it quickly seized. The market frenzy fostered unscrupulous accounting practices, undetected or ignored by overworked and compromised regulators. Lower capital gains tax rates fed the bubble, and the bubble fed Wall Street. When things didn't go as planned and financial institutions crumbled, the public picked up the pieces and footed the bill. Yet, we have not learned the more basic lessons: financial markets are not the font of wisdom, what is good for Wall Street may or may not be good for the rest of the society, and financial markets are shortsighted. A country that subjects itself single-mindedly to the discipline of financial markets does so at its own peril.[39]

ADAM SMITH (1723-1790), PIONEER ECONOMIC THINKER.

Americans have always had an unshakable faith in capitalism. The demise of communism and the roaring markets of the 1990s renewed that faith and brought it to new heights. There have always been a number of different flavors of capitalism; American capitalism is different from Japanese and European capitalism. America's success in the 1990s relative to those other versions of capitalism reinforced the belief that America's system was not just right for America but right for everyone else. Americans smugly believed that they had discovered the answer to the world's economic ills: neoliberal capitalism. They pushed this version of capitalism beyond American shores to the rest of the unsuspecting world.[40]

Questions to Consider

1. What is your opinion about the Efficient Market Theory?

SHORT-TERM THINKING

The United States has always prided itself in thinking about the future. The public judges presidential candidates on whether they can paint a glowing picture of the future. The public remembers Reagan for his impassioned call: "Morning in America." During the Democratic convention in 1992, Bill Clinton's theme was the Fleetwood Mac song "Don't Stop Thinking about Tomorrow." Cheering crowds clapped exuberantly as streamers descended from the rafters and the music blasted, driving the crowd into paroxysms of ecstasy. In 2008, Barack Obama campaigned on a message of hope for the future. Part of the American Dream is that the next generation will be better off than the present generation. Immigrants almost always cite the fact that they love America because a "better future" awaits them and their children. Yet, the future was not in the forefront for those involved in the lead-up to the financial crisis – far from it. Instead of thinking about the next generation, those in the financial sector fixated on the short-term. In particular, they zeroed in on short-term profits. They thought, "Let those in the future fend for themselves; there is money to made in the now."

All along the financial chain, financiers translated concern about business performance into a focus on short-term returns. With corporate management's pay dependent not on long-term returns and future stability of their company but on short-term stock market prices, they did what they could to drive up stock market prices – even if it entailed deceptive or even illegal accounting practices. Company demands for high quarterly returns from stock market analysts reinforced the short-term focus. The drive for short-term returns led banks to focus on how to generate more fees – and, in some cases, how to dodge accounting and financial regulations. The innovativeness that Wall Street proudly crowed about was dreaming up new products that would generate more income in the short term for its firms. The problem of high default rates these financial innovations posed seemed matters for the distant future. On the other hand, financial firms were not the least bit interested in innovations that might have helped ordinary people keep their homes when foreclosure was imminent or protect them from sudden rises in interest rates that would shatter their household budgets. Only the short-term counted; immediate financial rewards were not part of these long-term innovations.[41]

RECKLESSNESS: THE MASTER NARRATIVE

I live in New Mexico. Our population is composed of about 10 percent native peoples. Native communities don't have to conform to all federal laws; therefore, in the last couple decades many of them have built casinos on their land as a source of revenue. Even though the state is large in area, the fifth largest state in the United States, it seems as though there are casinos everywhere. In fact New Mexico has 20 of them, which ranks my state 15th among all of the 46 states that have casinos. Albuquerque, where I live, boasts 4 casinos. That means a lot of gambling. I wonder how our very poor state

SANDIA RESORT AND CASINO, SANDIA PUEBLO, LOCATED IN ALBUQUERQUE, NEW MEXICO, USA.

can support so many casinos; the parking lots are always full. But as I understand, many tourists and New Mexicans find gambling a very enjoyable pastime.

This gambling observation leads to a point I want to make about the financial crisis. Ever since the financial crisis of 2008, I have been thinking and rethinking the catastrophic chain of events that wreaked havoc on our economy and society. I will be looking at 10 flaws in the financial sector that contributed to the 2008 crisis in chapters 3 and 4, but I keep coming back to the nagging question, "Why did the financial sector take such crazy risks in the first place?" What made them literally gamble away their own and other people's money with a clear conscience? When asked what caused the financial crisis, many people without hesitation answer greed, pure and simple. I don't disagree with the answer, but I think there is more to it than simple greed. After all, greed is part of the human condition and has been for eons.

Greed during the lead up to the financial crisis seemed to be a different sort of greed than just a sordid behavior; in this case, society embedded greed within its acceptable social and cultural values and behaviors. This is a far more harmful type of greed because it is largely an acceptable and encouraged behavior in society at large. When reporters asked some of the Wall Street tycoons why they acted with such duplicitous behaviors, they replied that everyone else was doing so, and that they had to do so as well or risk a downturn in their business. Some replied that risk-taking is all part of the Wall Street culture to make money. No questions asked, it had to be done. This reasoning leads me to the question: "What is it in our American society that fosters an ethic of extreme risk-taking, greed, and other avaricious behaviors?" What is the underlying story or master narrative of our society that helped to shape this crisis?

Whether we know it or not, our national ethic or story shapes many of our views and behaviors, what I will call here the master narrative. Since I have taught U.S. history for many years, I see the narrative unfold starting before the founding of our nation. It certainly helped shape the thinking of the financial crisis. What is this narrative? Many Americans have a "frontier mentality." There is always an unknown to discover, conquer, control, and eventually rule. Settlers built the country by

"MANIFEST DESTINY". PAINTING (CIRCA 1872) BY JOHN GAST CALLED AMERICAN PROGRESS, IS AN ALLEGORICAL REPRESENTATION OF THE MODERNIZATION OF THE NEW WEST. COLUMBIA, A PERSONIFICATION OF THE U.S., LEADS CIVILIZATION AND SETTLERS WESTWARD.

expanding westward, conquering new territories, eliminating the native peoples, and growing a new country. Pioneers led the way, fearless of danger and ready to risk everything for new opportunities. It was the Manifest Destiny of the American nation to conquer. The cowboy archetype, taming the lawless West, has always been near and dear to the American psyche. They took inordinate risks, played high stakes gambles with their lives, and expanded into a territory with seemingly unlimited bounty. The narrative continued after World War II as the U.S. emerged as the overwhelming superpower of the age. Americans boasted they were the nation with the highest standard of living, were the first to reach the moon, and had the best system of government and economy. President Johnson was intent on conquering poverty, as well as the moon and the North Vietnamese people. The narrative continued with President Reagan, complete with cowboy hat, the ultimate rugged individual ready to conquer a new enemy: the government itself. Even President George W. Bush displayed manly hubris as he donned aviator gear and descended from a hovering helicopter unto a floating battleship, he swaggered to the cameras proclaiming "mission accomplished." He was referring to, prematurely as it turned out, that the mighty American military had subdued Iraq.

The heady days of the 1990s through the mid-2000s were a time of great triumphal optimism. The Soviet Union had collapsed. George H.W. Bush crowed it was his administration that brought the mighty Soviet Union to its knees, ignoring the fact that perhaps the Soviet Empire had fallen on its own accord, since it was rife with corruption, inefficiencies, stagnation, and a demoralized population. Neoliberal capitalism reigned supreme. The markets were the new "god," bestowing their wisdom onto a holy grail of the efficient market hypothesis. Overconfident financial wizards were the new "chosen ones," ready to impart their financial miracles for the masses. These privileged men were told they were "born to rule" the marketplace, with limitless fame and fortune their destiny. Hubris, according to the ancient Greeks, leads to the downfall of man. Hubris, unfortunately, was in ample supply during this giddy time.

CONCLUDING INSIGHTS:
AN OVERVIEW OF THE FINANCIAL SECTOR

Risk-taking is part of the American character. But understanding the other side of risk is not part of it. There is no back-up plan if risk-taking goes awry. There is never a thought that the frontier may have limits, or technology might not save us from all our problems, or markets may not be right in all cases. If there is a mess up, so the story goes, something or someone will come along as the savior. We tell ourselves it will always be so; it is part of our American consciousness. American movies are rife with saviors coming to the rescue of those in distress, whether it is the Lone Ranger, Superman, Wonder Woman, or Batman. In the case of the 2008 financial crisis, it was the government that rode to the rescue.

Americans don't want to understand that the national story they have been telling themselves is a lie. Nothing is limitless – with risks come consequences, Mother Nature always wins, what comes around goes around, with hubris comes humility, and with every action there is a reaction. These sayings balance risk with the notion that failure can result from risk-taking as well as success. And if failure does occur, there better be a back-up plan.

If the narrative is not changed, the same type of financial crisis will happen again. As I listen to the political candidates or financial experts, I don't hear a different narrative. In fact, the narrative has gone into hyper-drive instead of stall mode. Our story of endless growth, risky "opportunities," and high stakes gambling with Mother Nature has gone ballistic. Market excesses have tarnished our faith in them, but only slightly. Our faith in technology is still sound; in fact, in some quarters technology has emerged as the new god, rivaling the fallen market god. For some, the narrative has shifted to one that government didn't ride to the rescue after the financial crisis but that government caused the problem in the first place. We are slamming our foot on the accelerator of unfettered markets, just when we should be putting on the brakes.

Excessive risk-taking, without regard for the consequences, is the master narrative of the financial crisis. It is apparent everywhere. If we understand the narrative as part of the American national character, instead of merely a personality defect among a few "bad apples" on Wall Street, it is easier to see that we can change it. We need to replace the tired stories of limitless abundance and perpetual growth not only to avoid further financial crises, but also to curb our voracious appetite for nature's resources. I hope you will join me in stitching together a new national narrative, one that does not follow a reckless path, but one more in keeping with our place in the larger human and natural community and with the well-being of the next generations in mind. Understanding the excesses of the financial sector is a step in this process.

Let's turn in the next chapter to see a number of historical financial crises that have happened in the past. These crises are informative in helping us better understand and evaluate the 2008 financial crisis.

A BAD APPLE

Questions to Consider

1. What do you think a new national narrative should be? What values would it express?

CHAPTER TWO

Financial Crises

"Contrary to conventional wisdom, crises are not black swans but white swans: the elements of boom and bust are remarkably predictable."

Nouriel Roubini

PATTERNS OF FINANCIAL CRISES

Have you ever seen a black swan? Chances are the answer is no if you live in the Western hemisphere. They are rare in the Western hemisphere and breed mainly in the southeast and southwest regions of Australia. In the above quote economist Nouriel Roubini is using the metaphor of black and white swans that Nassim Taleb developed in a book called *The Black Swan: The Impact of the Highly Improbable*. The book and his theory behind it have relevance to this chapter on historical financial crises. Taleb's book focuses on the extreme impact of certain kinds of rare and unpredictable events (outliers) and the human tendency to find simplistic explanations for these events after they have occurred. This theory, in the last several years, has become known as the black swan theory. Taleb claims that almost all consequential events in history come from the unexpected – yet humans later convince themselves that these events are explainable.

Humans are often slow to recognize rare and novel events. Taleb uses the examples of World War I, the 9/11 attacks, the personal computer and the Internet as black swan events. We tend not to anticipate a black swan event partly because built into the very nature of human experience is the tendency to extend existing knowledge and experience to future events and experiences. To exacerbate this natural inclination, society has built much of our cultural education, both formal and otherwise, upon historical knowledge. Taleb contends that banks and trading firms are very vulnerable to hazardous black swan events and the market exposes them to losses beyond those that are predicted by what he calls their defective financial models. In fact, many people in the financial sector called the financial crisis of 2008 a black swan event.[1]

Roubini, on the other hand, argues in his short quote above that the financial crisis of 2008 was not a black swan event. Instead, it was a white swan event, which meant that it is common and happens frequently. It is merely because we are short-sighted in our thinking and ignorant of the lessons of history, that we would label the 2008 crisis a black swan event. According to Roubini, financial disasters proceed along a predictable path that follow expected patterns that have proven through history to repeat under slightly different circumstances.

Economists Carmen Reinhart and Kenneth Rogoff, in their book *This Time is Different: Eight Centuries of Financial Folly*, assembled historical data on financial crises, showing that while the details of currency crashes, banking panics, and debt defaults change, the broader trajectory of crises varies little from decade to decade, century to century.[2] Many bubbles, while fueled by concrete technological improvements, gain force from changes in the structure of finance. The desirable assets could be anything, but stocks, housing, and real estate are the most common. As the assets' price shoots skyward, optimists zealously attempt to defend this overvaluation. When confronted with the evidence of previous downturns, they proclaim, according to Reinhart and Rogoff: "This time is different."[3]

The financial crisis pattern tracks the following predictable path. As credit becomes increasingly cheap, because of low interest rates, and abundant, because of an expansionary

BLACK SWAN, WHICH REMAINED UNDOCUMENTED IN THE WEST UNTIL THE 18TH CENTURY.

money supply, the desirable asset becomes easier to buy. Demand rises and outstrips supply; prices accordingly rise. But that's just the beginning. Because the assets at the heart of the bubble can typically serve as **collateral** (a guarantee) for loans, and because the value of the collateral is rising, a speculator can borrow even more money with each passing day. Borrowers **leverage** themselves, meaning that they borrow money for investment which accumulates as debt.[4] This pattern played out like a charm from 2000 onward in countries such as the U.S. Spain, Ireland, and the UK: as home values rose markedly and wages stagnated, households used their homes as collateral in order to borrow more, most often in the form of a home equity loan.

A **home equity loan** is a loan secured by a primary residence or second home to the extent of the excess of the fair market value over the debt incurred in the purchase. If the fair market value of the house is $300,000 and the loan amount is $200,000, then the equity in the home is $100,000, which the borrower can use as collateral on another loan. Borrowers effectively used their homes as ATM machines. As housing prices climbed, borrowers could borrow more, using what they had purchased – home improvements and even second homes – as additional collateral. By the 4th quarter of 2005, home equity loans peaked at $1 trillion, enabling millions of households to live well beyond their means. In effect, many home owners turned into mini Wall Street tycoons, wheeling and dealing with borrowed money. At the same time, the household savings rate plunged to zero, and then went into negative territory for the first time since the Great Depression. This debt-financed consumption spurred the economy – households and firms purchasing goods and services fueled economic growth – all the while disguising the fact that all of this prosperity was riding on a bubble about to burst.[5]

The developments in the mid-2000s created a vicious cycle, a cycle seen before. As the economy grows, incomes rise and companies record higher profits. Worries about risk drops while the cost of borrowing falls and households and firms borrow and spend with greater abandon. At some point the bubble stops growing, typically when the supply for the bubble's asset exceeds the demand. Confidence that prices will keep rising vanishes and borrowed money becomes harder to find. This process began in the U.S. when the supply of new homes finally outstripped demand.[6]

When the boom becomes a bust, the results are also predictable. Roubini explains, "The falling value of the asset at the root of the bubble eventually triggers panicked **margin calls**, which are requests by banks or other financial institutions that borrowers put up more cash or collateral to compensate for falling prices. This, in turn, may force borrowers to sell off some of their assets at fire-sale (low) prices. Supplies of the asset soon far out-strip demand, prices fall further, and the value of the remaining collateral plunges, prompting further margin calls and still more attempts to reduce exposure."[7] Let's review a few important terms and definitions before going on to examine a few historical examples of financial crises.

Questions to Consider

1. Why can't the general public and Wall Street financiers recognize a bubble when there is one?

TERMS AND DEFINITIONS

A **bubble** is a type of investing phenomenon that occurs when investors put so much demand on a particular asset that they drive the price beyond any accurate or rational reflection of its actual worth. In the case of stocks, the performance of the underlying company should determine price, but when in the midst of a bubble, the price of stocks soars beyond the actual worth of the underlying company. When investing during a bubble, it often appears as though prices will rise forever, but since the prices do not represent anything substantial, they eventually pop. And when prices do pop, the money invested in the asset dissipates into the wind.[8]

A **crash** is a significant drop in the total value of a market. A crash almost always happens when a bubble pops, creating a situation where the majority of investors are trying to flee the market at the same time and consequently incurring massive losses. Attempting to avoid more losses, investors during a crash engage in **panic selling**, hoping to unload their declining stocks or other assets onto other investors, often at what are called **fire sale prices**, prices that are well below the previous price. This panic selling contributes to the declining market, which eventually crashes and affects everyone.[9]

It is important to note the distinction between a crash and a correction. A **correction** is supposedly the market's way of showing, through price adjustments, the actual value of an asset. As a general rule, a correction should not exceed a 20 percent loss of value in the market. Surprisingly, some commentators have erroneously labeled crashes as corrections, but a correction is not a crash if the steep drop in market price has halted within a reasonable period.[10]

Let's turn next to a sampling of crises that have occurred since the early 17th century. See if you recognize some of the following 10 patterns in the crises.

10 Financial Crisis Patterns

1. A popular or valuable asset is in short supply while its demand is high.

2. Asset prices rise as demand increases.

3. Outsiders enter the market and buy coveted assets seeking quick and high returns.

4. Over-investment in the desirable asset leads to a bubble.

5. When investors reach the tipping point, where supply is greater than demand, panic selling ensues.

6. There are more sellers than buyers, resulting in a sharp and swift decline in the price of the asset.

7. Those who borrowed from lenders to buy the inflated asset are unable to repay their loans.

8. Either the government bails out the lender or their loans go into default.

9. If severe enough, the total economy collapses, resulting in a recession or depression.

10. Unless the government takes steps to curb abuses, the bubble can be repeated.

Questions to Consider

1. Identify the 10 patterns in each of the financial crises described in the following section.

CRISES BEFORE 1980

Tulip Mania

I have a deal for you. I have a beautiful tulip bulb that will cost you a mere year's salary! Are you interested? If you were transported back to early 17th century Netherlands, your answer might be yes. You may think that the Dutch seem like reasonable people. Could they be so foolish as to engage in such gambling? But the Dutch cast reason and doubt aside in what has come to be known as "**tulip mania.**" With the emergence of the Netherlands as the world's first capitalist dynamo in the 16th and 17th centuries, a new kind of crisis made its appearance: the asset bubble. In 1630, tulip mania gripped the country. This was a period in the Dutch Golden Age, during which the contract prices for bulbs of the recently introduced tulip reached extraordinarily high levels and then suddenly collapsed. Economists generally consider it to be the first recorded speculative bubble. The term tulip mania is now often used metaphorically to refer to any large economic bubble.

Growers in the Ottoman Empire introduced the tulip to Europe in the mid-16th century, and it became very popular in the Netherlands. The flower rapidly became a coveted luxury item and a status symbol, and a profusion of varieties followed. As the flowers grew in popularity, professional growers paid higher and higher prices for certain bulbs. By 1634, in part as a result of demand from the neighboring French, speculators began to enter the market. In 1636, the Dutch created a type of formal futures market where contracts to buy bulbs at the end of the season were bought and sold. The immense popularity of tulips caught the attention of the entire nation, and many Dutch people eagerly engaged in the tulip trade. By 1635, a sale of 40 bulbs for 100,000 florins (also known as Dutch guilders) was recorded. By way of comparison, a ton of butter cost around 100 florins, a skilled laborer might earn 150 florins a year, and "eight fat swine" cost 240 florins.[11] By 1636, traders in many Dutch towns and cities traded tulips on financial exchanges. Some individuals suddenly grew rich. Every one imagined that the passion for tulips would last forever and that the wealthy from every part of the world would buy tulip bulbs from the Dutch at whatever price they asked. They believed the riches of Europe would flow to their fair country; wealth would proliferate and poverty would be banished forever. Nobles, citizens, farmers, mechanics, seamen, footmen, maidservants, even chimney sweeps and "old clotheswomen" dabbled in tulip speculation. At the peak of tulip mania in February 1637, some single tulip bulbs sold for more than 10 times the annual income of a skilled craftsman.[12]

People were purchasing bulbs at higher and higher prices, intending to re-sell them later for a nifty profit. However, such a scheme could not last unless someone was willing to pay these high prices and take possession of the bulbs. In February 1637, tulip traders could no longer find new buyers willing to pay increasingly inflated prices for their bulbs. As this realization set in, the demand for tulips collapsed, and prices plummeted – the speculative bubble burst. The crisis left the traders holding futures contracts to purchase tulips at a later date for prices now ten times greater than those on the open market, while others found themselves in possession of bulbs worth a fraction of the price they had paid for them. The panicked tulip speculators sought help from the Dutch government. Although they attempted to resolve the situation to the satisfaction of all parties, their efforts were unsuccessful. The mania ended with many individuals stuck with worthless tulip bulbs that they owned at the end of the crash – no court would enforce payment of a tulip bulb contract, since judges regarded them as gambling debts and thus not enforceable by law.[13]

A TULIP, KNOWN AS "THE VICEROY", DISPLAYED IN A 1637 DUTCH CATALOG. ITS BULB COST BETWEEN 3,000 AND 4,200 GUILDERS DEPENDING ON SIZE. A SKILLED CRAFTSMAN AT THE TIME EARNED ABOUT 300 GUILDERS A YEAR.

The South Sea Bubble

For the British, the 18th century was a time of prosperity. This meant that a large section of the British population had money to invest and were looking for places to put their money. The South Sea Company, founded in 1711, was a British joint-stock company that traded in South America. The British government granted the company a monopoly to the trade in Spain's South American colonies. The company had no problem in attracting investors when it purchased the rights to all the trade – mainly in slaves – in the South Seas. The first issue of stock didn't satisfy hardcore speculators, let alone the average investors, who were confident of the company's eventual profitability. The popular perception among the British was that Mexicans and South Americans were just waiting for someone to introduce them to the finery of wool and fleece in exchange for mounds of jewels and gold! Nobody questioned the repeated re-issues of stocks by the company – investors gobbled up the stock as fast as it was offered. Even though inexperienced management headed the company, the stocks continued to appreciate. To further lure gullible investors, management set up opulent offices in the most affluent quarters of town to give the illusion of success. Once potential investors saw the wealth the company was supposedly generating, they clamored for more stock in which to invest their money.[14]

The success of the South Sea Company stirred British pride, and, believing that British companies could not fail, money poured in from British investors. They were undeterred by the many indications that the company was too poorly run to break even. For example, whole shipments of wool were misdirected and left decaying in foreign ports. Eventually, the management team realized that the value of their own personal shares of stock did not reflect the actual value of the company or its dismal earnings. They secretly sold their shares of stocks in the summer of 1720 and hoped no one would leak the information to other shareholders. But secrets like that are not held for long, the bad news spread like wildfire, and the panic selling of worthless stock certificates ensued. After the price soared from 128½ pounds per share to over 1,000 in nine months, the bubble of overvalued stock burst and the price per share dropped to 124, dragging other stocks down with it and leaving many investors ruined.[15]

The prominent economic position of the British Empire and the government's aid in stabilizing the banking industry helped the economy avoid a complete crash. An inquiry by the

The Headlong Fools Plunge into South Sea Water.
But the Sly Long-heads Wade with Caution after.
The first are Drowning but the Wise Last
Venture no Deeper than the knees or Waist.

TREE CARICATURE FROM SOUTH SEA BUBBLE CARDS

British House of Commons found collusion by several government ministers in the scandal. As a result, the British government outlawed the issuing of stock certificates, a law that it did not repeal until 1825.[16]

Questions to Consider

1. How did hubris get in the way of British investors employing rational analysis of the South Sea Company?

Panics of the 1800s

Unregulated capitalism in the 1800s experienced periods of extreme booms and busts. The panics of 1819, 1825, 1837, 1866, 1873 and 1893 were the most notable. Many bubbles begin when a burst of innovation or technological progress heralds the dawn of a new economy. In the 1840s, Great Britain endured a mania driven by a new technology: the railroad. In 1830, the first commercially successful railroad began carrying passengers between Manchester and Liverpool, England; thereafter, investors bought shares in companies that would build even more profitable lines. During the height of the boom in 1845-1846, share prices of railroad stocks soared, and corporations built thousands of miles of track, much of it redundant and unnecessary. Even though most of the railway companies of the 1840s went bankrupt, they left behind a new transportation infrastructure that was essential to the nation's economic expansion throughout the 19th century.[17]

One of the most dramatic of the 19th century global meltdowns was the crisis of 1873. Typically, a crisis begins in core economies, when after excessive bank lending for speculative ventures those investments go bust, triggering a banking crisis.[18] The Panic of 1873 set off a severe international economic depression in Europe, the U.S,, and it even stretched to the Ottoman Empire in the Middle East. It lasted until 1879 and even to 1893 in some countries. The depression was known as the Great Depression until the 1930s, when the description great took on a new meaning of severity. In Europe it is now called the Long Depression and in the U.S. as the Panic of 1873. The fall in the international demand for silver caused the panic, along with industrial overproduction, and events in the U.S.

In the U.S. at this time, a boom in railroad construction followed the American Civil War (1861-1865) with over 56,000 miles (90,000 km) of new track criss crossing the country between 1866 and 1873. Government land grants and subsidies to the railroads drove much of the craze in railroad investment. The railroad industry was also booming from an infusion of cash from speculators, which added to the overbuilding of docks, factories and other facilities. At the same time, investors had put too much capital into projects offering no immediate returns. Germany's decision to cease minting silver coins in 1871 caused the demand and value of silver to plummet, thus hurting the U.S. min-

A BANK RUN ON THE FOURTH NATIONAL BANK, NO. 20 NASSAU STREET, NEW YORK CITY, 1873.

ing industry that mined much of the world's silver. In 1873, the U.S. Congress passed the Coinage Act, which changed the backing of its currency from both a gold and silver standard to solely the gold standard. Not only did the act depress silver prices, it also reduced the domestic money supply, since now only gold backed up money. These developments raised interest rates, since money was tight or in short supply, thereby hurting farmers and anyone else who normally borrowed money and carried heavy debt loads. The result from these and other factors contributed to a crisis in the American economy.

During this time, Jay Cooke & Company, a major player in the U.S. banking establishment, had invested heavily in the railroad industry. Reports circulated that the credit standing of Cooke's firm had significantly dropped resulting in halting the construction of another transcontinental railroad. In 1873, the firm declared bankruptcy, along with 89 of the country's 364 railroad companies. A total of 18,000 businesses failed between 1873 and 1875. Unemployment reached 14 percent by 1876. The crisis halted construction work, employers cut wages, real estate values fell and corporate profits vanished.[19]

The panic and depression of 1873 – 1896 hit all industrial nations with a vengeance. Most European countries experienced a drastic fall in prices. After the 1873 crisis, agricultural and industrial groups lobbied for protective tariffs that stimulated economic revival through state intervention in the economy. Germany, France, and others attempted to deal with their economic problems through the implementation of high protective tariffs, while the U.S. continued its high tariff policies that were already in place.

Up to that point, the Panic of 1893 was the worst economic crisis in U.S. history. Some historians say the Panic of 1893 was a continuation of the Panic of 1873, the era known as the Long Depression. But a period of significant economic expansion in the 1880s, driven by speculation in railroads, punctuated these dates. For our purposes, it is important to isolate the Panic of 1893 as a separate crisis and describe its dire effects, despite its similarities to the Panic of 1873.

The collapse of railroad overbuilding and shaky railroad financing marked the Panic of 1893, which set off a series of bank failures. One of the first signs of trouble was the bankruptcy in early 1893 of the Philadelphia and Reading Railroad, which had been greatly over-built. Compounding overbuilding and the railroad bubble was a run on the world's gold supply. Because people were withdrawing gold from banks and hoarding it, the decline of gold reserves stored in the U.S. Treasury fell to a dangerously low level. The dire situation forced President Cleveland to borrow $65 million in gold from the powerful Wall-Street banker J.P. Morgan in order to support the country's gold standard. In a nutshell, an ever-growing credit shortage created panic, which resulted in a depression. Over 15,000 businesses, 600 banks, and 74 railroads failed. In addition, about 17 percent to 19 percent of the workforce was unemployed at the Panic's peak. The huge spike in unemployment, combined with the loss of life savings kept in failed

KLONDIKE GOLD RUSH, PROSPECTORS IN A TENT CAMP WAITING FOR THE ICE ON YUKON RIVER TO BREAK UP, MAY 1898.

banks, meant that a once secure middle-class could not meet their mortgage obligations. Many walked away from recently built homes as a result. The U.S. economy began to recover in 1897 when the money supply expanded because of an influx of gold from the Klondike Gold Rush in northern Canada and finds in South Africa. The economy began 10 years of rapid growth, until the next panic, the Panic of 1907.[20]

The Crisis of 1907

The crisis of 1907 began in the U.S. after a speculative boom in stocks and real estate collapsed. So-called **trust companies** – lightly regulated commercial banks bound together by complicated chains of ownership – suffered runs on their reserves, and panic spread throughout the country. A loss of confidence among bank depositors, combined with the retraction of lending by a number of New York City banks, ended up resulting in a 50 percent drop in the stock market from where it had been in 1906. As the crisis spiraled out of control, the nation's most influential banker, J.P. Morgan, convened a series of emergency meetings with New York City's banking establishment to stop the bank runs. On the first weekend of November, Morgan, in a famous act of brinksmanship, invited fellow bankers to the private library in his brownstone mansion on Madison Avenue and 36th Street in New York City. When they failed to agree to come to one another's aid, he locked them in the room and pocketed the key. The bankers eventually agreed, and the crisis came to an end shortly thereafter. While Morgan received credit for averting a catastrophe, the events of 1907 persuaded many in the financial sector of the need for a central bank to provide lending support in future crises. In 1913, the Federal Reserve was born.[21]

A SWARM GATHERS ON WALL STREET DURING THE BANK PANIC IN OCTOBER 1907.

The Florida Land Boom of the 1920s

I have a personal connection with the Florida Real Estate Craze in the mid 1920s. No, I did not buy and sell real estate personally. But during this time my grandfather, Edward Jenner, owner of Jenner Construction from Davenport, Iowa, built roads and bridges in the Miami, Florida area and the island keys jutting south of the mainland. My grandfather packed up his family – his wife, my grandmother, Hulda Herbst Jenner, and their two young children, Clarence and, my mother, Ruth – for a construction stint in what many thought to be paradise at the time. My mother had fond memories of innocently playing on sandy beaches as building and land sales took off like wildfire. I don't think my grandfather was involved in big-time land speculation, but since it was the craze at the time, I wouldn't doubt if he, like thousands of others, engaged somewhat in the fantasy of getting rich quick.

The 1920s was a time of great prosperity for many individuals in the United States. During this time, Florida became a popular destination and residence for people who wanted to escape the cold winters of the north. The population grew steadily, but housing couldn't match the demand, causing prices to double and triple in some cases. News of anything doubling and tripling in price always attracts speculators, and they began to swarm into the region. Once people began pumping huge amounts of money into the real estate market, it took off like a future Cape Canaveral rocket. Soon nearly everyone in Florida was either a real estate investor or a real estate agent. The Florida land boom of the 1920s was Florida's first real estate bubble.[22] Others would follow.

For awhile there was a frenzy of buying and selling. Land prices quadrupled in less than a year. Land bought for $800,000 could, within a year, be resold for $4 million. The land boom so inflated prices that to buy a condo-style property in 1926, you had to pay the same as the price ($4 million) of a gated, luxury home in Miami today – without adjusting for inflation! Eventually, as always happens, there were no "greater fools" to buy the overpriced land, and prices began to correct. Speculators finally realized the boom was coming to an end and began to sell their properties while they could. Then everybody realized the boom was over. Panic selling ensued. With thousands of sellers and very few buyers, prices came crashing down, and then went down even lower. The hurricane of 1926 ingloriously ended Florida's land boom. The story includes many parallels to the modern real estate boom, including the entry of outside speculators into the fray, easy credit access for buyers, and rapidly-appreciating property values.[23] The hurricane also wiped out my grandfather's road-building project. Finding the economic situation in Florida too unreliable, he retreated back to Davenport, Iowa to continue building roads throughout the region until his retirement in the early 1950s.

The Roaring 1920s and the Stock Market Crash of 1929

"Anyone who bought stocks in mid-1929 and held onto them saw most of his or her adult life pass by before getting back to even." ... *Richard M. Salsman*

The Roaring Twenties, the decade that led up to the Stock Market Crash of October 1929, was a time of wealth and excess. The crash followed a speculative boom that had taken hold in the late *1920s*, which had enticed hundreds of thousands of Americans to invest heavily in the stock market. A significant number of them were borrowing money on margin to buy more stocks, which meant that by August 1929, brokers were routinely lending small investors more than two-thirds of the face value of the stocks they were buying. Over $8.5 billion was out on loan, which at the time, was more than the entire amount of currency circulating in the U.S. economy.[24] The rising share prices bolstered the confidence of more people to invest in the stock market, they were sure their share prices would continue to go up. Speculation fueled further rises in the market and inflated an economic bubble. With margin buying, investors stood to lose large sums of money if the market turned down – or even failed to advance quickly enough.[25] It was a crisis waiting to happen.

By 1929, Charles Mitchell, President of the National City Bank (which would later become Citibank), had popularized the idea of selling stocks and bonds directly to smaller investors. Mitchell and a small group of bankers, brokers, and speculators manipulated the stock market, grew wealthy and helped spark the economic boom. Ironically, their successes made them folk heroes of the day. In

1929, while the market was rising, seemingly without limits, there were few critics. Based on eight years of continued prosperity, presidents and economists alike confidently predicted that America would soon enter a time when there would be no more poverty, no more depressions – a "New Era" when everyone could be rich. Instead, it was the rich who became richer.[26]

Almost everyone believed the stock market was a no-risk world, where everything went up. Many people poured all their savings into it without learning about the system or the underlying companies they were investing in. With the flood of naïve investors into the market, it was ripe for some manipulation and swindling. Investment bankers, brokers, traders, and sometimes business owners banded together to manipulate stock prices, and when the prices went up, they got out of the market with gains. They did this by deviously acquiring large chunks of stock between them and then trading the stocks among each other for slightly more gains each time. When the public noticed the rising stock prices on the ticker tape, people decided it was an opportune time to buy. The market manipulators would then sell off their overpriced shares for a healthy profit. The deception left buyers holding stocks worth less than they paid for them. On and on the cycle went as fraudulent investors turned a profit by selling the manipulated, over-priced shares to someone who wanted to have a rising stock. During the speculative craze, a number of academics, including Roger Babson, were predicting a crash, but for every bit of cautionary advice, there were four bullish academics guaranteeing the endless growth of the American stock market.[27]

The commercial real estate market also boomed and collapsed in the 1920s. Issuance of commercial mortgage-backed securities financed the construction of most of the U.S. skyscrapers in the 1920s and led to overbuilding and then widespread vacancies. The price declines in the mortgage-backed securities market in the late 1920s preceded the crash of the stock market. Widespread economic optimism after World War I fueled demand for office space, boosting average commercial rents nationally 168 percent through 1924. The 1920s kicked off a speculative commercial real estate construction frenzy not matched until the mid-2000s. New York and Chicago were the primary focus of the real estate run-up. New York developers constructed more office buildings taller than 70 meters – 235 in all – between 1922 and 1931 than in any other ten-year period before or since. The purpose of this construction boom was for investors to capitalize on rents from multiple tenants to generate profits; previously companies had built and occupied their own buildings. Demand was such that traders created a real estate securities exchange in 1929, and commercial mortgage-backed securities quickly grew into one of the largest classes of investment assets of the 1920s, raising more than $4.1 billion from 1,090 bond offerings between 1919 and 1931. Among the reasons for this rapid growth was the presence of small investors who, it turned out, relied on poorly supported assessments of asset values in a market with little regulatory oversight. At the market's peak in May 1928, easy access to capital spurred massive overbuilding and then resulted in empty structures, which led to defaults and finally a widespread collapse in the bond prices. By April 1933, bond prices fell to a low of 24.75 cents on the dollar (par value is 100 cents on the dollar), resulting in defaults of many real estate companies. These were toxic real estate securities 1930s style, similar to what they were in the post 2008 crisis. The real estate bond market soon vanished, as did many of the bond houses that created them, among them many of the most trusted names on Wall Street at the time.[28]

In the late 1920s many believed that the stock market would continue to rise indefinitely. Shortly before the crash, economist Irving Fisher famously proclaimed, "Stock prices have reached what looks like a permanently high plateau." The market had been on a six-year run that saw the Dow Jones Industrial Average increase in value fivefold, peaking at 381 points on September 3, 1929. A string of terrible days followed, with more than a 40 percent drop in the market at the end of October 1929. "Black Thursday," October 24, 1929, shook the optimism and financial gains of the great bull market, when share prices abruptly lost 11 percent of their value at the opening bell. On October 28, "Black Monday," more investors decided to get out of the market, and the slide continued with a record loss in the Dow for the day of 38 points, or 13 percent. The next day, the infamous "Black Tuesday," October 29, 1929, traders exchanged about 16 million shares, and the Dow lost an additional 30 points, or 12 percent. The volume of stocks traded on October 29, 1929 was a record that was not broken for nearly 40 years. The market continued to decline until July 1932, when it bottomed out, down nearly 90 percent from its 1929 highs.[29]

The fall in share prices of stocks on October 24 and 29, 1929, were practically instantaneous in all financial markets, except Japan. The Stock Market Crash of 1929 was the most devastating stock market crash in U.S. history. It had a major impact on the U.S. and world economy. It signaled the beginning of the 12-year Great Depression. During the crash of 1929, as the crisis spun out of control, the Federal Reserve stood idly by. Rather than pursuing an expansionary monetary policy, in which the Fed pumped money into the economy, it tightened the economic reins, making a bad situation even worse. As a result, the money supply sharply contracted between 1929 and 1933, leading to a severe credit crunch that turned a stock market bust into a banking crisis and eventually into a severe economic depression. The U.S. Treasury secretary Andrew Mellon believed that the financial panic would "purge the rottenness out of the system. High costs of living and high living will come down. People will work harder, live a more moral life." In addition, the U.S. raised protective tariffs with the passage of the Smoot-Hawley Tariff, triggering a series of retaliatory tariffs across the world, which contributed to a breakdown of world trade.[30]

In the early 1930s, most of the economists believed that the economy was capable of regulating itself. Moreover, they assumed that full employment is the natural state of things, and that when wages were too high, the economy will naturally contract. As unemployment rises, wages will start to fall. The conventional wisdom was that as wages fall, entrepreneurs will start to hire again, lured by the prospect of increased profits from low wages. The cycle then begins anew.[31] But this cycle did not begin anew. Instead, the most severe depression in modern history ensued. The roaring 1920s captured the unbounded optimism of the age; it was a time when the stock market epitomized the false promise of permanent prosperity. It did not last forever.

Questions to Consider

1. What was the American government's reaction to the stock market crash in October 1929?

2. What do you think would have been a more appropriate response? ?

CROWD AT NEW YORK'S AMERICAN UNION BANK DURING A BANK RUN EARLY IN THE GREAT DEPRESSION

DEPRESSION ERA REGULATIONS 1930-1980

The key question to ask about this period in history is why, after an average of one every 13 years, was there not a comparable depression for 79 years, from 1929 to 2008? We can find the answer in New Deal reforms. The Franklin D. Roosevelt (FDR) administration enacted the New Deal to counteract the conditions that led to the Great Depression. During the Great Depression, democratic forces gained the upper hand over the financial markets, which the largest banks and financiers previously dominated. The FDR administration realized the financial markets had to be tightly controlled. For example, currency speculation only deepened the Depression and had to be strictly limited. New Deal reformers established the **Glass-Steagall Act** in 1933, which the government designed to protect average depositors by separating commercial and investment banking. They enacted progressive taxation to limit concentration of wealth among the super-rich and to increase the wealth of working people through programs such as Social Security, wage laws, and support of unions. In the depression-era U.S., economic stability also rested on the passage of the **Federal Deposit Insurance Corporation** (FDIC), a government sponsored deposit insurance program to stop bank runs. New Deal reforms regulated the financial system that contributed to the stability of the era. These domestic and international restrictions kept financial excesses and bubbles under control for over a half a century.[32] And it worked pretty well.

The golden era of global postwar growth (1948-1973) skirted major financial crises for over 25 years. A reason for the stability of the period was the Bretton Woods agreements forged by the Allies in 1944 towards the end of World War II. These agreements set up strict rules for global finance, rules that kept financiers in check for more than a quarter century. Since the U.S. was the leading economy of the time, the agreement established the dollar as the exchange standard. In this system, every participating nation could exchange their currency for dollars at a fixed rate. The result was a period of remarkable economic growth and stability.

The theory behind this long period of economic stability was the work of British economist John Maynard Keynes. His most famous work was *The General Theory of Employment, Interest and Money*, published in 1936. In this complex book he parted ways with economists of the classical and neoclassical schools, and approached the problem from an entirely different perspective. What really determines employment levels, he argued, is aggregate demand – the collective demand for goods and services within a particular economy; if companies cut wages and fire workers, people will consume less, and demand will falter. The argument essentially countered the era's conventional wisdom. Keynesian theory held that as demand drops, businesses will become more reluctant to invest, which will lead to further wage cuts or layoffs. Likewise, ordinary consumers will save more and spend less, which dampens demand still further, a conundrum known as the "paradox of thrift." Keynes theorized that this self-fulfilling cycle would continue as workers remained unemployed and factories shuttered. Then, as demand falls below the supply of goods, the downturn would force firms to

SENATOR CARTER GLASS (D.) AND REP. HENRY B. STEAGALL (D.), CO-SPONSORS OF THE GLASS–STEAGALL ACT.

cut prices to sell the inventory of unsold goods; this price deflation would lead to a further fall in their profits and cash flows.[33] Keynes also had an active hand in shaping the policies of the Bretton Woods agreement and the post-war economic order.

FINANCIAL CRISES: 1970s ONWARD

The golden age of capitalism came to a screeching halt in the mid-1970s. A new economic phenomenon seized core economic countries: **stagflation** – the coexistence of low growth with high inflation. The root causes of stagflation were due to global productive capacity outrunning global demand, which was constrained by continuing deep inequalities in income distribution. Also, the reconstruction of Germany and Japan and the rapid growth of industrializing economies like Brazil, Taiwan, and South Korea added tremendous new productive capacity and increased global competition, while demand remained limited. The massive oil price rises of the 1970s further aggravated stagflation.[34]

Contributing to the crisis was that from the late 1960s onward, the U.S. was printing more and more money to fund President Johnson's ambitious social programs at home and the war in Vietnam. Where there had once been a dollar shortage in the world, there was now a dollar glut. The U.S. was supposed to be the anchor of the global financial system, but its gold reserves were dwindling and the dollar's value in gold was untenable. In 1971, President Nixon severed the agreement that linked the dollar to gold. In effect, U.S. creditors realized that there wasn't enough gold to back up the dollars in circulation. When that happened, the Bretton Woods agreement collapsed and the dollar depreciated. The system further broke down in 1973 when the financial markets devalued the dollar again. Instead of the dollar/gold standard, the world moved to a system of flexible exchange rates where it remains today.[35]

By the late 1970s, neoliberals, who had been kept on the economic margins by the dominance of Keynesian thought, worked to regain the advantage they held in the pre-depression era. They spread a new faith to a worried public that emphasized self-regulated markets, free of what they called government's "burdensome regulations." They lobbied against progressive taxes, unions, and social welfare programs. The new conventional wisdom of neoliberals was to let the wealthy invest in businesses, which would then trickle down to workers. Their mantra was "a rising tide will lift all boats." This revived economic philosophy from the early 20th century rapidly spread. Thus began a period of deregulation, tax reductions for the wealthy, and privatization of publicly held assets. And on Wall Street, the money tap was open, but it did not trickle down.[36]

The crisis-free era of global capitalism would abruptly change when the neoliberal economic philosophy gained more and more traction. Stiglitz counts 124 global financial crises from the period 1970 to 2007.[37] The following is a brief overview of some of the more notable crises during this period. The U.S. expe-

AN AMERICAN MARINE INVESTIGATING A VIET CONG SUSPECT DURING THE VIETNAM WAR (1955-1975).

rienced a banking crisis, rooted in the deregulated savings and loan industry, beginning in 1984. It cost American taxpayers about $500 billion to rescue the industry. During the late 1980s and early 1990s, following a surge in capital inflows (lending from abroad) and soaring real estate prices, the Scandinavian countries experienced some of the worst banking crises the wealthy economies had known since World War II. In 1992, Japan's asset price bubble burst (mainly real estate) and ushered in a decade-long banking crisis. Around the same time, with the collapse of the Soviet bloc, several formerly communist countries in Eastern Europe joined the ranks of nations facing banking sector problems. As the second half of the 1990s approached, emerging markets faced a fresh round of banking crises. The legendary Asian crisis of 1997-1998 followed problems in Mexico and Argentina (1994-1995), and then troubles arose in Russia and Colombia. The upswing in banking crises enveloped Argentina in 2001 and Uruguay in 2002, after which a brief tranquil period ensued. This reprieve came to an abrupt halt in the summer of 2007 when the subprime crisis in the U.S. began in earnest, soon transforming itself into a global financial crisis. The U.S. crisis was firmly rooted in the real estate bubble pumped up by a massive influx of cheap foreign capital, the Fed's expansionary money policy, and an increasingly permissive regulatory policy that helped propel escalating housing prices.[38] Since we cannot cover all of the financial crises, I will highlight a few in the pages below.

The Dot-com Bubble (1995-2000)

The boom and bust cycle called the **dot-com bubble** was a speculative bubble roughly covering the years 1995–2000. A new technology – the internet – was the craze in the 1990s that promised many positive applications. The period was marked by the founding and, in many cases, failure of a group of new Internet-based companies commonly referred to as dot-coms. Companies were seeing their stock prices shoot up if they simply added an "e" prefix to their name or a ".com" to the end. A combination of rapidly increasing stock prices, market confidence that the companies would turn future profits, individual speculation in stocks, and widely available venture capital created an environment in which many investors were willing to overlook traditional measurements of what made a successful business.

A DOT-COM CASUALTY. THE PETS.COM SOCK PUPPET. THE COMPANY WAS FOUNDED IN AUG. 1998, AND DEFUNCT IN NOV. 2000.

Perhaps one of the most infamous dot-com companies was WorldCom, a long-distance telephone and internet-services provider that became notorious for using fraudulent accounting practices to increase its stock price. The company filed for bankruptcy in 2002, and the courts convicted former CEO Bernard Ebbers of fraud and conspiracy. The table on the next page lists just a few of the many dot-com companies.

The disconnect between the real economy and the virtual economy of finance was evident in the dot-com bubble. With profits in the real economy stagnating, the smart money flocked to the financial sector where investors squeezed out profits. The rapid rise in the stock values of Internet firms which, like Amazon.com, still had to turn a profit exemplified the workings of this virtual economy. Never before had a U.S. economic expansion become so dependent upon the stock market's ascent. But stock prices could only proceed to a point before reality bit back and enforced a correction.[39]

The peak of the bubble occurred on March 10, 2000, when stocks tumbled on the NASDQ stock exchange. The dot-com bubble fully burst in 2001, ultimately wiping out a whopping $5 trillion in the market value of technology companies from March 2000 to October 2002.[40] When the bubble collapsed only about 50 percent of new companies made it through 2004, but like the railroads in the 19th century, surviving was a vast new communications infrastructure of coaxial cable lines, cell phone towers, and other technologies.[41] The tragic events of 9/11 added to the stock market collapse. The economy avoided a long recession, but it was only by encouraging another bubble to form and grow: the housing bubble.

Dot-com Bubble Companies

- The Learning Company – bought by Mattel in 1999 for $3.5 billion, sold for $27.3 million in 2000.

- pets.com: sold pet supplies to retail customers before entering bankruptcy in 2000.

- Webvan: an online grocer, operated on a "credit and delivery" system; bankrupt in 2001.

- Boo.com: spent $188 million in 6 months creating a global online fashion store; bankrupt in 2000.

- InfoSpace: March 2000 stock $1,305 per share, April, 2001 stock crashed to $22 a share.

Questions to Consider

1. What is a lesson we can learn from the Dot-com bubble?

Japan's Asset Price Bubble (1980s onward)

World War II devastated Japan's economy. However, it launched, with American assistance early on, a remarkable recovery to achieve the coveted status as the number 3 economy in the world today. After the war, Japanese industry competed in a low-tech world market offering low prices and poor quality. In the 1960s, consumers sneeringly referred to products made in Japan as "junk." However, Japan quickly moved into ever more sophisticated markets by honing worker's skills and importing more advanced technology from around the world. By the 1980s, Japanese brand names such as Toyota and Sony had become famous for their high quality and reasonable prices. In the 1980s, America thought of Japan much as it does China today – as a rival for global economic dominance. Then, in 1990, the Japanese economy entered a period of stagnation.

In 1952, finance Minister Hayato Ikeda created a financial model to fund the growth of companies like Toyota and Sony. In this model, banks, rather than the stock exchange, would be the main source of capital for industry. The British and American model of capitalism built upon the Dutch invention in the 17th century – the joint stock company. In this Western model, stock exchanges raise money through the sale of shares of stock. The stock exchange publicly lists most large corporations because this is the best way to access large pools of capital. Ikeda thought that this system focused too sharply on short-term profits to satisfy shareholders, rather than on long-term planning. He reasoned that the Japanese model of bank lending to corporations would solve these problems.[42]

The Japanese government played a role in directing its banks to establish close, some say even cozy, relationships with their industrial borrowers, and freely lent to them for the long term. Banks used the funds from Japanese citizens, who were unsurpassed savers rather than consumers, for lending. The main purpose of the stock market, instead of raising capital for enterprises, was to allow industries and banks to hold shares of stock in each other, which they thought made the system even more stable.[43]

Despite Western skepticism, Ikeda's model seemed to be working. Japan ran trade surpluses year after year, as it focused on export-led growth, much like China does today. By the 1980s, Japan was the world's largest creditor nation, a distinction once held by the U.S. The government's deliberate policy to keep the value of the yen low and their exports competitive helped Japan achieve economic success, it was not just their industrial innovation and productivity alone. The U.S., experiencing troublesome trade deficits, began to lean on Japan to raise the value of the yen in order to reduce their trade surplus. Japan finally agreed in 1985, when senior officials from the world's leading economies met at the Plaza Hotel in New York City to decide what to do. The following agreement, known as the **Plaza Accord**, directed the value of the Japanese currency to rise steadily against the dollar.[44]

As a result of the Plaza Accord, the spending power of Japanese companies in the U.S. and the rest of the world heated up. Since the yen was now worth more overseas, it sparked a wave of real-estate and other asset purchases abroad. Fearing the loss of competitiveness because a rising yen would lead to a drop in higher priced exports and an economic slump, the Bank of Japan repeatedly cut interest rates to stop the yen from appreciating further, a move that would also provide cheap credit to industry. It was at this point in Japan that a bubble in shares of stock and real estate started to inflate, driven by cheap and plentiful credit. In addition, in keeping with neoliberal principles, the U.S. pressured the Japanese to diversify and deregulate their financial sector. As a result Japanese banks, looking for new ways to make money, invested heavily in real estate, which they viewed as a fail-safe investment. They also began experimenting with sophisticated financial instruments, such as derivatives. At the same time, the banks continued to lend to their long-established clients, without much due diligence regarding their credit worthiness or the prospect for returns.[45] This was uncharted water for Japanese banks, but since the days of Ikeda, the Japanese government had been active in directing the economy, and borrowers and lenders may have assumed that the government would never let the banks fail.[46]

Asset prices in Japan spiraled upward. By 1990, the value of all shares traded on Japanese stock exchanges was greater than stocks traded in the U.S., a country with an economy twice Japan's size. Real-estate prices soared as well. At the peak of Japan's real estate boom, the land beneath and surrounding Tokyo's Imperial Pal-

AERIAL PHOTOGRAPH OF IMPERIAL PALACE OF JAPAN IN 1979.

ace – several hundred acres in total – had by some estimates market value equivalent to all the real estate in California. Real estate in Tokyo was so valuable it was selling by the square meter. Unbelievably, choice properties, such as in Tokyo's Ginza district, were fetching over 100 million yen (approximately $1 million) per square meter ($93,000 per square foot).[47]

At the end of 1989, the Bank of Japan decided it was time to pop the inflated bubble. It began to raise interest rates steadily from 2.5 percent to 6 percent in August 1990. The strategy worked. By October 1990, the Nikkei 225 Stock Exchange had fallen by nearly 50 percent from its peak and real-estate prices were in a tailspin, eventually falling 70 percent. As the economy slowed, Japanese companies that had invested heavily in real estate turned to their banks seeking short-term loans to ease their cash-flow woes. Fearing the potential bankruptcy of their clients, the banks lent freely, broadening their exposure to the sinking real-estate market. The weak economy hit the banks on all sides; real-estate collateral that was declining in value backed 80 percent of the loans that the banks had made. And much of the bank's own reserve capital, which they had always kept to a minimum to encourage lending, was also declining in value as stock prices fell.[48]

Toxic assets were piling up in Japanese banks. Yet their managers refused to confront reality. Instead bankers opted to wait until the crisis blew over, and real-estate prices would rise again, effectively hiding the true extent of their losses. Bankers hid revealing files away from regulators and the public, and they parked troubled assets in subsidiary companies where they kept the information off the company's accounting balance sheet.[49]

Meanwhile, as worries about the reliability of the banks spread, depositors withdrew their money, putting it in postal savings banks (government banks) or under their futons. This only deepened the crisis in the banking system. In 1993, regulators forced Japanese banks to acknowledge $120 billion of bad loans against only $34 billion of capital reserves. Most observers thought this underestimated their bad loans, yet no agreement on how to resolve the crisis came forth. Equally, the banks did not have the capital and the government did not have the determination to clean up the

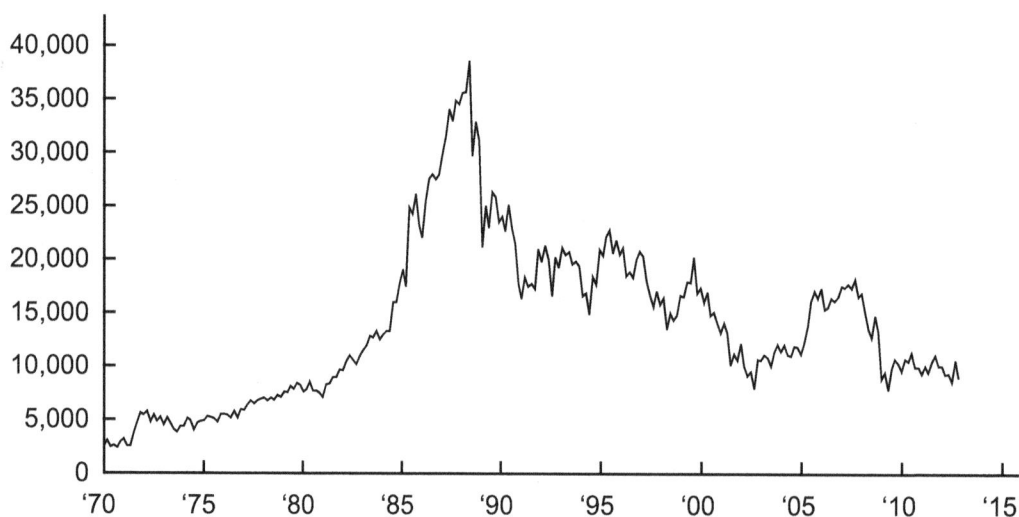

THE NIKKEI 225, JAPAN'S STOCK MARKET INDEX, PEAKED ON DECEMBER 29, 1989 AT 39,957.
IT CLOSED ON MARCH 10, 2009 AT 7,054.

toxic assets. The result was a stalemate as banks continued to hide bad loans off their balance sheets and pay dividends, as if everything was normal.[50]

This state of denial could not last forever. The problem spread to larger mortgage lenders, which the government saved with a bailout using taxpayers' money. The government feared that letting them fail would lead to **contagion**, which could spread across the entire financial sector and lead to the collapse of many financial companies. Since Japan does not have a government guaranteed Federal Deposit Insurance Corporation (FDIC) as in the U.S., spooked savers continued to pull their money out of the banks.[51]

Unlike the U.S. in the 1930s, the Japanese economy did not melt down. It experienced stagnation, not depression. The central bank of Japan kept interest rates high for several months when the bubble first burst in 1990, fearing that asset prices would take off again if it cut rates too quickly. Confidence had all but evaporated by the time the bank lowered rates again, which failed to have any impact even as interest rates reached zero. The bubble's deflation lasted for more than a decade with stock prices initially bottoming out in 2003, although they would descend even further during the global crisis in 2008.[52] On March 10, 2009, the Japanese Nikkei 225 stock market index reached a 27-year low of 7054.98. The Japanese asset price bubble contributed to what the Japanese refer to as their "Lost Decade."

> ### Questions to Consider
> 1. What do you think was the main cause of Japan's economic woes?
> 2. How would you have solved this problem?

The East Asian Financial Crisis of 1997-98

Gripping much of East Asia beginning in July 1997, the **East Asian financial crisis** was a period in which financial institutions suddenly lost a large part of the value of their assets. The crisis raised fears of a worldwide economic meltdown due to financial contagion. The reasons for the crisis follow the patterns set out in other financial crises.

It was during this time that the International Monetary Fund (IMF) and the U.S. Treasury Department targeted East Asia for market liberalization. They pushed for rapid financial and capital **market liberalization**, another name for the opening up of countries' markets to the inflow of money from other countries for investment and the deregulation of banks. Market liberalization was a two-edged sword, but with one edge far sharper than the other. When markets were doing well, capital flowed in, and even though only a fraction went into productive investment, the economy grew. But often the good times got out of hand, and what followed was an onslaught of speculative money that quickly flowed in and out of a country, leaving economic havoc in its wake. Through history speculators have repeated this pattern time and time again. Although the U.S. is able to bear the ups and downs of markets reasonably well, the consequences for developing countries

> ### Major Events of the Asian Financial Crisis of 1997-98
> 1. Financial liberalization at the urging of the IMF and the U.S. Treasury Department.
> 2. Entry of foreign funds seeking quick and high returns, mainly in real estate and the stock market.
> 3. Over-investment, leading to a bubble.
> 4. Panicky withdrawal of funds leading to a fall in stock and real estate prices.
> 5. Bailout of foreign speculators by the IMF.
> 6. Collapse of the real economy – recession throughout East Asia in 1998.

are far more serious. The result was the developing countries lost far more as capital flowed out than they gained as capital flowed in. South Korea in 1993, the Asian financial crisis of 1997, followed by crises in Russia and Brazil, made it clear that something was terribly wrong.[53]

Global money traders are notoriously fickle. In the 1990s, East Asia was the next new investment destination. The economies of Thailand, Malaysia, Indonesia, Singapore, the Philippines, and South Korea were booming. The East Asian countries had managed very high growth rates by violating the principles of neoliberalism. They practiced a managed version of capitalism. It relied on close ties between local business and government, very low interest rates, high domestic savings, and a degree of consensual planning. They also closed their economies to foreign financial speculation.

The East Asian tigers, as the media called them, were simply the best investment opportunities in the late 1980s and early 1990s. They had disciplined work forces, low wages, pliable yet reliable governments, and a focus on producing goods destined for export, not domestic consumption. From 1985 to 1996, Thailand's economy grew at an average rate of over 9 percent per year, the highest economic growth rate of any country at the time. Inflation was kept reasonably low, within a range of 3.4 – 5.7 percent. They pegged the baht, their local currency, at 25 to the U.S. dollar.[54] International investment flooded into East Asia in the 1980s and 1990s because East Asia was a more profitable place to invest than anywhere else, and there was a mass of global wealth looking for a place to park itself. Rolling in foreign exchange yen from decades of trade surpluses, Japan, early on, was the biggest investor in the region. With an appreciating yen it was cheap for Japanese corporations to buy foreign currencies or build subsidiaries in other Asian countries. Long-term Japanese strategy called for transferring manufacturing to subsidiaries abroad to take advantage of cheaper foreign labor. In short, the Japanese were busy rebuilding what they once called, prior to World War II, the "Japanese Asian Co-Prosperity Sphere."[55]

The U.S. Treasury Department and IMF pressured these countries to liberalize their economies and open them up to more foreign investment. Once these relatively small countries succumbed to neoliberal principles, their currencies became objects of speculation. They cast aside managed capitalism, which had served them well for years. In the late 1990s traders and investors poured money into the newly liberalized economies of East Asia, creating a brief, artificial boom. Awash with money, Thailand went on a spending spree. Skyscrapers shot up in Bangkok, and so did real-estate prices. Unlike Mexico 20 years previously, private companies, not the government, were borrowing money. According to optimistic investors, Thailand's public finances were in good order, so the highly-leveraged borrowing was not a problem.[56]

But the frenzied growth did not last forever. There was a problem with the storied Asian development model: it suffered from a problem known as the "**fallacy of composition**." The first Asian export-oriented economies, such as South Korea, competed with high-cost Western producers. Their low-cost labor, low taxes, and lax environmental laws allowed them to under-price their competition and still make a tidy profit. But as more export-oriented countries entered the export game, increased competition meant a slice into high profit margins. As the East Asian exporting economies competed more and more with each other, rather than with Western producers, the export game started to slow. Regional recession became a greater likelihood. Investments lost their luster and became less profitable than expected by both lender and borrower – a situation that leads to problems in any highly leveraged credit system – even if there are no further complications.[57] But there were exacerbating complications. In the following textbox Robin Hahnel succinctly explains the problems in East Asia which contributed to the crisis.

The East Asian Financial Crisis[58]

Many Asian banks "borrowed dollars short" and loaned local currency "long." This meant Asian banks borrowed dollars from international investors at high interest rates that fell due for repayment quickly. The banks used the dollars to buy local currency and make loans to Asian businesses at even higher interest rates, but these loans did not come due for longer periods of time. As long as new short-term dollar loans were available to the Asian banks, and as long as the Asian businesses were enjoying booming sales and high profit margins, the arrangement worked just fine for all concerned. The bubble kept growing. International lenders got rapid turnover and high yields on their dollar investments. Asian banks earned high profits from a high volume of business conducted with a large **spread** (the difference) between the interest rate they charged Asian businesses and the interest rate they paid international investors. And Asian businesses expanded their profit margins by leveraging their own financial investment with seemingly unlimited borrowed money. As long as the local currency remained reasonably stable vis-a-vis the dollar, which it would as long as export sales were strong, the businesses repaid loans in local currency which were then converted to dollars and used to repay the dollar-based loans without any problem. This is just the happy coincidence of events that textbooks love to use to illustrate the benefits of credit systems. But what happens when something goes wrong?

When competition among exporting countries led to falling export sales, Asian businesses could not repay their high interest loans from Asian banks. Moreover, falling export sales lowered international demand for the Asian currencies leading to depreciation, which made dollars more expensive for Asian banks to buy. For both reasons, Asian banks could not repay their short-run dollar debts in the usual manner – by selling local currency from repaid loans for dollars. Instead the falling economy forced Asian banks to pay dollar lender Peter by borrowing even more from some new dollar lender Paul in the international capital markets. But this only helps if the underlying problem with Asian export businesses is short lived. If it persists, as it did, the stop-gap solution only aggravates the problem farther down the road because there are still more dollar debts now to Paul as well as Peter.

When the Asian banks finally couldn't meet payments on their dollar loans, it was too late. Their outstanding debt was too big and too short-term. As they scrambled to convert what local currency they had into dollars to meet their payment deadlines, they further depreciated the local currency. When the international investors and currency speculators and local wealthy elites caught on to what was happening, they obeyed Rule number 2: Panic. As new dollar loans dried up overnight, they dumped more local currency on the exchange market, causing further depreciation. While it is true that the devaluations could have made manufactured exports cheaper and more attractive to buyers abroad, it was already too late to save the exporting companies. Their previous actions already saddled them with too much bad debt and they couldn't get new credit from their local banks, which were also saddled with too much bad debt, and, in turn, they couldn't get new credit from the international capital markets. At this point there was no possibility that the high-flying borrowers could

THE SUKHUMVIT AREA OF BANGKOK. THAILAND WAS THE EPICENTER OF THE ASIAN FINANCIAL CRISIS

pay off the dollar loans owed to international investors Peter or Paul, since the bottom had fallen out of the local currency, making the dollars necessary for repayment prohibitively expensive. Moreover, factories couldn't produce exports for sale because they had no money to buy the imported inputs needed to make them, a condition made worse as depreciating local currencies multiplied the price of those inputs.

In hindsight, the Asian bankers were foolish to borrow hard currency short and lend local currency long. But they were no more foolish than international lenders who made unsecured dollar loans to Asian banks. The Asian governments were foolish not to see the fallacy of composition problem in the export-led growth model. But they were no more foolish than the economists at the IMF and World Bank who encouraged it. With hindsight it is easy to pass around blame. But the underlying problem lay in the dangers lurking in the liberalized international credit system that encouraged the logic of speculative wealth.

In a matter of a few short weeks during the summer of 1997, the thriving countries of East Asia saw their economies overwhelmed by a financial tsunami. First Thailand and Indonesia, and then South Korea and Malaysia saw investors panic and then watched capital flee. Their currencies plummeted in value and their biggest companies wrestled with bankruptcy.[59] This caused a run against these countries' currencies. In the summer of 1997, Thailand's central bank could no longer defend its currency, the baht, and it abruptly fell by about 25 percent. The "hot" speculative money that poured into the region for quick returns found that the so-called East Asian miracle had peaked. The money, even more quickly, poured out. Asian currency devaluations spread rapidly to Malaysia, Indonesia, the Philippines, and even the strong economy of South Korea. When the crisis hit South Korea, ordinary citizens carried gifts of family gold to Korean banks to help them meet foreign debt payments and thereby avoid "shaming" the nation. A creditor's dream.[60]

The trouble did not end. Capital started to flow out of countries across Southeast Asia as investors worried that others in the region might be vulnerable. Only Hong Kong was able to fight off a speculative attack. The crisis then moved on from Asia, as panic spread to all the emerging markets. For example, Russia, which had just started to receive large sums of international capital, defaulted on its debts.[61]

Deep recessions took place throughout the emerging markets. Shell-shocked government officials, like the prime minister of Malaysia, Mahathir Mohamad, blamed the excesses of speculative hedge funds operators such as the American financier George Soros, whom he called a "moron" and a "criminal." By then, the crisis-hit governments had decided to blame the international capital markets much more broadly and to take steps to ensure that they did not fall victim to them again. Malaysia, for one, introduced capital controls to make the flow of international funds in and out of the country less volatile.[62]

The emerging-markets financial crisis of 1997 and 1998 challenged the prevailing conventional wisdom of the **International Monetary Fund** (IMF) and U.S. Treasury Department that the quickest route to prosperity was for developing countries to open up their economies to inflows of international capital.[63] This influential world financial institution was part of the Bretton Woods agreement in 1944. The IMF regulates an international monetary system based on convertible currencies, lends to countries experiencing temporary balance of payment problems, and facilitates global trade, while leaving sovereign governments in charge of their own monetary, fiscal, and international investment policies. After the IMF and prominent economists everywhere held up these countries as models of successful development, these groups suddenly denounced them for their lack of transparency, poor accounting standards and crony capitalism.[64] According to economist Walden Bello, "The IMF helped bring about the crisis by pushing the Asian countries to eliminate capital controls and liberalize their financial sectors, promoting both the massive entry of speculative capital as well as its destabilizing exit at the slightest sign of crisis. The Fund [IMF] then pushed governments to cut expenditures,…when it should have been pushing for greater government spending to counteract the collapse of the private sector."[65]

The IMF's rescue plan imposed harsh conditions on the crisis-hit countries. It demanded that these countries enforce austerity measures and allow foreign investors to buy up their businesses at depressed stock prices. The IMF did not intend to rescue the collapsing economies, but to compensate foreign financial institutions for their losses – a development that has become a textbook example of "**moral hazard**," or the encouragement of irresponsible behavior. The other part of the story was that the IMF insisted that these countries repay their debts. The only way they could do so was to export like crazy. The plunge in the value of their currencies, most significantly against the dollar, opened up this route of recovery to the Asian countries. The result was that goods from the region became very cheap to American consumers, yielding a flood of imports to the United States and Europe.[66]

Reckless lending may have played a major part in the crisis, but the governments of the crisis countries were not entirely blameless. In Thailand, **crony capitalism** based on murky political connections between government and business had led to widespread misuse of the money borrowed from abroad and moral hazard for lenders.[67] All told, the crisis wiped out $7 trillion in investor wealth and contributed to the U.S. recession of 2001.[68]

Thailand paid off its IMF debt in 2003. Along with Brazil, Venezuela, Argentina, and Indonesia, they declared their "financial independence" from the IMF. Other countries likewise decided to stay away from IMF lending, preferring to build up their foreign exchange reserves to defend themselves against external developments rather than contract new IMF loans. This was one of the reasons for the IMF's budget crisis over the last few years, for most of its income came from debt payments made by the larger developing countries.[69]

> **Questions to Consider**
>
> 1. How did the policies of the International Monetary Fund (IMF) and the U.S. Treasury Department contribute to the East Asian financial crisis?
> 2. How do these policies affect your daily life?

The Argentine Financial Crisis (1999-2001)

The **Argentine economic crisis** was a financial situation that affected Argentina's economy during the late 1990s and early 2000s. Technically, the critical period ran from 1999 and ended in 2002, but the origins of the collapse of Argentina's economy can be found in actions before, and the aftermath continued into the 2000s.

In 1991, after a bout of hyper inflation that plagued the country in the 1980s, Argentina pegged its currency to the dollar at a rate of one peso to one dollar. Any citizen could go to a bank and convert any amount of domestic currency to dollars. To secure this exchange the Central Bank of Argentina had to keep its U.S. dollar foreign exchange reserves at the same level as the cash in circulation. The initial aim of such measures was to ensure the acceptance of domestic currency, since during the peaks of hyperinflation in 1989-1990 business people had started to reject the peso as payment demanding U.S. dollars instead. Bello claimed that the peso-dollar convertibility effectively meant that Argentina "voluntarily gave up any meaningful control over the domestic impact of a volatile global economy. This system tied the quantity of pesos in circulation to the quantity of in-coming dollars. This policy effectively handed over control of Argentina's monetary policy to the U.S. Federal Reserve. This was, effectively, the dollarization of the country's currency."[70] As a result of the convertibility law, inflation dropped sharply and prices stabilized.

Bello and others argue that Argentina's financial crisis stemmed from its faithfulness to neoliberalism. Argentina had been the poster child of neoliberalism, Latin-style. It brought down its trade barriers faster than most other countries in Latin America and opened up its economy to overseas financial investment more drastically. It followed a privatization program involving the sale of 400 state enterprises − including airlines, oil companies, steel, insurance, telecommunications, postal services, and petrochemicals − about 7 percent of the nation's annual domestic product.[71] The U.S. Treasury Department and the IMF either urged or approved of all of these measures.

Despite this adherence to neoliberal principles, Argentina still had external debts to pay, and it needed to keep borrowing money. As the dollar rose in value, so did the peso. This caused Argentine-made exports to become expensive both globally and locally, while the fixed exchange rate made imports cheap. This resulted in a constant flight of pesos away from the country and a loss of Argentine industries, which contributed to an increase in unemployment. Raising tariff barriers against imports was not an option, owing to Argentina's commitment to the neoliberal tenet of free trade. The influx of foreign currency following the privatization of state companies in the 1990s had dried up by the end of the decade. Argentina spiraled into debt. They borrowed heavily from the IMF to finance the widening trade gap during the 1990s, but the country showed no true signs of being able to repay the debt. The IMF, however, kept lending money to Argentina and postponing its debt payment schedules. The more it borrowed, the higher the interest rates rose as international creditors grew more alarmed about Argentina's economic situation. Money began leaving the country. Banks desperately needed capital for lending, but foreign control of the banks controlled the outflow of much-needed capital; thus they were unable to lend to Argentineans.[72]

The crisis unfolded with lightening speed in late 2001. The crisis forced Argentina to go to the IMF once again for money to service its mounting debt. After repeatedly providing loans, the IMF refused this time. The government defaulted on its $100 billion debt. Argentines lost confidence in their financial system and staged a run on banks. The crisis forced the government to severely restrict cash withdrawals and transfers of money out of the country. The cash economy, upon which lower-wage workers such as maids and taxi drivers depended, ground to a halt. Businesses collapsed, people lost their jobs, and capital left the country. Riots broke out in the streets of the capital, Buenos Aires, 27 people were killed. Unable to provide the U.S. dollars needed to back bank deposits, the government announced an end to the currency peg, and the peso collapsed, causing many Argentines to lose large portions of their savings. Left to float freely on the market, the peso eventually fell about two thirds in value, while GDP plunged 11 percent in 2002 and unemployment hit 25 percent.[73]

DEPOSITORS PROTEST THE FREEZING OF THEIR ACCOUNTS. THEIR MOSTLY DOLLAR-DENOMINATED ACCOUNTS WERE CONVERTED TO PESOS AT LESS THAN HALF THEIR NEW VALUE, BUENOS AIRES, ARGENTINA

Riots and other forms of citizen unrest toppled one president and government after another. President Nestor Kirchner inherited a bankrupt country upon his election as Argentine president in 2003. The economy was in a depression, and the crisis pushed 53 percent of Argentines below the poverty line. What was once the richest country in Latin America in terms of per capita income plunged below that of Peru and parts of Central America. Kirchner saw the choice as putting the interests of the creditors first or prioritizing economic recovery. He offered to settle Argentina's debts with its creditors, but at a steep discount. He would write off 70-75 percent of the debt, repaying only 25-30 cents on the dollar. The bondholders, who lent Argentina money, screamed and demanded that the IMF do something to Kirchner. But he stood fast, and repeated his offer. He warned the bondholders that this was a one-time offer, and they had to accept the deal or lose the rights to any repayment. He told the creditors that he would not tax poverty-ridden Argentines to pay off the debt to the wealthy and invited them to visit his country's slums to "experience poverty first hand." Faced with his determination, the IMF stood by helplessly, while a majority of the bondholders angrily acquiesced and accepted his terms. In December 2005, Kirchner paid off the country's debt to the IMF in full and booted it out of Argentina.[74]

For over two decades, since the periphery countries' debt crisis in the early 1980s, developing country governments had considered defying the creditors. There had been a few quiet defaults on payments, but Kirchner was the first to publicly threaten the lenders with a unilateral **haircut** (reduction in repayment) and make good on his promise. The country also escaped its massive debts simply by renouncing them, waiting four years before negotiating partial repayment at a steep loss to creditors. Litigation continues to this day in courts around the world to recover portions of the sum, leaving Argentina effectively locked out of international credit markets. Creditors and the IMF feared that other countries might soon follow the example set by Argentina. Kirchner's actions contributed to the erosion of the credibility and power of the IMF in the middle of the 2000s and onward.[75]

Argentina did not collapse. Instead, it was not long before it staged a comeback. It grew by a remarkable 10 percent per year over the next four years fueled by its robust agriculture and manufacturing sectors and abundant natural resources. The weakened peso and a boom in world commodity prices fueled exports. The high price of soybeans in the international market produced an injection of foreign currency, with China becoming a major buyer. Many workers at collapsed businesses faced a sudden loss of employment and no source of income. Many decided to reopen businesses on their own, without the owners and their capital, as self-managed cooperatives. Former workers have now legally purchased some of their employers' businesses for nominal fees, while other businesses remain "occupied" by workers who have no legal standing with the state. The Argentine government is considering a Law of Expropriation that would transfer some occupied businesses to their worker-managers.[76]

A central reason for the high rate of growth was that the government reinvested its money in the national economy. It formerly relied on foreign institutions for investment funds. Kirchner's administration initiated a historic debt program to throw off what they perceived as the "shackles of neoliberalism."[77]

Questions to Consider

1. What did Argentinean President Kirchner mean when he said he was throwing off the "shackles of neoliberalism?" Do you agree or disagree with this statement?

CONCLUDING INSIGHTS: FINANCIAL CRISES

In this concluding insight section, let's go back to the quote at the beginning of the chapter by Nouriel Roubini: "Contrary to conventional wisdom, crises are not black swans but white swans: the elements of boom and bust are remarkably predictable." Do you think the financial crisis of 2007-2008 was a black or white swan event? Some supporters of neoliberalism were quick to point out that the financial crisis was a black swan event – no one saw it coming they claimed. Many cried that it took most of those in the financial sector by a complete surprise. But from our brief look at several financial crises through history – from 17th century Netherlands and the bubble in tulip bulbs to the late 1920s stock market in the U.S. to the 1990s and real estate in Bangkok, Thailand – the crises repeat the 10 patterns again and again. These patterns are predictable and emerge so clearly that financial crises can be none other than white swan events. It is only our human emotions that step in the way of rational thinking and claim that this bubble is not like the others, "this time is different."

Questions to Consider

1. Do you think the financial crisis of 2007-2008 was a black or white swan event?

CHAPTER THREE

Ten Fatal Flaws in the Financial Sector: Part I

"I don't think this is just a financial panic; I believe that it represents the failure of a whole model of banking, of an overgrown financial sector that did more harm than good."

Paul Krugman, "The Market Mystique," NewYorkTimes, March 26, 2009

UNCOVERING FLAWS IN THE FINANCIAL SECTOR

According to my estimation, there are fundamental flaws in today's financial system. The 2008 financial crisis and Great Recession revealed that in a big way. Too many people think of the reason for the crisis as excessive greed exhibited by bankers. They did act greedily, but be wary of overly simplistic explanations for the crisis. It was not the result of just greed alone. Bankers acted greedily because the crisis gave them incentives and opportunities to do so. Some neoliberals say it was a mere blip on the road to continuous world economic growth. In fact, many argue that the crisis was a result of too much government interference in the economy instead of not enough. Neoliberals figure that if Americans had a more competitive work ethic and more cutting-edge skills, high unemployment rates would decline. Single answer explanations, although they make good headlines, are not going to get us to the understanding we need about the complicated financial crisis that sent shockwaves rippling through our global economy.

Uncovering the flaws in the financial system is like peeling back an onion. Each explanation gives rise to further questions at a deeper level. For example, growth in the U.S. economy was not sustainable in the 2000s; government, business, and consumers built the economy on a mountain of debt. Government bailouts rescued banks from their lending practice follies – not only in the U.S. but also in Ireland, Greece, Thailand, Korea, Indonesia, Mexico, Brazil, Argentina, and Russia; the list is almost endless. Governments repeatedly have the thankless task of saving financial markets from their own mistakes. Those who concluded that all was well with the global economy made the wrong inference, but the error only became obvious when a crisis so large that everyone could not ignore it occurred in the U.S.[1]

This crisis was different from others in the last 30 plus years – it was in the U.S. Most Americans like to think of their country as an engine of global economic growth, an exporter of sound economic policies – not recessions and bailouts.[2] Yet, that is exactly what happened. There are multiple reasons why the financial system has performed so badly in the last 30 years and in the 2000s, in particular. I have organized these reasons into what I call 10 fatal flaws in the financial sector. Once again, these flaws are all interconnected and hard to separate out for analysis. However, it is much easier to look at these flaws separately with the understanding that all these flaws are part of a system – the financial system. We need to look at these flaws in depth if solutions are to be constructed.

These 10 fatal flaws in the financial sector I see as the most egregious, and have a negative impact on 90 percent of all Americans, as well as the world. These are not all the flaws that I could have listed, but organizing them into these categories should give at least a basic understanding of what conditions contributed to the 2008 financial crisis and are still around today. I will be using the United States as the platform for how these 10 fatal flaws have played

Ten Fatal Flaws in the Financial Sector

Fatal Flaw #1.	Too Big to Fail Banks (TBTF)
Fatal Flaw #2.	Unchecked Deregulation
Fatal Flaw #3.	A "Markets Know Best" Federal Reserve
Fatal Flaw #4.	A Real Estate Bubble and Out of Control Lending
Fatal Flaw #5.	Dicey Financial Products
Fatal Flaw #6.	Financial Speculative Mania
Fatal Flaw #7.	Moral Hazard and Lack of Transparency
Fatal Flaw #8.	Deceptive Rating Agencies
Fatal Flaw #9.	Bloated Compensation Plans

out. However, readers from other countries should be mindful that these flaws are also present in many countries, especially those ascribing to neoliberal principles, including Europe. System thinking principles are helpful when examining and evaluating the 10 fatal flaws: all of the parts or flaws interact and influence each other.

Questions to Consider

1. What 10 benefits of the financial sector would you list?

FATAL FLAW #1: TOO BIG TO FAIL BANKS (TBTF)

I would bet that almost 100 percent of you have some type of bank account. It seems a necessity in our high-tech cashless society. We have our organization's checking account at a credit union in Albuquerque, New Mexico. I like the idea that they are a nonprofit credit-union that helps its members with loans and low-cost checking. But it is big and has many branches. No one knows my name, and tellers always ask for my identification when I make a transaction. From the late 1970s through the 1980s, I banked at Dewey State Bank, in Dewey, Illinois. It was a small, "no-frills" bank in a farming community, aptly adjoining the local grain elevator. Everyone knew everyone else. In fact, I would call, and employees would recognize my voice and instantly know who was calling. When I did business at the bank, the president would come out of his office to say hello and personally give a treat to my toddler daughter. His wife, whose family started the bank in the early 20th century, was my son's English teacher. The bank's claim to fame was that it survived the Great Depression. Indeed, it has even survived the banking mergers of the last 30 years and recently celebrated its 100th anniversary. But Dewey State Bank is an anomaly; it is far from typical of the banking industry today.

At the heart of it, banking is a simple business. Before the arrival of modern innovations in finance, lenders lived in a straightforward world. There was a running joke in the past that tells a lot about how banks operated: it was according to the 3-6-3 rule. Bankers paid their depositors 3 percent interest, lent it out at 6 percent, and lined up to tee off at the golf course by 3 p.m. Customers deposit money in a bank in return for interest; the bank lends that money to other people at a higher rate of interest. It wasn't glamorous, but it was a guaranteed way of making steady money and creating credit in the economy. However, this depended upon banks following one all-important rule: they had to be careful to whom they lent money. The quality of the loans was crucial, because those loans were the bank's earning assets. Bankers and banking were boring. That's exactly what the people who entrusted their money to them wanted. Ordinary citizens didn't want someone to take their money and gamble with it. They didn't want the CEO of their bank to have a yacht and five lavish houses around the world.[3] They wanted CEOs to serve the needs of the community.

At the core of it, banking is essentially creating more money by loaning it out. If you have a bank and your clients deposit $100 with you, your money supply can double by simply loaning it to someone else. Maybe the person who borrowed it spends part of it and leaves the rest in his/her own bank account, which the bank loans to someone else, and so the process goes. An initial sum of currency can be "grown" into a much bigger money supply. The banking system takes money in excess of its reserve requirements and creates new money by loaning it out.[4] Banks take in deposits and invest the money in a variety of assets, from ordinary loans to complex derivative deals. They make their money on the spreads, or the difference in what interest they pay depositors and the interest they loan to borrowers.

There are basically two types of banks: investment banks and commercial banks. **Investment banks** issue bonds and shares of stock, issue other complex financial instruments, trade on capital markets, and put together mergers and acquisitions. **Commercial banks** lend out the money deposited in them. The two types of banks have cleverly been called the piggy bank and the casino; the piggy banks are the commercial banks, and the investment banks are the casinos. Investment banks issue stocks, and if a company whose stock they have issued needs cash, it becomes very tempting to make a loan, which can create a problem. If the casino activities of the investment banks get out of hand, the bankers can endanger the piggy bank deposits of the general public. This is just what happened during the 1920s, which contributed to the stock market crash of 1929 and the ensuing Great Depression. This catastrophe resulted in the passage of the Glass-Steagall Act during the depths of the Great Depression in 1933, which forced retail banks to split from investment banks. The Glass-Steagall Act addressed a very real problem and was successful in regulating the banking system for almost 70 years.[5]

As part of the Glass-Steagall Act, the government stepped in and set up the Federal Deposit Insurance Corporation (FDIC) to insure deposits. During the Depression, depositors were fearful that banks would close, and all their hard-earned savings would be lost. With the FDIC people would feel that the government protected their money, even if there were rumors that a bank was facing difficulties. Once the government provided this insurance, it had to make sure that banks did not take undue risks with depositors' savings. To make sure that the banks didn't speculate in the marketplace and lose money knowing the government would then have to pick up the tab, the government regulated the banks, ensuring that they did not undertake excessive risk.

Several different policies and procedures monitored the banks for excessive risk-taking. For example, in the post-war years, banks required homebuyers to have a 20 percent down payment before they could purchase a house. The bank would then loan the borrower 80 percent of the value of the house they were purchasing. An independent appraiser hired by the bank provided an evaluation of the house's value by comparing it to similar houses that recently sold in the neighborhood. The likelihood that an 80 percent mortgage would wind up exceeding the value of the house was very small – prices would have to drop by 20 percent, which was highly unlikely (until recently). Bankers understood rightly that a mortgage that was "**underwater**" (a mortgage that is more than the house is worth) had a large risk of nonpayment. Usually, the worst that could happen was that the borrower lost his/her house. The system worked pretty well. The reality that homeowners usually had to put up 20 percent of a home's value to get a loan dampened their aspirations for a home beyond their financial means.

FDIC SEAL, FOUNDED IN 1933.

Previously, regulated banking provided an important check on U.S. corporate activity. By carefully monitoring a corporation's loan portfolio, banks helped prevent bankruptcies and excesses in the business world.[6] Accountants, rating agencies, and other agencies also had a system of checks and balances, much like our three branches of government – by which each monitored the other's activities and reduced risk.

When the U.S. and global economy started to phase in neoliberal ideas in the 1980s, things began to change. Some in the banking industry complained they were feeling constrained by what they perceived were excessive regulations of their industry and wanted to earn higher profits. The Reagan administration in the 1980s enthusiastically responded to the domestic banking industry's desire to remove regulations on its operations and expand worldwide. As part of the Uruguay Round (1986-1994) of international trade talks, the pro-bank forces came up with a nontraditional area for trade: financial services. The idea was that the government should give banks free rein globally and that foreign-owned banks operating outside their home countries should enjoy exactly the same rights and privileges as domestic ones. This was part of the broader agenda of what is called "**liberalizing**" the international financial sector from all kinds of national regulations.[7]

As the government loosened regulations and the culture of banking changed, bankers began to look for new ways to generate profits. They found the answer in a simple word: fees. For example, when consumers make purchases with credit cards, approximately two cents of each dollar goes not to the retailer but to the credit card companies that run the payment network and the banks which supply the credit for such cards branded Visa and MasterCard. These "interchange fees" bring in over $35 billion in profit to the credit card companies in the U.S. alone, and they reflect the strong market power of the banks and credit card companies over the various big and small retailers. The 2 percent charge comes to about $31,000 for a typical convenience store, just below the average per-store yearly profit of $36,000.[8] Visa has about 50 percent of the debit-credit card market, and MasterCard has 25 percent, which grants them strong bargaining positions. The U.S. has the highest interchange fees in the world. The *Wall Street Journal's* description was that "these fees...have been paradoxically tending upward in recent years when the industry's costs due to technology and economies of scale have been falling."[9]

Since the early 2000s, the market share of the five largest banks grew from 8 percent in 1995 to 30 percent today.[10] Exemplifying the concentration of wealth and power in a few banks is the trade in derivatives (more on derivatives later). There are 1,030 commercial banks in the U.S. that trade derivatives but five banks – JP Morgan Chase, Citigroup, Goldman Sachs, Bank of America and Wells Fargo – control 97 percent of all the derivative trades. These five banks hold assets of more than 60 percent of U.S. gross domestic product (GDP): $8.6 trillion. According to radio host and au-

BANK OF AMERICA CORPORATE CENTER, LOCATED IN THE HEART OF CHARLOTTE, NORTH CAROLINA. IT IS THE 2ND LARGEST BANK HOLDING COMPANY IN THE U.S. BY ASSETS AND 5TH LARGEST COMPANY IN THE U.S.

thor Thom Hartman, "That's not just too big to fail, that's monopoly capitalism and monopolies like this lock out competition and destroy markets."[11]

"Shadow" banks are another dimension of the banking industry. **Shadow banks** are financial institutions that lend money to people just like traditional banks do. The difference between the two is that in a traditional bank, money comes from depositors, while in a shadow banking system the money comes from investors, who want to invest to earn a return on their money. Also, the government regulates traditional banks and it does not regulate the shadow banking system. The investors in shadow banking are corporations, investment banks, and money market funds, and the borrowers are financial firms. Shadow banking institutions are typically intermediaries between investors and borrowers.[12] For example, an investor – like a pension fund – may have a stash of money sitting idly in an account and be willing to lend that money for a certain rate of interest, while a corporation may be searching for funds to borrow. The shadow banking institution will channel funds from the investor, the pension fund in this case, to the borrower, the corporation, profiting either from fees or from the spread, the difference in interest rates between what it pays the investor and what it receives from the borrower. Shadow banking comes in all shapes and sizes: nonbank mortgage lenders, structured investment vehicles, conduits, commercial paper, hedge funds, "repos," or repurchase agreements, money market funds, private equity funds, and others.[13] The volume of transactions in the shadow banking system grew dramatically after the year 2000. By late 2007, the size of shadow banking in the U.S. exceeded $10 trillion. By late 2009, as a result of the financial crisis, the number had shrunk to under $6 trillion.[14]

The shadow banking system was at the heart of the financial crisis. One of the reasons for this is that traditional banks are subject to government regulation and can, if need be, borrow from the Federal Reserve as a "lender of last resort." Shadow banks do not have access to the Fed's "discount window," or the authority to borrow from the government. Therefore, when the financial crisis hit, the lending and borrowing done in the shadow banking system froze, and the demand for money exceeded the supply. For example, the investment bank Lehman Brothers in September 2008, was unable to borrow enough money from the shadow banking system to meet its short-term needs. Since the government didn't step in to save Lehman Brothers with emergency loans, it went bankrupt.

The effective abandonment of regulatory principles since the 1980s has resulted in a remarkable monopolistic concentration of the banking sector. For example, the Fed kept approving financial mergers that created even bigger banks in the midst of the 2008 crisis. The first was JP Morgan Chase's acquisition of Bear Stearns in March 2008 for $1.2 billion, followed by Bank of America's September 2008 purchase of Merrill Lynch, initially valued at $50 billion, JP Morgan Chase acquired Washington Mutual for $1.9 billion in September 2008, and Wells Fargo bought Wachovia in a $12.7 billion deal announced in October 2008.[15] The megabanks achieved too-big-to-fail status on steroids. According to economic journalist Robert Weissman, "While this should have meant they be treated as public utilities requiring heightened regulation and risk control, the deregulatory frenzy of the time enabled them to combine size, and reckless high-risk investments."[16]

The financial sector is among the highest-contributing industries to U.S. political candidates, with total 2008 campaign contributions, according to the Center For Public Integrity, approaching half a billion dollars. This industry uses its deep pockets to fund electoral campaigns and congressional lobbying in order to influence public policies that benefit it. Banking institutions receive many favors from the government representatives; since many personnel from the financial industry go on to serve in key governmental posts. For example, one of the most powerful investment banks, Gold-

man Sachs, has had two of its former CEOs go on to become Secretary of the Treasury: Robert Rubin (1993-1999) under the Bill Clinton administration and Henry "Hank" Paulson (2006-2009) under the George W. Bush administration. This is why the influential Senator Dick Durbin from Illinois said of Congress, "The banks own the place."[17]

Questions to Consider

1. What did Senator Dick Durbin from Illinois mean when he said of Congress, "The banks own the place?" Do you agree or disagree with him?
2. Why do the banks need to "own" Congress in the first place?

FATAL FLAW #2: UNCHECKED DEREGULATION

Deregulation is the removal or simplification of government rules and regulations that manage market forces. It does not mean elimination of laws against fraud, but rather eliminating or reducing government regulations on how business conducts its affairs, thereby, moving toward a neoliberal form of capitalism. According to neoliberals, the rationale for deregulation is that fewer and simpler regulations will lead to a higher level of competitiveness and productivity, more efficiency, lower overall prices, and increased growth rates. To those advocating for managed capitalism, deregulation is necessary to rein in the excesses of market forces that cause disproportionate concentration of wealth and less prosperity for the vast majority of a nation's citizens. Neoliberals have carried out a well-orchestrated deregulation campaign in many sectors of the economy since the 1980s; however, in this section, I will only mention a few of the many acts passed by the federal government to deregulate the financial sector.

WELLS FARGO CENTER IN MINNEAPOLIS, MINNESOTA, USA. ONE OF MANY LARGE BUILDINGS OCCUPIED BY WELLS FARGO THROUGHOUT THE U.S. IT IS THE FOURTH LARGEST BANK IN THE U.S. BY ASSETS AND THE LARGEST BANK BY MARKET CAPITALIZATION IN 2011.

Before the 1980s, as mentioned in the previous section, American commercial banking was a small-scale affair. State-chartered banks were prohibited by state laws from running branches outside their home state or sometimes even outside their home county. Nationally chartered banks were likewise limited, and federal law allowed interstate acquisitions only if a state legislature specifically decided to permit out-of-state banks to purchase local branches. No states allowed such acquisitions until 1975, when Maine and other states began passing legislation allowing some interstate banking. The passage in 1994 of the **Riegle-Neal Act** capped the trend; the act removed the remaining restrictions on interstate banking and allowed direct, cross-state banking mergers. This geographic deregulation allowed commercial banks to make extensive acquisitions, in-state and out. When Wells Fargo acquired another large California bank, Crocker National, in 1986, up to that time it was the largest bank merger in U.S. history. Since "the regulatory light was green," a single banking company could now operate across the large U.S. market.[18]

In the 1990s, the efforts of the banking lobby to deregulate the financial sector even more were finally beginning to pay off for them. Banks saw the potential for earning huge profits. Drawing upon the philosophy of free market competition, banks lobbied for the removal of what they considered to be "barriers" keeping American banks, investment banks, and insurance companies from merging – as their European counterparts were able to do. They argued that too much regulation had kept the U.S. banking system from reaching its full, globally-competitive potential. President Clinton's Treasury Secretary, Robert Rubin, led the refrain that Congress should repeal the Glass-Steagall Act. In 1995, he pleaded that without the repeal of Glass-Steagall, the U.S. was destined to lose out in the global marketplace. He stoked an already illusory fear that if the U.S. banking industry didn't have the same opportunities and structure as existed abroad, banks would move their most profitable businesses across the ocean.[19] The banks won.

The hyper-competition that arose between key industry players in the late 1990s further spurred merger mania. Mergers and acquisitions between banks became an increasingly high-stakes game of one-upmanship. Chemical and Chase Banks merged in 1995 in a deal worth 1.4 times their book value. The banking landscape was fast becoming a competitive game between a handful of very large banks. Among the teams in the financial big leagues were Citigroup, JPMorgan Chase, Bank of America, Washington Mutual, and Wachovia, which in October 2006 acquired Golden West Financial Corporation for $26 billion.[20] In 1998, the financial industry put Glass-Steagall Act to the test when Citibank chairman Sandy Weill orchestrated the merger of his bank with Travelers Insurance, Primerica, a financial products firm, and the investment banking giant Salomon Smith Barney. The merger was openly illegal, but it had the implicit backing of Fed Chairman Alan Greenspan and Rubin. According to journalist Matt Taibbi, it was a "dangerous concentration of capital in the hands of a single megacompany."[21] But the financial sector saw it as a blessing.

INTERIOR OF CHEMICAL BANK, (NYC) 1824-1996, ACQUIRED CHASE MANHATTAN BANK IN 1996 AND ASSUMED THE CHASE NAME, NOW THE CORE OF JP MORGAN CHASE.

November 12, 1999 marked the final death blow to the 66 year-old Glass-Steagall Act, which separated commercial banks (which lend money) and investment banks (which organize the sale of bonds and equities). Glass-Steagall, which contributed to banking stability and economic prosperity for decades, was now history. The new act, the **Gramm, Leach, Biley Act** or the **Financial Services Modernization Act**, was the culmination of the banking and financial-services industries' years-long massive lobbying campaign to reduce regulation in their sector. Banks could now offer investment, commercial banking, and insurance services all under one roof. The result was the infusion of the investment bank speculative culture into the world of commercial banking. With the repeal of Glass-Steagall, the conditions were ripe for banks to invest monies from checking and savings accounts into high-flying financial instruments, such as mortgage-backed securities. These investment gambles led many of the banks to ruin and rocked the financial markets in 2008. The consequences of the repeal of Glass-Steagall were not readily apparent at the time but would come to light a few short years later as corporate and banking scandals emerged.[22] Yet another bill to further deregulate the financial sector was just around the corner.

The passage of the Commodity Future's Modernization Act of 2000 granted the financial sector another blessing. The high angel of dispensing blessings to the financial sector was Senator Phil Gramm from Texas. As chairman of the U.S. Senate Committee on Banking between 1995 and 2000, he was not content with just the passage of his landmark Gramm-Leach-Bliley Act in 1999 (deregulated banks). A director in the Commodity Futures Trading Commission told the following eerie scenario about the passage of the act to author David Faber in an interview.

Financial Services Modernization Act[23]

It was Friday night, December 15, 2000. The Presidential and Congressional elections had taken place. Congress was going off for the Christmas recess and ending that Congressional session. They had before them an 11,000-page Omnibus Appropriation Bill to fund the entire federal government for fiscal year 2001. Senator Gramm walks to the floor that night and puts a floor rider (addition) on it, a 262-page bill called The Commodity Futures Modernization Act of 2000. This Act further deregulates the market. I don't believe anyone in Congress besides Senator Gramm, and sometimes I wonder whether even Senator Gramm, understood what they were doing. No hand in Congress wrote this piece of legislation. Wall Street wrote it. And six ways from Sunday, it deregulated these markets, not only from federal oversight, but from state oversight as well. President Clinton quietly signed the controversial act of important consequences into law on December 21, 2000.

The **Commodities Futures Modernization Act** of 2000 officially marked the deregulation of financial products known as over-the-counter derivatives that would be at the heart of the financial crisis of 2008. The bill was not without its critics. One in particular stands out as a future seer of the problems that an unregulated derivative market could unleash: Brooksley Borne. From 1996-1999 she headed the Commodity Futures Trading Commission (CFTC) under President Clinton's administration. She saw the potential dangers of unregulated financial markets and sought to exert regulatory control over them. But fierce opposition from Treasury Secretary Robert Rubin and Fed Chair Alan Greenspan, who aggressively pushed for a more deregulatory approach, quashed her efforts. With Borne out of the way, the scene was now set for the use of financial derivatives in many types of

BROOKSLEY BORNE, HEAD OF COMMODITIES FUTURE TRADING COMMISSION 1996-1999. SHE WARNED OF THE DERIVATIVES MARKET.

financial products (see flaw #6).[24] The act not only prevented the federal government from regulating risky financial instruments, it even prevented the states from regulating them using gaming laws – which otherwise might easily have applied, since so many of these new financial wagers were the same as racetrack bets.[25]

Senator Phil Gramm of Texas

Senator Gramm, the orchestra leader of deregulating the financial sector, went on from his service as senator to be the senior economic adviser to Republican John McCain's failed presidential campaign from the summer of 2007 until July 18, 2008. His tenure as economic advisor ended abruptly due to his remarks in a revealing July 9, 2008 interview on McCain's economic plans. Although the signs of a recession were all around, Gramm emphatically stated the nation was not in a recession. He explained, "You've heard of mental depression; this is a mental recession." He added, "We have sort of become a nation of whiners, you just hear this constant whining, complaining about a loss of competitiveness, America in decline." Gramm's comments immediately became a campaign issue, forcing McCain to fire him. McCain's opponent, Senator Barack Obama, cleverly replied on the campaign trail, "America already has one Dr. Phil (TV talk show personality). We don't need another one when it comes to the economy. ... This economic downturn is not in your head."[26] Retiring from the Senate in 2009, at the time of this writing, UBS AG, a Swiss global financial services company headquartered in Switzerland, employed Gramm as a Vice Chairman of the Investment Bank division.

When deregulation allowed investment and commercial banks to merge together, the investment banking culture came out on top. There was a high demand for the kind of high returns that investors could gain only through high leverage and big risk-taking deals. There was another consequence of deregulation: a more concentrated and less competitive banking system that ever larger banks dominated. One of the hallmarks of America's banking system in the past had been the high level of competition, with a myriad of banks serving different communities and different niches in the market. This is no longer the case.

In 1975, the Securities and Exchange Commission (SEC) passed a rule requiring investment banks to maintain a debt to-net capital ratio of 15 to 1 or less. In simpler terms, this meant that for every $15 borrowed, the bank had to have $1 in deposits to cover potential losses. This limited the amount of borrowed money the investment banks could use to lend out or for investments. In 2004, amidst the deregulation frenzy, the SEC succumbed to a push from the big investment banks – led by Goldman Sachs, and its then-chair, Henry Paulson (who would later become Treasury Secretary)

ALAN GREENSPAN, (CENTER), ROBERT RUBIN (LEFT), AND LARRY SUMMERS (RIGHT) ALL OPPOSED BORNE'S REFORM AGENDA. THEY LANDED ON THE COVER OF TIME MAGAZINE IN FEBRUARY 1999. (COVER CREDIT: MICHAEL O'NEILL)

– and authorized investment banks to have net capital requirements based on their own risk assessment models. With this new autonomy, as expected, investment banks pushed ratios to as high as 40 to 1. This meant that a bank only had to have $1 in bank reserves for every $40 they borrowed. This high debt to capital ratio used by many investment banks made them more vulnerable when the housing bubble finally popped.[27]

Even in a deregulated environment, the banking regulators still had authority to rein in predatory lending abuses. Such enforcement activity would have protected homeowners and lessened, though not prevented, the financial crisis. But the regulators sat on their hands. The Federal Reserve took only three formal actions against subprime lenders from 2002 to 2007. The Office of Comptroller of the Currency, which has authority over almost 1,800 banks, only took three consumer-protection enforcement actions from 2004 to 2006.[28] Even among regulators, deregulation was the watchword of the day.

Wall Street's capacity to turn out more and more sophisticated financial instruments ran ahead of government's regulatory will. This was not because government was incapable of regulating, but the dominant neoliberal deregulatory ideology blinded the government to regulatory action. The idea that deregulation of the marketplace was the best way and only way to create wealth was golden. Wall Street people believed that the marketplace would regulate itself, outside governmental agencies were a hindrance and merely got in the way.[29] As the pattern of speculation, systemic risk, and costly bailouts kept repeating itself in the late 1990s and 2000s, it might seem as though regulators and legislators would have learned a valuable lesson: deregulation was not working. But so much money was at stake that the political elite either cheered on the whole affair or looked the other way.[30]

Questions to Consider

1. What group/s do you think benefit the most from financial deregulation? Explain.
2. What group/s do not benefit from financial deregulation? Explain

---

FATAL FLAW #3:
A "MARKETS KNOW BEST" FEDERAL RESERVE

We like to think of money as something tangible – a fist full of dollars means you've got money to spend. It seems strange, then, to think of money in the U.S. as simply debts of the Federal Reserve that are in circulation, and checks written as debts of banking institutions. The **Federal Reserve** (the Fed) is the **central bank** of the U.S. and it consists of a Board of Governors and 12 Federal Reserve Banks spread around the country. Although all 12 banks are supposedly equal, the New York Fed carries more clout. It's the Fed's job to oversee the American banking system and manage the money supply with the goal of promoting full employment, steady, healthy economic growth, and stable prices.[31] Since the U.S. is the world's largest and most influential economy, the Fed's policies and actions have worldwide impact. In the past, it was common for national economies to back up their currency with something of market value, most commonly gold or silver. Those days are gone. Today governments have to manage their money according to the level of economic activity they engage in at home and abroad, and that can be tricky.[32]

Functions of the Federal Reserve

1. **The Banker's Bank**
   This means the central banks do for local banks what local banks do for their customers. The Fed accepts deposits from and makes loans to its member banks. Under extreme conditions the Fed is a "banker of last resort," which means it will lend to local banks that are in serious financial trouble.

2. **Managing the Money Supply**
   They manage the country's money supply and keep the dollar stable. One way is to try to influence the supply and demand of currency. When the Fed decides it's time to stimulate the economy with more dollars, it buys government securities from member banks, which puts more money into the economy. When it is time to slow down the growth rate or keep inflation from getting out of hand, the Fed sells government securities to banks, which "soaks up" currency, thereby reducing the supply of money.

3. **Managing Interest Rates**
   The Fed tries to indirectly influence interest rates in the economy. It signals its interest-rate intention through the borrowing rates it charges member banks. The Fed charges this rate, plus interest, to bank clients. Private financial institutions do most of the lending, the largest of which are multinational corporations that deal with central banks, like the U.S. Fed, from many countries.[33]

THE MARRINER S. ECCLES FEDERAL RESERVE BOARD BUILDING IN WASHINGTON D.C

When I was a child I loved to play the game Monopoly. I coerced my grandmother to play the game with me for hours on end. I thought I was so smart, since I would usually win. I always imagined the Monopoly money as real money. I would wheel and deal until all the play money ended up in my stack, but the money actually had no intrinsic value, just as our currency today has no intrinsic value.

If our currency has no intrinsic value, what makes it more valuable than the Monopoly money I played with? A combination of three things gives value to money: its status as legal tender, its acceptability, and its scarcity. The dollar is the legal tender of the U.S. because the government says so. Acceptability – knowing that everyone will accept the money in exchange for goods and services – is vital. Scarcity means that because governments reserve the right to issue money, they have control over the supply.[34] It is very tempting to politicians to try and slide more money into circulation in an attempt to increase wealth and alleviate political problems. When the government expands the money supply in a haphazard way, the value of money decreases and inflation may occur. **Inflation** is when price levels rise and the value of money drops. When it occurs, to buy the same amount of goods and services requires more money than before. Moderate inflation isn't a real problem if incomes rise as well. In most of the world's economies, economists assume that there will be some inflation, usually 2 to 3 percent is well within an acceptable rate.[35] If inflation spirals out of control, it can wreak havoc on a nation's economy.

I visited Brazil in 1987, amidst one of its infamous inflationary spirals. Upon arriving we had time to look through the airport gift stores. In one of the stores, I spotted several moderately priced but unusual pieces of jewelry I thought would be ideal gifts to give to family and friends. I wanted to purchase them right away but decided against it since we hadn't even started our trip yet. I thought, "I will keep these in mind if I don't see anything better on the tour." Back at the airport after the tour, I decided to go back to the same store to pick up some of the jewelry items I liked so well two weeks earlier. To my surprise, the jewelry had practically doubled in price! Inflation was out of control. Resentful that prices had spiraled upward so fast, I decided to forgo my purchases.

There are tools with which the government can calibrate the American economy. Congress and the president focus on **fiscal policy**, which relates to decisions on spending and taxes, while the Fed enacts **monetary policy**, influencing the flow or availability of money and credit. "**Fine-tuning**" the economy is how people typically refer to the Fed's actions in raising or lowering interest rates. The Fed's principle tool is "printing" money, a process by which the Fed attempts to expand the economy by making cash available for lending by buying bank securities.[36] At the time of this writing, the Fed is not worried about inflation; it's worried that the economy is in an extended recession. In response, the Fed has set a low interest rate, at the time of this writing hovering just above 0 percent, and has flooded the economy with money, buying up short-term government debt. Where does it get the money? It creates it out of thin air. Money does grow on trees if it is the Fed tree. For example, the Fed effectively writes a check for $10 billion and gives it to the sellers of government debt. These sellers deposit the money they've received from the Fed in various banks. Now these banks can use it to make loans worth several times that amount. Money is suddenly more available, and as a consequence, credit is easier to obtain. More to the point, it's cheaper, too: the net effect of adding money to the economy is that interest rates will fall.[37]

On the other hand, if the Fed is worried about inflation and wants to keep the economy from over-expanding, often called overheating, it sells, for example, $10 billion worth of short-term government debt. By doing so, it effectively removes money from the banking system because the purchasers of the debt have to write checks drawn on their respective banks, which the Fed then cashes and keeps. The banking system and the larger economy are now out that $10 billion. Because banks use every dollar on deposit to create many more dollars' worth of loans, the real hit to the banking system – and by extension, the money supply – is something approaching $25 billion or $30 billion because of the way in which banks loan out money using leverage. In this way, the Fed has tightened the money supply and made credit harder to obtain: it has effectively raised the cost of borrowing. Money, like any other commodity, responds to the laws of supply and demand, and now that the supply is lower, borrowing money costs more. Interest rates go up because lenders can now command a higher rate.[38]

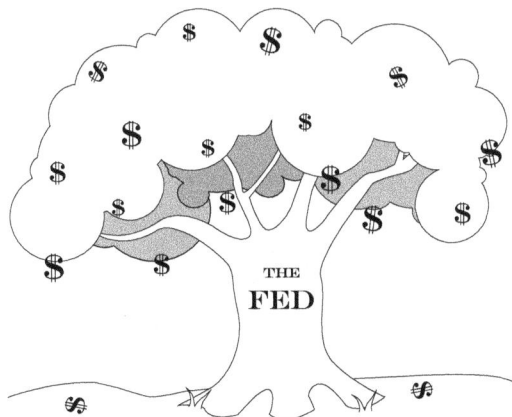

MONEY GROWING ON THE FED TREE.

At this point, you may think that the Federal Reserve is a good institution and wonder why I would consider it one of the flaws in the financial sector. I think it is a good institution, as well, but the reason I listed it as a flaw is because of the actions and philosophy of the Federal Reserve Chairman from 1987 to 2006:

Alan Greenspan. He articulated a libertarian ideology, which made him loath to use the powers of the government to regulate the market place. Instead, he thought the market knew best, better than the government or highly trained individuals. Therefore, from the beginning of his term he was ambivalent about government's role in regulating the financial industry, the very task the President appointed him to do. However, paradoxically, during his term he repeatedly abandoned his "markets know best" philosophy when it came time to bailing out banks and the financial sector, but he would follow his philosophy to the letter when it came time to prick a bubble or regulate financial speculation.

The sheriff riding-to-the rescue role of the Federal Reserve and the Treasury in bailing out financial institutions during the speculative 1980s and 1990s was the opposite of what deregulation was supposed to do – an ideology that purportedly disdained the need for government. Four months after Greenspan's appointment to chair the Federal Reserve in 1987, the stock market crashed, and he immediately donned his cowboy hat to ride to the rescue in the savings and loan debacle. Out the window went any principled opposition to government intervention in the economy.

Greenspan seemed to have had little interest in long-standing thinking that considered it best for the Fed to step in to prevent bubbles from forming in the first place. Cleverly summarizing this belief, former Fed chairman William McChesney Martin once said that the job of the central bank was "to take away the punch bowl just as the party gets going." Greenspan was unwilling to take the punch bowl away. In 1996, as the stock market spiraled into a giddy bubble focused on tech and Internet stocks, he warned of "irrational exuberance," then did next to nothing to stop the bubble from inflating. When the dot-com bubble finally popped in 2000, Greenspan poured plenty more alcohol into the metaphorical punch bowl, channeling more money into the economy, which ratcheted up the formation of another bubble: the housing bubble.[39]

Financiers believed that the Fed would always ride to the rescue of reckless traders who were ruined after a bubble collapsed. According to Roubini, "It created moral hazard on a grand scale, and Greenspan deserves blame for it. He also deserves blame for refusing to use the power of the Federal Reserve to regulate markets. For example, in 1994, Congress passed the **Home Ownership and Equity Protection Act** in order to crack down on predatory lending practices. Under its terms, Greenspan could have regulated subprime lending, but he refused to do so."[40] The earlier postwar decades prohibited the kinds of speculative activities that got the banks into trouble after the 1980s. For example, there was no such thing as currency speculation in an era of fixed exchange rates and capital controls. There was no such thing as Savings and Loan speculation in junk bonds, given that they were explicitly charted to make only mortgage loans and only in a local area.[41]

In 2001, the economy was on the verge of serious recession. The dot-com bubble had burst and 9/11 had spooked markets, resulting in their steep decline. Greenspan, who had encouraged deficit reduction under the Clinton administration, suddenly changed course. To him, deficits didn't matter anymore. The Fed took a "lose money" policy and supported a

THE PUNCH BOWL

stimulative budget based on large deficits. The need for cheap money was required to recapitalize banks still recovering from earlier bouts of speculative excess. Coupled with the convenient willingness of foreign central banks to keep lending the U.S. money to prevent the fragile economy from sinking into deflation and depression, the American economy was awash in money.[42] It was ripe for another speculative bubble.

The administration of George W. Bush (2001-2009) used the short recession following the collapse of the dot-com bubble as a reason to push its agenda of tax cuts, especially favoring the wealthy. Congress did not design the tax cuts to stimulate the economy and did so only to a limited extent. The burden of restoring the economy to full employment shifted from the federal government to the Fed's "lose money" monetary policy. Accordingly, Greenspan lowered interest rates, flooding the market with **liquidity** (money). With so much excess money in the economy, not surprisingly the lower interest rates did not lead to more investment in plants and equipment. Since money is always looking for higher rates of return, a housing bubble replaced the tech bubble. A consumption and real-estate boom followed.[43]

The deadly combination of very low interest rates, large deficits, and ever-increasing foreign borrowing kept the economy growing at acceptable rates in the years after the dot-com crash, but in the short term the high rates of growth disguised the economy's underlying weaknesses. In the years preceding the 2008 crisis, the Federal Reserve had kept interest rates low. Cheap money can lead to an investment boom in plants and equipment, strong growth, and sustained prosperity or a speculative bubble. In the U.S. and rest of the world, it led to a housing and speculative bubble. According to Stiglitz, "That's not the way the market is supposed to behave. Markets are supposed to allocate capital to its most productive use. But historically, there have been repeated instances of banks using other people's money to engage in excessive risk-taking and to lend to those who can't repay. It is one of the reasons for regulation."[44]

Greenspan kept up his "markets know best" philosophy, despite warning signs of an impending crisis. But the financial sector doesn't really want to accept the consequences when the "markets know best" policy plays out. They hate regulation of risky practices but depend on bailouts after the fact. It is the government that permits the current strategy of self-enrichment by ever riskier behavior to persist without producing a 1929 scale depression. The key player in this financial drama is the Federal Reserve.[45]

PRESIDENT GEORGE W. BUSH PRESENTS THE PRESIDENTIAL MEDAL OF FREEDOM TO ALAN GREENSPAN, ON NOVEMBER 9, 2005 IN THE WHITE HOUSE.

FATAL FLAW #4: A REAL ESTATE BUBBLE AND OUT OF CONTROL LENDING

As we can see from the three previous flaws, the ingredients for some type of bubble were mixing together. But what would be the asset darling of the newly forming bubble? The dot-com bubble had just burst, and tulip bulbs didn't seem to have a particular appeal at the time. Maybe real estate in Florida – now that sounded more appealing, especially since, unlike the 1920s, air-conditioning had been invented. Real estate had always proven to be a great bubble asset, so real estate it would be.

Do you or your parents own a house? Many Americans consider home ownership to be the American Dream. But not just any old house, a house with all the latest gadgets and decorating style. I recently watched a show on the HGTV channel where home buyers were searching for an upgraded house. As the youngish, affluent couple toured a spacious home overlooking a golf course, they were constantly pointing out the slightly dated decorating appointments. When they reached the kitchen, the woman impatiently tapped on the kitchen countertop and insisted, "These have got to go!"The real estate agent meekly protested that the sellers had just installed the countertops a few years ago. She quickly turned to confront him and admonished him for his outdated taste in countertop design. He deftly retracted his previous comments, and murmured that, indeed, she was the one in the know as far as countertops were concerned. The couple ended up buying the house, agreeing with each other that a substantial amount needed to be set aside for a "cosmetic house face-lift."

I tell this story because it reflects the attitude that was indispensable in creating a housing bubble. Americans love home ownership; it serves as a primary individual status symbol, as well as the largest financial investment. Americans were willing participants in buying and selling real estate that contributed to the bubble. Yet for many decades Americans have purchased homes according to the rigid lending standards set by mortgage lenders described in the banking section.

I remember when my family built our first home. I was taken in, like the couple on HGTV, with all the latest home appointments. I wanted them all. I especially had my sights set on the brushed nickel bathroom faucets, instead of just the plain polished nickel. They looked so elegant in the showroom. Yet, our budget would not allow another upgrade. I already went over budget with my decision to get the raised-panel oak cabinets built by the Amish in central Illinois, instead of the plain-faced cabinets they offered for the budget-minded shopper. Restraint was now in order. I grudgingly consented to purchasing the polished nickel faucets. After a few weeks in the house I forgot all about the texture of the bathroom faucets. Nor did my family or guests ever comment on their pedestrian look. In hindsight, I wondered why I had been so obsessed with wanting them.

Affluent homebuyers wanting to upgrade to houses that were beyond their means, however, did not solely create the real estate bubble. Many politicians attributed the high foreclosure rates to individuals simply buying too much house for their income, or in many cases, no income at all. In my case, even if I hadn't been able to finally exhibit some self-restraint in the cost of my first home, the lender would not have approved a loan that was more than our income would allow. But during the housing bubble years, checks and balances on the system were out the window; government had removed many regulations and regulators ignored many of the ones still remaining. It was a time of deregulation, and the market was supposed to restrain over-exuberance.

If it wasn't just individuals going house wild, what really made this housing bubble the worst in recorded memory? Using a systems ap-

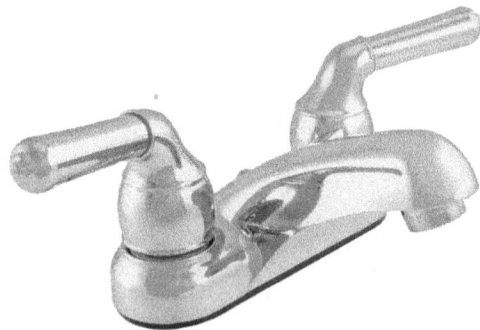

proach, there were many interconnected factors contributing to the housing bubble. Hopefully, this section will help sort out the run-up of house prices and the subsequent crash that contributed to our financial crisis and economic woes since 2008.

Several decades ago banks that made home loans followed the "originate and hold" model. A prospective homeowner would apply for a mortgage, and the bank would lend the money, then sit back and collect payments on the principal and interest. The bank that originated the mortgage held the mortgage; it was strictly a transaction between the homeowner and the bank.[46] If a borrower defaulted on his/her loan, the bank bore the consequences. If a borrower had trouble – say, he lost his job – the bank might help him along. Banks knew when it paid to extend credit and when it was necessary to foreclose – something they did not do lightly. Foreclosures were few and far between.

To understand real estate lending even further, let's look at two important financial institutions: Fannie Mae and Freddie Mac. In 1938, during the Great Depression, the government created **Fannie Mae (Federal National Mortgage Association)** and they gave it a mandate to buy mortgages from lenders, thereby freeing up capital in order that those lenders could extend more mortgages. With an initial budget of a billion dollars in capital, Fannie Mae modestly started to buy up mortgages. It eventually sold bonds to investors in order to raise more capital and buy more mortgages. The bonds were an easy sell to investors because people were sure that the government would pay them back since Fannie Mae was a government-sponsored entity (GSE). Even after it went public in 1968, it was able to raise capital cheaply. By 1982, Fannie Mae was funding one out of every seven mortgages made in the U.S.[47] By then it had company, a little brother. The government launched **Freddie Mac (Federal Home Loan Mortgage Corporation)** in 1970 to expand the secondary mortgage market. Well into the 1980s, Fannie Mae and Freddie Mac held most of the mortgages they bought.

Fannie Mae and Freddie Mac had strict rules about who they could lend money to and under what terms, even though they didn't lend directly to the public but to the financial institutions that actually own the mortgages. Mortgages which conformed to their rules were known as "**conforming loans.**" The mortgage lenders sandwiched in between Fannie and Freddie and the general borrowing public had even more rules. There were restrictions based on credit history, on the appraisal of the house, and so on. But this "**originate and hold**" model was beginning to change in the 1970s with a new scheme. Another institution with a cute name in the mortgage lending business was being born.

The Government National Mortgage Association (Ginnie Mae), another GSE, put together the first mortgage-backed securities. Ginnie Mae pooled the mortgages it had originated, issued them as bonds, and then sold these pools of bonds as a mortgage-backed security to investors on the open market. Rather than waiting 30 years to make back the proceeds from a mortgage, Ginnie Mae received a lump sum up front from the purchasers of the bond. Investors buying these new bonds received a certain portion of the revenue stream from the thousands of homeowners paying off their mortgages. This secondary mortgage market seemed like a win-win situation for everyone; it increased the supply of money available for mortgage lending for new home purchases, and it appeared to be a sound investment choice.[48]

Financiers dubbed this ground-breaking new process **securitization**. Now financiers could pool and convert **illiquid assets** – assets not easily or quickly converted into money – like mortgages –

into **liquid assets** – assets easily and quickly converted into money – that were tradable on the open market. Financers called these new financial instruments **mortgage-backed securities**, since the collateral behind the loans were home mortgages. In time, other GSEs like Freddie Mac and Fannie Mae joined the securitization business. Investment banks, brokerages, and even home builders jumped on the securitization band wagon to gobble up profitable pools of the growing numbers of home mortgages. Investors around the world snapped them up with the comforting knowledge that home prices never went down in the U.S. Though mortgage-backed securities were popular in the 1980s, it was not until the 1990s that they really took off. Now the mortgage model was "**originate and distribute**" rather than "originate and hold."[49]

The securitization method was a sound economic principle as long as the buyers of the securities could accurately assess the risk. But according to Roubini there lurked a fundamental flaw in the process, "(I)f you're a bank selling off newly minted mortgages via the securitization pipeline, your primary objective is to unload as many mortgages as quickly as possible. Each sale gives you more money with which to make more loans. Unfortunately, because the bank no longer faces the consequences of making bad loans, it has much less incentive to properly monitor the underlying risk of the mortgages it originates." With this process a bank is more likely to pass a bad mortgage along down the line like a hot potato.[50]

Those "nonconforming" loan customers that Fannie Mae shunned were another thorny issue in the real estate industry; they had no place to go for lending. This changed, too. It started with the **Community Reinvestment Act** in 1977, which Congress designed to encourage commercial banks and savings associations to help meet the needs of borrowers in all segments of their communities, including low-and moderate-income neighborhoods. A huge new market in nonconforming mortgages, which didn't fit Fannie and Freddie's strict borrowing criteria, grew. Mortgage lending to "underserved" communities was a principled policy in which lower-income, higher-risk groups – mostly minorities – were, because of government policy, given a chance to get mortgages. Although they still had to meet certain qualifications to get loans, the lending policy seemed to work. Mortgage

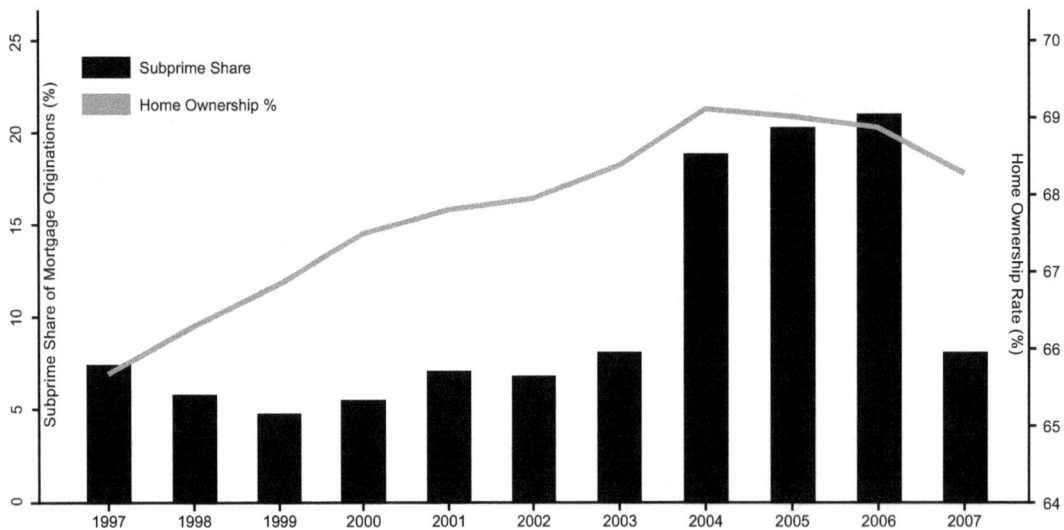

U.S. SUBPRIME LENDING EXPANDED SIGNIFICANTLY 2004 - 2006

lenders quickly realized that there was a new market in riskier and, therefore, more profitable lending among poorer and supposedly less creditworthy borrowers. Cautiously, lenders began extending mortgages to this new group of creditors. These nonconforming mortgages came to be known as "**subprime**" mortgages, a name which was confusing in one respect because subprime loans actually meant the borrowers paid a higher interest rate rather than a lower one, as the term subprime implies. From 2002 to 2006, subprime loan originations went from 8.6 percent of all mortgages to 20.1 percent.[51]

As securitization became more commonplace in the 1990s and 2000s, lenders no longer scrutinized borrowers' loan applications as carefully as in the past. Many different types of mortgages were available to both subprime and conventional borrowers. One was the 100 percent mortgage, in which banks would lend 100 percent or more of the value of the house. With no money down, homeowners were irresistibly tempted to buy more expensive houses than they could afford. They were posed to make a killing in the booming real estate market; at least they thought they were. Like the sophisticated financial experts, they, too, thought that house prices would never go down. And because bankers and mortgage originators collected fees for servicing the loans regardless of the outcome, they had little incentive to curb this recklessness.[52] Among the strangest of the new loan products were the so-called "liar loans." To get one of these loans, individuals were not required to prove their income, and in many cases borrowers lied about their income or failed to provide written confirmation of their salary. Most infamous of all were the "NINJA loans" in which a borrower had No Income, No Job, and no Assets. In many cases, borrowers were encouraged by loan officers to overstate their income. In other cases, the loan officers did the overstating, and the borrower only discovered the "mistake" at the closing. This was all in the service of a simple refrain: the larger the house, the larger the loan, the greater the lender's service fees.[53] Lending practices had gone wild.

Low interest rates and lax regulation fed the housing bubble. Low interest rates were a result of Fed Chairman Greenspan's expansionist money supply policy and lax regulations because of the deregulation climate. Lower rates meant that it was cheaper for banks to borrow more money. It also meant that lenders had more funds to lend out. However, low prime loan rates weren't earning much profit for lenders. To make up for it, lenders extended riskier, subprime loans at higher rates to sketchier borrowers. With cheap money readily available, lenders were able to fund more mortgages for those riskier borrowers. If some loans didn't go well, it wouldn't matter. If banks had to foreclose, lenders bet that they could either sell the mortgaged homes for a higher price, which would more than cover the defaulted loans, or convince the borrowers to take out home equity loans backed by the homes' presumably rising value.[54]

As housing prices soared, homeowners could take money out of their houses in the form of home equity loans or by refinancing. The fall in interest rates helped this trend. Lenders started to refinance mortgages in record numbers. Lenders encouraged borrowers

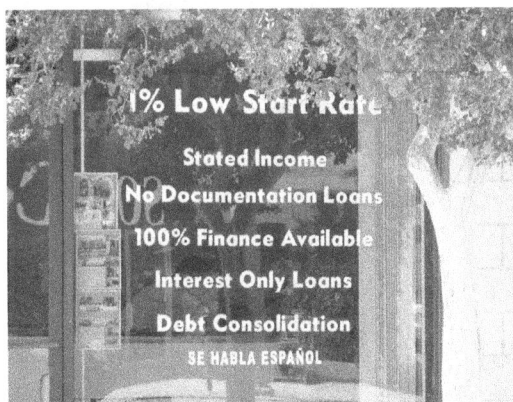

A SUBPRIME MORTGAGE CENTER

to refinance their mortgages and withdraw their excess equity in their homes. Although some people chose to keep their mortgages the same size and simply lower their monthly payments, many others saw a golden opportunity to capture equity that had built up in their homes by increasing the amount of their mortgages. Because their interest rate would be lower than before, their monthly payment might not rise at all, while they would find themselves with a pile of cash they could spend on whatever they desired.[55] These mortgage equity withdrawals, which in one year hit $975 billion, 7 percent of GDP, allowed borrowers to make a down payment on a new car and still have some money left over for retirement.[56] Homeowners had their own ATM machine with seemingly no limit: their home.

Low interest rates and lax lending standards meant it was cheaper than ever for a family to buy a first home. In response, mortgage companies introduced new products: adjustable rate mortgages (ARMs), interest only mortgages (only interest on the loan was paid), and promotional "teaser rates" that would have a low introductory rate and then go up in the next few years. With all this credit readily available and demand skyrocketing, prices began to go up. This is called **asset price inflation** – simply put, it means that instead of stock or bond prices going up, other categories of assets go up in price.[57] This encouraged speculation in residential housing units. House prices started to rise by double digit rates. Real estate prices rose by 50 per cent, with the run-ups close to 80 per cent in the key bubble areas of the West Coast, the East Coast, north of Washington, D.C., and Florida. Economist Dean Baker estimated that the run-up in house prices created more than $5 trillion in real estate wealth compared to a scenario where house prices follow their normal growth rate.[58] All this served to encourage speculation, and the rise in house prices made the owners feel rich; the result was a consumption boom in the mid-2000s.

These so-called "innovative" mortgages had several flaws. First, lenders assumed that it would be easy to refinance these loans because house prices would continue to rise at the same rapid rate. After all, ever since the end of World War II, house prices had never declined; everyone considered it to be a near economic impossibility. However, the real income adjusted for inflation of most Americans has been stagnating since the 1980s; the median household income in 2005 was nearly 3 percent lower than in 1999. Meanwhile, home prices had been rising far faster than inflation or real income. To confirm the widespread expectation that home prices would continue to rise, from 1999 to 2005 home prices increased by 42 percent.[59] Yet, these trends were not sustainable. Stiglitz noted, "The economy was out of kilter: two-thirds to three-fourths of the economy was housing related: constructing new houses or buying contents to fill them, or borrowing against old houses to finance consumption. It was unsustainable – and it wasn't sustained."[60]

Another problem was that the mortgage originators securitized these various mortgag-

IN THE MID-2000s, A HOME WAS ONE'S PERSONAL ATM

es with other assets, creating complex derivative products called "**collateralized debt obligations**" (CDO's). Different layers of middlemen understated the risk of these products in order to offload them as quickly as possible to other banks and institutional investors. These institutions, in turn, dumped these securities onto other banks and foreign financial institutions. The idea was to make a sale quickly and make a tidy profit, while foisting the risk on the suckers down the line.[61]

When lenders exercised sensible scrutiny of a borrower's qualifications, as they did in the past, home mortgages seldom defaulted and dependable collateral protected default. It was an easy formula. So safe were Savings and Loans that in its first 47 years from 1934-1981, the Federal Savings and Loan Insurance Corporation had had to pay claims of just $630 million on bad loans. All that would change with deregulation and lax enforcement.[62] For Lehman Brothers, Merrill Lynch, Fannie Mae, Freddie Mac, and Bear Stearns, the losses represented by these toxic securities simply overwhelmed their reserves and brought them down.[63]

In the era leading up to the 2008 crisis, real estate offered a seemingly risk-free path to fortune. Willing buyers saw the opportunity to make a quick buck in real estate, mortgage lenders got rich on fees, and investment bankers clamored for more mortgage-backed securities to sell to investors. They were all giddy from the metaphorical punch bowl that served up a seemingly continuous supply of addictive intoxicants. But when the Fed finally raised interest rates, resulting in higher rates on subprime loans, adjustable-rate mortgages, and other housing loans, the party was officially over. We are still cleaning up the confetti and streamers celebrating the big bash. Years later, we are still feeling the repercussions.

Questions to Consider

1. What was the fatal flaw in the real-estate lending process in the mid-2000s?
2. Why wasn't this flaw recognized and corrected?

FATAL FLAW #5: MOUNTAINS OF DEBT

What is debt? **Debt** is simply something that a person owes or that one is bound to pay to or perform for another. There are different forms of debt that we will cover in this section: government debt, financial sector debt, consumer debt, and trade deficits. Debt is an important component in a dynamic, modern economy. But on the down side, debt may also spiral out of control.

A MOUNTAIN OF DEBT

During and after World War II, the Fed had large national debt and low interest rates, but the debt financed investment in productive assets, such as real homes, factories, and farms. Since the 21st century, as we have seen, low interest rates and a deregulated financial economy financed a speculative bubble of unproductive toxic assets. From the late 1990s until the credit crunch of 2007, funds from China, South Korea, and other developing countries poured into this country as a result of trade imbalances (see trade deficits below) and loans. These countries lent funds to U.S. consumers, corporations, and banks who built up a mountain of debt. In turn, this debt was spent inflating the latest bubble in the stock market or housing.[64]

This cycle of debt and bubbles is not new in world history. We introduced in chapter 2 the basic message, according to economists Carmen Reinhart and Kenneth Rogoff in their book *This Time is Different: Eight Centuries of Financial Folly*, "We have been here before." They state that no matter how different the latest financial frenzy or crisis always appears to be, there are usually remarkable similarities with past experience from other countries and from history. They go on to state, "Recognizing these analogies and precedents is an essential step toward improving our global financial system, both to reduce the risk of future crisis and to better handle catastrophes when they happen. If there is one common theme to the vast range of crises, it is that excessive debt accumulation, whether it is by the government, banks, corporations, or consumers, often poses greater systemic risks than it seems during a boom." Large-scale buildups of debt, particularly when debt is short term and needs to be constantly refinanced, pose systemic risks because it makes an economy vulnerable to crises of confidence. They go on to offer this chilling advice: "Debt-fueled booms all too often provide false affirmation of a government's policies, a financial institution's ability to make outsized profits or a country's living standard. Most of the booms end badly." Although debt is a crucial element to all economies, balancing the risk and opportunities of debt is always a challenge, a challenge everyone must always remember.[65]

Government Debt and Trade Deficits

Let's first look at government debt; this is what a particular country owes to others. Most countries have some type of debt. At the time of this writing in April 2013, the U.S. has a total national debt to the tune of $16.8 trillion.[66] Although this is a staggering sum, the U.S. is the world's largest economy. Is it too much debt? Of course, there are conflicting opinions.

Throughout most of the 20th century, America was the world's premier financier. Even during World War II, when spending was at record levels, high tax rates and the sale of government bonds to its citizens financed much of the debt. Americans, at that point, had a very high savings rate and were able to lend vast sums of money to their government as a patriotic duty. The government repaid the loans with interest. But that has changed. Since the start of the 21st century, the flow of capital has reversed. While the U.S. personal savings rate has turned negative, leading up to the financial crash, the Chinese were saving an astonishing 59 percent of their income.[67]

During the 1990s, the Bill Clinton administration focused on reducing the yearly budget deficits. Every year since the 1950s, the U.S. government would spend more than it received in taxes and other forms of income. The amounts were so monstrous under the Reagan and Bush I administrations that economic advisors pushed for a balanced budget amendment to the constitution, which did not pass. Clinton focused on reducing the deficit and did so with modest increases in the tax rates of most Americans – in particular, higher income individuals. Because the Cold War ended when the Soviet Union collapsed, he also reduced the sizable defense budget. The result was a balanced budget in 1999 and 2000 (taking away Social Security from the equation).[68] That quickly changed with the Bush II and Obama administrations. With a tax cut in 2001, especially for high-income Americans, two costly wars, and a financial crisis in 2007-2008, the yearly budget deficits and the total national debt have ballooned.

During the 2000s, the U.S. imported more goods than it exported, leading to a trade deficit. Although the U.S. had mountains of debt, China, Japan, Germany, and a range of emerging economies had a surplus of dollars from trade imbalances and the savings of their citizens. All that savings had to be invested somewhere, since under the mattress has not been found to be a good option. In the end, the surplus of savings from other countries went into purchasing debt generated by the U.S., and the U.S. government had lots of debt to finance. However, the low interest rates on the federal government's short-term and long-term debt predisposed investors to prefer debt paying a higher return. They purchased, for example, the higher paying debt of Fannie Mae and Freddie Mac, along with the mortgage-backed securities guaranteed by those institutions. After all, the U.S. Treasury implicitly guaranteed their debt. Estimates vary, but between 40 and 50 percent of the debt securities generated by American financial institutions ended up in the portfolios of foreign investors. In other words, the income stream from credit card debt, home equity loans, auto loans, student loans, and mortgages ended up in the portfolios of foreign investors via the process of securitization. By making these purchases, foreign creditors helped finance American consumers' borrowing binge that drove the bubble.[69] Complicit Chinese lenders assured the U.S. government that they could keep borrowing money cheaply, which implied that Americans consumers could continue spending even more.

The International Monetary Fund (IMF) and others warn countries that trade deficits are harmful to their economies, but the sum of the world's trade deficits must equal the sum of the surpluses. If a few countries, like Japan and China, insist on having a surplus, other countries must have a deficit. It is simple arithmetic. The deficits are like hot potatoes – one country wants to pass them along to another country. When a country finds itself with a large deficit, it faces a crisis. The only thing that keeps the system working is that the U.S. has been the borrower of last resort. As other countries strive to eliminate their deficits, America is willing and able to run the huge deficits that make the global arithmetic add up.[70]

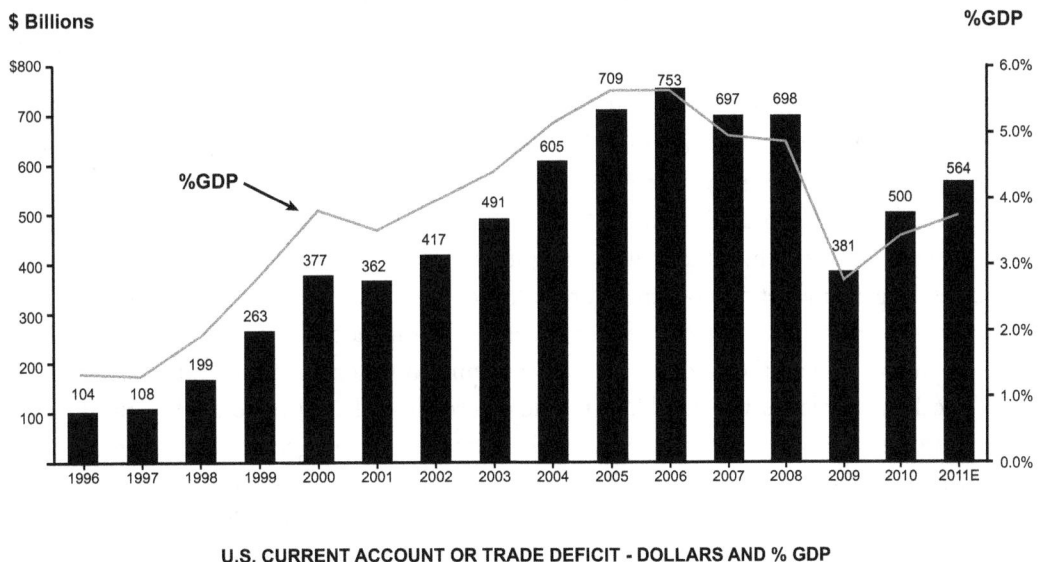

U.S. CURRENT ACCOUNT OR TRADE DEFICIT - DOLLARS AND % GDP

Many blamed the U.S. trade deficit on unfair trade policies, such as China dumping goods at below cost. According to Stiglitz, this was not the cause of high trade deficits but, it was "caused by the high exchange rate, what the U.S. Treasury hailed as the 'strong dollar'." He goes on to explain that the high exchange rate was the result of the relationship between savings and investment. Since the 1980s, America had saved too little. To finance its investments it had to borrow from abroad, with the huge influx of money driving up the dollar's exchange rate. During the 1980s and early 1990s, much of this foreign borrowing went to finance a consumption binge, with the government at the center. If the borrowing had been for investment in infrastructure and other productive assets, the borrowing would have been acceptable. But it wasn't. After the Reagan tax cut of 1981, the government spent more than it received year after year and, having to make up the shortfall, borrowed much of the money from abroad. The Clinton administration inherited ballooning budget deficits, but eventually balanced it. However, American households did not save anymore (see below). Once again, the country had to borrow massively from abroad, this time to finance investments – some of which turned out to be speculative, toxic assets.[71]

Financial Sector Debt

When discussing corporate debt, it is interesting to examine the ideas of a previously little-known economist, whose views on debt and the economy suddenly became very popular in 2007: Hyman Minsky. Indeed, the "Minsky moment" had become a fashionable catch phrase on Wall Street at the time. It refers to the time when the market forces over-indebted investors to sell even their solid investments to make good on their loans, sparking sharp declines in financial markets, while the demand for cash can force central bankers to lend a hand as the lenders of last resort.[72] This needs a little more explanation.

Mr. Minksy, who died in 1996 at the age of 77, was a tall man with unruly hair who wore well-worn, rumpled suits. He was a professor of economics at Washington University in St. Louis, Missouri, and built his theories on the foundation that John Maynard Keynes had laid. Although he was born in Chicago, the Chicago School of Economics had little use for a Keynesian disciple. Minsky claimed that capitalism was by its very nature unstable and prone to collapse. He wrote, "Instability is an inherent and inescapable flaw of capitalism." Instability, according to Minsky, originates in the very financial institutions that make capitalism possible. Paradoxically, the innovation and vitality of capitalism contain the potential for runaway expansion, powered by an investment boom. Minsky showed that as banks and other financial institutions became increasingly complex and interdependent, they could crash the entire system. Minsky's argument centered on how financiers accumulated, distributed, and valued debt.[73]

At its core, Minsky's hypothesis was straightforward: When times are good, investors take on risk; the longer times stay good, the more risk they take on, until they've taken on too much. Eventually, they reach a point where the cash generated by their assets is no longer sufficient to pay off the mountains of debt they took on to acquire them. Losses on such speculative assets prompt lenders to call in their loans, which is likely to lead to a collapse of asset values. When the downturn forces investors to sell even their less-speculative investments to make good on their loans, this move causes markets to spiral lower. At this point, the Minsky moment has arrived.[74]

The non-government sector's accumulation of debt, according to Minsky, is a key mechanism that pushes an economy towards a crisis. He identified three types of borrowers that contribute to the accumulation of debt: hedge borrowers, speculative borrowers, and Ponzi borrowers. Hedge borrowers are those who can make payments on both the interest and the principal of their debts from their current cash flow. Speculative borrowers are those whose income will cover interest payments but not the principal; they have to repeatedly roll over their debts, selling new debt to pay off old. Ponzi borrowers (our old friend from chapter 1) are the most unstable because their income covers neither the principal nor the interest payments. Their only choice is to keep borrowing, hoping for a rise in the value of the assets they purchased with borrowed money.[75] Because of the unlikelihood of speculative and Ponzi borrowers' gaining enough money to pay both interest and principal, much of this type of finance is fraudulent. As with a line of dominoes, collapse of the speculative borrowers can then bring down even hedge borrowers, who are unable to find loans despite the apparent soundness of the underlying investments.

Leverage is the use of debt to supplement investment. Minsky grasped an essential truth about leverage: an economy would become vulnerable to collapse should its various players resort to debt to finance their activities. He believed that the greater the reliance on debt and leverage, the more fragile the financial system.[76] This theory of too much reliance on debt in the 2008 financial crisis is borne out by journalist Naomi Prins who claimed, "It wasn't the subprime market collapse that wrecked the banks and the greater economy; it was all of the borrowing on top of the subprime loans that did the deed."[77]

As a result of the Gramm, Leach, Biley Act in 1999 that repealed the Glass-Steagal Act of 1933, the government removed the "fire wall" separating investment banks and commercial banks. Although some investment banks preferred to remain insulated from commercial banks, the problem was that investment banks couldn't compete with the money and leverage of the commercial banks, which had access to their customers' deposits as collateral. The solution for the investment-only banks was to raise their own leverage limits, so they could borrow more money for speculative activities without having to post as much collateral or capital to secure the transaction. However, investment banks felt stymied by a Securities Exchange Commission (SEC) rule that had been set up in 1975 requiring broker-dealers to cap their debt-to-net capital ratio at 12 to 1. In other words, they could only borrow $12 worth of debt for every one dollar of real capital, or equity, that they had to hold on reserve or as collateral. On April 28, 2004, the biggest investment banks – those with more than $5 billion in assets – Lehman Brothers, Bear Stearns, Merrill Lynch, J.P. Morgan, and Goldman Sachs – got approval from the Securities Exchange Commission (SEC) to increase their official leverage from 12 to 1 to 30 to 1. The SEC even allowed the broker dealers to increase their debt-to-net capital ratios sometimes, as in the case of Merrill Lynch, to as high as 40 to 1.[78] The result of this change was a hedonistic bout of borrowing and debt that substantially contributed to the financial crisis of 2008.

Consumer Debt

The coming together of America's raging consumerism with the strategic, export-led growth policies of many other countries, such as China and Germany, had produced a world with virtually one net consumer: the United States. In the 2000s, American consumers merrily consumed about $700 billion a year more than the U.S. produced. All other major economies were net sellers, depending on American-bound exports for much or all of their growth. Because America consumes more than it makes, it must borrow from abroad to finance its excess consumption. A few foreign central banks provide the financing by buying U.S. Treasury bills and other U.S. assets, such as the Abu Dhabi owned parking meters in Chicago.[79]

The richest country in the world – the U.S. – was living beyond its means, way beyond its means. And, paradoxically, the strength of the U.S. economy and the world's economy depended on this consumption. The global economy needed ever-increasing consumption to grow, but how could this continue when the incomes of many Americans had been stagnating for so long? Americans came up with an ingenious solution: borrow and consume as if their incomes were growing. And borrow they did. Average savings rates fell to zero, which meant that many poor Americans had a largely negative savings rate.[80]

How Americans Kept Buying: Three Coping Mechanisms[81]

1. Women moved into paid work. In 1966, 20 percent of mothers with young children worked outside the home. By the late 1990s the proportion had risen to 60 percent. For married women with children under the age of 6, it rose from 12 percent in the 1960s to 55 percent by the late 1990s.

2. Everyone worked longer hours. In 2000, before the downturn, the typical American worker put in more than 2,200 hours a year – 350 hours more than the average European or Japanese worked. Compared to 1979, Americans put in 500 additional hours of paid work a year, a full 12 weeks more.

3. Draw down savings and borrow. From 1948-1973, the American middle class saved about 9 percent of their after-tax incomes each year. By the late 1980s they saved 7 percent, in 1994, 6 percent, and only 2.6 percent in 2008.

In the 2000s, the low interests rates meant that it was easy for businesses to raise money cheaply, easy for consumers to borrow money, and easy for borrowers to take out mortgages. By historic standards, household debt exploded. During the post-war years, debt averaged 50-55 percent of annual after-tax income (including mortgages), but starting in 1980 debt took off. In 2001, American owed

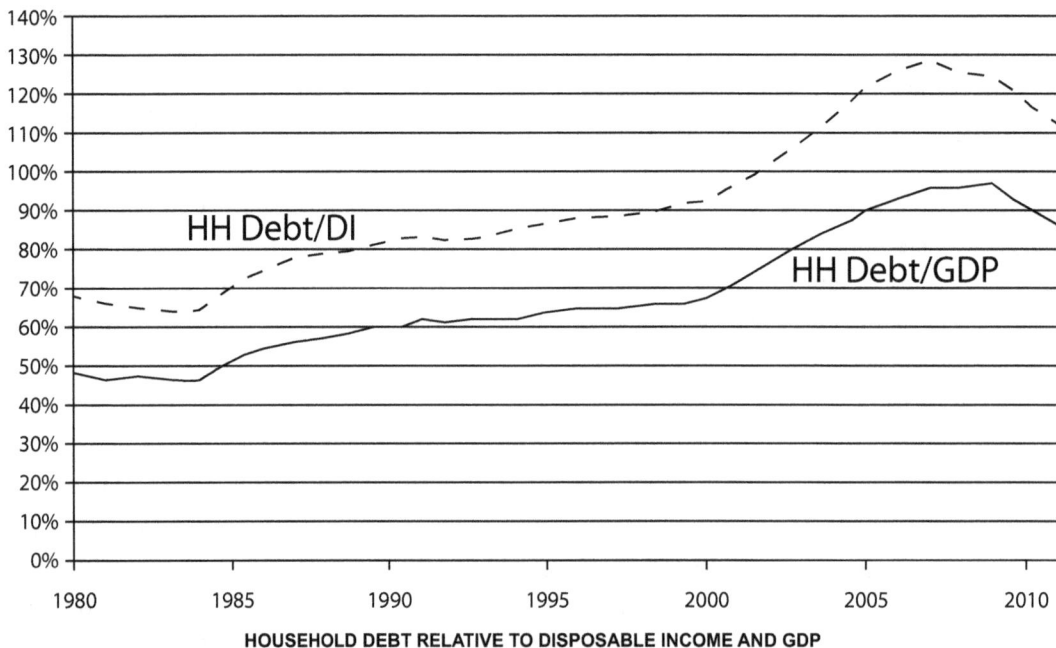

HOUSEHOLD DEBT RELATIVE TO DISPOSABLE INCOME AND GDP

as much as their entire after-tax income. But low interest rates made borrowing so easy that by 2007, many households owed an astonishing 138 percent of after-tax income.[82]

Americans borrowed anywhere and everywhere. Credit card solicitations flooded mailboxes. You didn't even need a job to get a credit card. Auto loans, college loans, credit card loans, and mortgage debt all exploded. Consumers refinanced their homes with even larger mortgages and used their home as collateral for additional loans. As long as housing prices continued to rise, it seemed a painless way to get money to make up for decades of stagnating wages.

Consumption was inordinately fueling the American economy. In 1980, the average home sold for $64,600; by 2006 it was $246,500. Between 2002 and 2007, American households extracted $2.3 trillion in equity from their houses, putting themselves ever more deeply into the hole. A typical new home built in the U.S. in 2007 was 2,500 square feet, about 50 percent bigger than its 1,780 square foot counterpart built in 1977 – even though median incomes barely rose. Another example was the typical wedding which cost $11,213 in 1980, while that figure rose in 2007 to $28,082 (adjusted for inflation).[83] Just before the downturn, personal consumption in America equaled almost 70 percent of the country's GDP (more than 75 percent if you include the purchase of homes). By contrast, personal consumption constituted only 65 percent of the British economy, 55 percent of Germany's, and 52 percent of Japan's. During the post-war years in the U.S. it constituted 62 percent.[84] Consumption was at epidemic levels.

As financial instability increased, so did the number of people who got into trouble by borrowing too much. The number of people filing for bankruptcy has increased in most English-speaking countries, most notably in the U.S., where, in the early 2000s, more than 2 million people declared bankruptcy every year. During these years, Americans were more likely to go bankrupt than to get divorced. The most immediate causes of bankruptcy were job losses and unexpected health care costs. But the underlying cause was a culture of indebtedness. As long as the crisis was primarily confined to the housing markets, the number of bankruptcies rose only gradually. But, with soaring unemployment and the end of easy access to credit, bankruptcy filings increased. In 2009, there were 1.4 million consumer bankruptcy filings, and 1.5 million in 2010. Reliance on access to credit to manage household budgets is encouraged by rather liberal bankruptcy laws in the U.S. compared to other countries, which act as a kind of substitute for a more equal tax-welfare system. Within the U.S., the states with the least progressive tax systems have typically had the most generous bankruptcy laws. In Europe the inverse is the case – bankruptcy laws are stricter than in the U.S. but their social safety net is more generous.[85]

Questions to Consider

1. Why is so much debt encouraged or acceptable in the U.S. and other countries? What benefits are there associated with a country built on debt? Drawbacks.
2. Do you have personal debt? Has it enhanced your life or is it a hindrance to your life?

CONCLUDING INSIGHTS:
FATAL FLAWS IN THE FINANCIAL SECTOR PART I

The fundamental problem is that Americans no longer have the purchasing power to buy what the U.S. economy is capable of producing. In other words, overproduction is causing excess supply, while overall demand is weak. The reason is that through governmental policy such as taxes and legislation, along with economic globalization, a larger and larger portion of total income and wealth has been flowing upward to the very wealthiest. What is broken is the basic bargain of the post-war years between government, labor, and business, linking pay to production. If this bargain was in place, wages would not have stagnated and debt would not have catapulted upward. One of the solutions to the financial crisis is to restore the bargain.[86] In other words, if wages accompany rising productivity levels, they would go up. There would be more money in the pockets of the 99 percent, and more demand for the goods and service produced. But, on the other hand, there would be less in the bank accounts of the 1 percent. Since the 1 percent is in the driver's seat of devising the government's economic policy, this historical bargain remains comatose.

Let's move on to the next five fatal flaws in the financial sector in the next chapter.

CHAPTER FOUR

Ten Fatal Flaws in the Financial Sector: Part II

"I have found very little evidence that vast amounts of innovation in financial markets in recent years have had a visible effect on the productivity of the economy."

Paul Volcker former chair of the Federal Reserve

In chapter 3 we examined five of the 10 fatal flaws in the financial sector – too big to fail banks, unchecked deregulation, a "markets knows best" Federal Reserve, a real estate bubble, and out of control lending. This chapter continues with the remaining five fatal flaws.

FATAL FLAW #6: DICEY FINANCIAL PRODUCTS

The **neoclassical economic order**, the forerunner of neoliberalism today, was a system of capitalism from the mid-19th century to 1914. Its supporters advocated for minimal government involvement in the economy, the gold standard, and the business sector heavily influenced political policy. During this time the financial sector joined savers who had surplus funds with entrepreneurs who had need of their funds to invest in production. This usually meant that the rich countries of the time – U.S., Britain, and France – lent money to the middle and periphery countries for investment in infrastructure and new businesses. The U.S. through three-quarters of the 20th century was the world's largest creditor. It was the world's piggy bank. Beginning in the 1980s, with government policy geared toward feeding the financial sector, and lowering taxes, especially on the wealthy, all this would change.

In 1944, the **Bretton Woods** financial system promoted a capitalist, political and economic order. One of its tenets is it restricted moving capital from one country to another to seek differentials in interest and foreign exchange rates in different capital markets. For example, if Germany was paying higher interest rates on its government bonds than France, investors were restricted from quickly moving capital around to capture those higher rates. The purpose of these restrictions, proposed by John Maynard Keynes and others, was that free-flowing capital would disrupt the economic stability of countries – flowing in and out too quickly – and cause more harm than good. However, with the crisis of the 1970s and the urging of the financial sector, these conservative economic policies changed. Also, technological changes made it possible for these complicated exchanges to take place swiftly and cheaply. The gold-dollar foundation of currency exchange, another Bretton Woods agreement, collapsed in 1971 and with it the restriction on the movement of capital across national borders. Financial capital was now "free" to move to areas where it could gain the highest return. The result was the rapid globalization of speculative capital circulating around the world, honing in on financial instruments, such as currency rate differences, which financers were able to take advantage of. This volatile movement of capital resulted in its "liberation" from the fetters of the post-war order, as supporters of financial deregulation echoed. It was also a source of economic instability.[1]

Since the 1970s, as a result of these and other global financial changes, there has been a tremendous burst of speculative activity that has made finance the most profitable sector of the global economy. The 1980s and 1990s witnessed the development of ever more sophisticated financial instruments, such as futures, swaps, options, and other derivatives, where profits came not from trading assets but from speculation on the underlying assets. In 1950, the financial sector contributed 3 percent to American national income, while in 2011 that increased to 9 percent. In comparison, all government services contributed 15 percent. One indicator of the super-profitability of the financial sector relative to other sectors of the economy, like trade, industry, and agriculture, is the fact that 40 percent of the total profits of all U.S. financial and nonfinancial corporations is accounted for by the financial sector, although it is responsible for only 5 percent of U.S. gross domestic product (GDP).[2]

You might be wondering at this point how the financial sector could make so much profit, yet contribute so little to the GDP. If you did wonder this, you are getting to the heart of the flaws in the financial sector. The rest of this section will be describing the different financial products that the financial sector has concocted to make its exorbitant profits. If you thought that the financial sector was all about providing and arranging financing for great businesses, such as Apple, Paramount Pictures, Microsoft, General Motors, musical groups, home purchases, or basketball franchises, think again. Unfortunately, it is not as simple as that. These financial products are complicated, opaque, and combined with other products to create layer upon layer of different products that financiers have chopped up, reconfigured, repackaged and sold to investors, some very naïve investors, around the world. If France is famous for its fine cheese and wine and Germany for its finely engineered cars, then Wall Street has been known for its "innovative" financial products, until 2008 when it collapsed. This section on "Dicey Financial Products" is difficult. I have tried to make it as understandable as possible without over-simplifying. If you don't understand every detail, that is fine. If you grasp the fact that these financial products were (and still are) so complex that to know what is being sold and the risk involved in the product is impossible for just about everyone, then you are getting to the point of this section.

Securitization

Going back to the section on the real estate and housing industry in chapter 3, you will remember (hopefully) how Wall Street made mortgage loans into securities, a process known as securitization. As a refresher, securitization is the process of converting illiquid assets (not easily converted into money) that could be pooled and transformed into liquid assets (easily converted into money) and, thus, tradable on the open market. The securitized mortgages had been sliced and diced, packaged and repackaged, and passed on as supposedly highly-rated investments by rating agencies to all manner of banks and investment funds around the world.

Wall Street revived the securitization industry because it proved to be its big profit center. Wall Street's old-fashioned business – making loans and helping business get started and grow – was much less profitable. The profits in stock brokering along with those in more conventional sorts of bond brokering, had been squashed by Internet competition. Thus, to stay afloat in the competitive world of finance and make the big bucks, the securitization gravy train was the answer. Never mind that it was wrecking the global economy, and would only last for a short-time – the glitter of fortune was too tempting to resist for thousands of financiers on Wall Street. The minute the market stopped buying the securitized junk that the investment banks were offering, they were in trouble.[3]

With securitization, financiers bundled together a group of mortgages and sold them to investors anywhere in the world. The investors who bought the securities might not even know where the houses were located that were packaged in their investment portfolio. Community banks lent mostly to members of the community, so if the town's factory shut down, many in the community would be unable to meet their mortgage payments, and the bank might face bankruptcy. Thus, securitization offered one big advantage – it diversified and shared risks. With securitization, diversification was easy for investors; they could buy shares in bundles of mortgages, and investment banks could even combine multiple bundles of mortgages. Financiers commonly assumed at the time that mortgages from different geographic regions would not experience housing downturns at the same time; thus, they geographically spread out the risks. But securitization did not account for all sorts of risk. An increase in interest rates would pose problems throughout the country, not just in one geographic region. Also, information about the origination of the mortgage was obscure. The buyer of the security knew little about the borrower or about the bank or firm that had originated the mortgage. And because the originator of the loan didn't bear the short-term consequences of his/her lending mistakes, incentives for doing a good job of credit assessment of the borrower were removed.[4] Yet, Wall Street ignored these risks as the feeding trough of riches brought out the impulse to make money anyway and anyhow.

Securitizing was not just in home mortgages, but also in commercial real estate mortgages, in consumer/credit card debt, and in car, student, and corporate loans. The resulting bonds securitized from these loans – asset-backed securities – proved popular, and securitization soon spread elsewhere. By the time the crisis hit, securitization had been applied to airplane leases, revenues from forests and mines, delinquent tax liens, radio tower revenues, boat loans, state and local government revenues, and even the royalties of rock bands.[5]

Financers sold the securities as bonds. Bonds have been around for many years and are not new financial products. For governments and for many corporations, bonds are the single most important way to raise money. A **bond** is a debt security, in which the authorized issuer owes the holders of the bond a debt and is obliged to pay interest and/or to repay the principal at a later date. A bond repays an agreed-upon rate of interest until it matures, and all of these facets are fixed – the price of the bond, the rate of interest it pays, and the date when it matures. Around 2008, the total value of the global bond market was in the region of $50 trillion.[6] Bonds vary widely as to whether they are a risky or a safe form of investment. Bonds considered to be a safe investment carry a lower interest rate than high risk bonds that carry a higher rate of interest. Therefore, Wall Street was eager to put together the mortgage-backed securities into packages that returned a higher rate of interest than ordinary, low-yielding bonds. And they did. Excessive risk coupled with excessive leverage had created what seemed like high returns – and they were high for awhile. Wall Street thought that by repackaging the mortgages and passing them on to numerous investors, they were sharing the risk and protecting themselves.[7]

Securitization of the hottest financial-products in the field provided a textbook example of the risks generated by the new innovations. Investors buying a mortgage-backed security are, in effect, lending to homeowners, about whom they know nothing. They trust the bank that sells them the product to have checked it out, and the bank trusts the mortgage originator. However, the mortgage originators focused on the quantity of mortgages originated, not the quality. They originated massive numbers of truly lousy mortgages. The banks like to blame the mortgage originators, but just a cursory glance at the mortgages should have revealed the in-

BOND CERTIFICATE FOR THE STATE OF
SOUTH CAROLINA ISSUED IN 1873.

herent risks. The fact is that banks didn't want to know. They merely wanted to pass on the securities backed by the mortgages that they created as fast as they could, down the money-greased pipeline to unsuspecting investors.[8]

Questions to Consider

1. How did the advent of securitization change the way the financial system worked? Did this change help the average person?

Predatory Lending

Since the demand for these mortgage-backed securities was so strong, even the poor, who lenders had in the past excluded from the housing market, were prime borrowing prospects. By the early to mid-2000s, house lending had taken a new turn; no longer was the motive to help place poor-but-reliable people into their own home, but instead it became a predatory practice driven by money. Mortgage lenders were frantically searching for people, anybody with a pulse, to sign up. An epidemic began of what came to be called "**predatory lending**." This meant that mortgage lenders were doing everything they could to sign up borrowers with subprime mortgages that carried higher-than-ordinary, interest rates. The lenders created mortgage debt that they sold to investment banks for securitization and then the banks passed on the securitized debt to willing investors. Some of this happened in the UK, Ireland, Spain and elsewhere, but the overwhelming bulk of predatory lending activity happened in the U.S.[9]

Bankers had gone into the "moving" business – taking mortgages from the mortgage originators, repackaging them, and moving them onto the books of pension funds and other investors. That was where the fees were the highest, as opposed to the "storage" business – originating mortgages and then holding on to them – which had been the traditional business model for banks.[10] The bankers gave no thought as to how dangerous some of the financial instruments were to the rest of us.

Even though some in the media simplified the 2008 crisis as solely caused by a sub-prime mortgage debacle, it was not. If merely sub-prime mortgage defaults caused the crisis, it would have been relatively easy to solve. The government could have bought and paid off every single sub-prime mortgage in the country, and it would have only cost $1.4 trillion. This seems like an astronomical figure, but compared to the $13 plus trillion estimated to ultimately have been spent on the bailouts, it was a manageable amount.[11]

Questions to Consider

1. Why did predatory lending develop during the financial crisis?
2. What are the ethical and moral dimensions of predatory lending?

Five Financial Products

If it wasn't just the sub-prime mortgages and their gullible borrowers, what caused such a catastrophic economic meltdown? It was the additional debt that financiers piled onto the sub-prime mortgages. Now that is hard to wrap our heads around. There was debt on top of debt? In order to understand this a little better, although it is complicated, let's look at some of the financial products that Wall Street has concocted that contributed to the financial crisis of 2008.

1. Hedge Funds

A **hedge fund** is a private pool of capital actively managed by an investment adviser. Hedge funds are only open for investment to a limited number of investors who typically invest a minimum range from about $250,000 to $10 million. These investors can be institutions, such as pension funds, university endowments and foundations, sovereign wealth funds, or high net-worth individuals.[12] According to Hedge Fund Research (HFR), in 2011, investors added $1.917 trillion to hedge funds around the world.[13] The funds generally invest in a diverse range of assets and employ a variety of investment strategies that aim to achieve a positive return on investment, whether markets are rising or falling. Hedge funds often take large risks on speculative strategies through various bets – on housing, oil, weather, pork bellies, wheat futures, or whatever. Since hedge funds are not limited to buying securities, they can potentially profit in any market environment, including one with sharply declining prices using shorting (selling) strategies. Because they move billions of dollars in and out of markets quickly, hedge funds can have a significant impact on the day-to-day markets.[14]

Hedge fund managers typically invest their own money in the fund they manage, which serves to align their interests with investors in the fund. They make fees, typically 2 percent management fees based on the value of investments, plus 20 percent performance fees. Hedge funds borrow money against these assets from commercial and investment banks to make even bigger speculative wagers. The thinking goes: the more you bet right, the more money you make.[15] Before the crisis, hedge funds were largely unregulated pools of investment capital. Regulations passed in the U.S and Europe after the 2008 credit crisis are intended to increase government oversight of hedge funds.

2. Derivatives

A **derivative** is a security whose price is dependent upon or derived from one or more underlying asset. The derivative itself is merely a contract between two or more parties. Fluctuations in the underlying asset determine the derivative's value. The most common underlying assets include stocks, bonds, commodities, currencies, interest rates and market indexes. Most derivatives have high leverage. Traders generally use derivatives as an instrument to hedge or circumvent risk but they also use them for speculation. Derivatives are a long standing feature of financial markets. Speculation on tulip derivatives was a feature of the Dutch tulip bulb bubble in 1637. One of the oldest derivatives is rice futures, which have been traded on the Dojima Rice Exchange, located in Osaka, Japan, since the 18th century.[16]

It's no coincidence that traders first extensively used derivatives in commodities markets. In 1864, in the United States, the Chicago Board of Trade (CBOT) listed the first ever futures contracts. In 1919, the industry reorganized the Chicago Butter and Egg Board, a spin-off of the CBOT, to allow futures trading. At their simplest, **futures trading** is where a farmer will agree to a price for his/her next harvest months in advance. The future price of the harvest is thus a derivative, which can itself

CHICAGO BOARD OF TRADE BUILDING, , BUILT IN 1930, THE CBOT WAS ESTABLISHED IN 1848, THE WORLD'S OLDEST FUTURES AND OPTIONS EXCHANGE.

be sold. The name comes from the fact that a derivative's value derives from an underlying product, the farmer's crop in this case. For years, derivatives have existed as useful tools of this type. The future's contract assures farmers of the price for their harvest long before the crops are in. They are immensely practical and basically not too complicated. They have been around for a long time.[17]

Today the simplest forms of derivatives are options and futures. An **option** gives a trader the right, but not the obligation, to either buy or sell something at a specified future date for a specified price. Since derivatives are difficult to understand (I am struggling with this myself), the following example by journalist John Lancaster might help in explaining the concept.

Do you want a Ferrari?[18]

Let's say, you want to buy a car, but not any old car, a Ferrari. They cost a lot of money so you are going to strategize on how to purchase it. Let's say you have decided to spend $500 on an option to buy a Ferrari for $50,000 in a year's time. When the year is up, the Ferrari is on sale for $60,000 – so your option is now worth $10,000, because that's how much money you can make by exercising the option – that is buying the car and then selling it for its current price. Conversely, if in a year's time the Ferrari is on sale for $40,000, exercising your option would leave you out of pocket by $10,000 – so you just let it go, and your only loss is the $500 premium (as it's called). You could alternatively have bought the right to sell the Ferrari for $50,000 – in which case your preferences would be reversed and you'd be hoping that the price had dropped. In that event you'd buy the car for $40,000 and immediately sell it for $10,000 more. Futures are the same as options, except that they bring with them the obligation to buy or sell at the specified price: with a future contract, you are committed to the deal. It follows that futures are much riskier than options.

FERRARI ROAD CARS ARE SEEN AS A SYMBOL OF SPEED, LUXURY AND WEALTH.

It quickly became obvious in Chicago and elsewhere that there was a huge potential market in the field of financial derivatives. But there was a major drawback: no one could work out how to price them. The interacting factors of time, risk, interest rates, and price volatility were so complex that they defeated the best mathematicians, until Fischer Black and Myron Scholes calculated their ground-breaking formula in 1973. Coincidentally, it was one month after the Chicago Board Options Exchange had opened for business. The revolutionary aspect of their formula was an equation that calculated the price of financial derivatives based on the value of the underlying assets. It was a defining moment in applying mathematical formulas to market pricing. Within months, traders were using these new inventions, and the worldwide derivatives business took off like a rocket.

Today economists count the total market in derivative products around the world in the hundreds of trillions of dollars. Nobody knows the exact figure, but the notional amount certainly exceeds the total value of the all the world's economic output, roughly $66 trillion, by a huge factor – perhaps tenfold.[19] The **notional value** is the total value of a leveraged position's assets. For example, an investor buys 250 units of a Standard and Poors (S&P) 500 Index futures contract that is trading at $1,000 a unit. The single futures contract is similar to investing $250,000 (250 x $1,000). Therefore, $250,000 is the notional value underlying the futures contract.[20] Even if the investor borrows the $250,000, the notional value remains the same. Notional values can spiral far, far away from the underlying value of the real assets.

Even once someone explains it, the concept still seems contrary to common sense that the market for products deriving from real things should be inconceivably vaster than the market for the actual things themselves. It is difficult for most of us to understand a derivatives contract or any of the range of closely related instruments. These are all products that traders initially designed to transfer or hedge risks – similar to purchasing a form of insurance against the prospect of prices fluctuating. The farmer selling his next season's crop might not have understood a modern financial derivative, but s/he would have recognized the use of it. In an ideal world, traders would use derivatives for only one thing: to reduce risk. Because traders buy derivatives on margin – that is, not for the full cost of the underlying asset but for the advancement premium, as in the hypothetical Ferrari example – derivatives offer a cheap and flexible form of insurance against things going wrong.[21]

Derivatives are a double-edged sword. As mentioned, the name says much about the essence of derivatives: the value is derived from some other asset. On one hand, traders use derivatives to manage risk. If Southwest Airlines is worried about the rising price of fuel, it can insure against that risk by buying oil on the futures market, locking in a price today for oil to be delivered in six months. Using derivatives Southwest can, in effect, take out an "insurance policy" against the risk that the price will go up. On the other hand, a derivative is a speculative bet. For example, the bet that the price of a stock will be greater than ten dollars next Monday is a derivative. A bet that the market value of a bet that a stock will be greater than ten dollars next Monday is a derivative based on a derivative. There are an infinite and imaginative number of such products that one could invent.[22] And, indeed, in the 2000s, the financial sector had a heyday in concocting speculative derivatives that were far removed from their supposed mission of helping businesses grow and prosper.

Derivatives have worked just fine for decades, enabling people to "hedge" against risk as in the case of the farmers and the airlines. They could hedge against fluctuations in the prices of their crops in advance of a harvest, giving them peace of mind they would otherwise lack. But in recent years derivatives have grown into something altogether different, thanks to the rise of new varieties of derivatives, such as the CDS (see below).[23] Some derivatives have gone from being a means of hedging risk to a purely speculative instrument, akin to making wagers and bets in Las Vegas. Yet, the activities in Las Vegas are pure and simple gambling; investors do not promote them as safe financial investments for a secure retirement. But that is how financiers promoted many of the speculative derivatives: promises of safe investments, instead of speculative instruments with massive amounts of leverage and risk.

Today's derivatives are the closest thing to rocket science ever invented. These complex and opaque instruments are a long, long way from a farmer's single quote for next season's wheat crop. PhDs in advanced mathematics swarm around the derivative business, devising new formulas and inventions that no one can understand. The products created are way over

AIRLINES, SUCH AS SOUTHWEST, USE DERIVATIVES TO LOCK IN FUTURE FUEL COSTS.

the heads of the average person, and sometimes, it seems, over the heads of the people who buy and sell them.[24]

Modern derivatives are the most powerful and most complicated financial instruments ever devised. And they are everywhere. Traders buy and sell more than a $1 trillion worth of derivatives every day, many of them in London. Every single thing which traders can exchange as derivatives they trade. In the words of the legendary billionaire investor, Warren Buffet, "The range of derivatives contracts is limited only by the imagination of man (or sometimes, so it seems, madmen). Say you want to write a contract speculating on the number of twins to be born in Nebraska in 2020. No problem – at a price, you will easily find an obliging counterparty." Buffet doesn't like derivatives; he prefers to know what's going on in the companies he invests in, and derivatives make that effectively impossible. Buffet prophetically said in 2002, "The derivatives genie is now well out of the bottle, and these instruments will almost certainly multiply in variety and number until some event makes their toxicity clear. However, the derivatives business continues to expand virtually unchecked. Central banks and governments have so far found no effective way to control, or even monitor, the risks posed by these contracts."[25] Financial leaders claimed they had "created value," by devising derivatives, but what they mostly created was a house of cards.

3. Collateralized Debt Obligation (CDO)

A **Collateralized Debt Obligation CDO** is a pool of debt that a group of borrowers is paying back, which financiers add together and then sell as a set of bonds paying a range of different interest rates. There are two streams of revenue, one from the fees to set up the deal and another from the debt and interest repayment.[26] Michael Milken in 1987 invented the first CDO at the now-defunct investment bank Drexel, Burnham Lambert. The CDO at the time was basically a security made up of a bunch of what were called **junk bonds**, a bond rated double B or lower because of its high default risk. A notable "innovation" of the 1980s, these junk bonds allowed companies that investment banks would not previously have considered credit worthy to issue debt. This debt, which paid higher yields to reflect greater risk, became a huge source of funds for "**leveraged buyouts**" (LBOs), through which investors borrowed money to launch (often hostile) takeover bids for public companies listed on the stock exchange.[27]

After the implosion of the junk bond market in 1990, the use of CDOs went dormant for nearly a decade. But the stuffing, slicing and dicing of any security that contained **credit risk** – the possibility that a person or a company might default on payments – into another security reemerged as a highly profitable business in the late 1990s. The four years from 2002 to 2006 saw a new wave of CDO stuffing using sub-prime and other risky mortgages. These CDOs were essentially a reincarnation of the lucrative financial gimmicks from the 1980s junk bond era.[28] Journalist Michael Lewis has concluded, that "it was impossible to get to the bottom of exactly what was inside a CDO – which meant that no investor could possibly know either. Far too many people were taking far too many financial statements on faith." Nevertheless, the CDO market climbed from nearly nothing in 1996 to $2 trillion by 2008.[29]

If the regular CDO market was not complicated enough, investment "gurus" began to design CDOs of CDOs, pools of pools of structured debt, chopped and sliced and then chopped and sliced again; the underlying assets were none other than people with shaky credit who were struggling to pay back their loans. The new CDOs of CDOs were known as CDO^2, or CDO squared.[30] It is a good exercise to try and think for a moment what actually makes up a typical CDO^2. Warning: this may scare you. Start with a thousand different individual loans – commercial and residential mortgages, credit card receivables, and small business, auto, student, and corporate loans. Package these loans together into an asset-backed security (ABS). Take that ABS and combine it with 99 other ABSs so that you have a hundred of them. That's your CDO. Now take that CDO and combine it with another 99 different CDOs, each of which has its own unique mix of ABSs and underlying assets. Want to pour your retirement savings into this "investment"? Do the math: in theory, the purchaser of this CDO^2 is supposed to somehow get a handle on the health of ten million underlying loans. Is this going to happen? Of course not![31]

Tranche is a French word meaning slice or portion. In the world of investing, it describes a security that financers can split up into smaller pieces and then sell to investors. Financiers often use the term tranche to describe a specific class of bonds within an offering, wherein each tranche offers varying degrees of risk to the investor.[32] The safer tranches are less lucrative with a lower interest rate, and the riskier tranches are more lucrative having a higher interest rate.[33] Sometimes the tranches are called towers.

In the meantime, investment bank Goldman Sachs had created an exclusive CDO, a security so opaque and complex that it would remain forever misunderstood by investors and rating agencies. They had invented the CDO to redistribute the risk of corporate and government bond defaults and now Goldman Sachs was refiguring it to disguise the risk of subprime mortgage loans. They gathered together thousands of subprime loans into a tower of bonds, in which both risk and return diminished as you climbed the tower. The packagers of the CDO assumed that it would be extremely unlikely that all the loans in the CDO would go bad together. The riskiest loans were at the bottom of the tower and had the lowest credit rating, such as a triple B rating. Without getting into the details of these towers, the point was to get the rating agencies to rate most of the tower the highest possible rating – triple A. With money flying in every direction, rating agencies, who were paid fat fees by Goldman Sachs and other Wall Street firms for each deal they rated, to no one's surprise, pronounced 80 percent of the CDO's tower of debt triple A.

You may wonder, at this point, how all those involved could get by with such a bold and deceptive scheme. This certainly would be a good question to ask of those on Wall Street inventing these CDOs. But the last thing the financial sector wanted was anyone who asked lots of tough questions. For Wall Street, the CDO scheme was a machine that turned lead into gold.[34]

4. Credit Default Swaps (CDSs)

Here's another financial "innovation" that will boggle your mind: credit default swaps. A **credit default swap** (CDS) is a form of insurance. The buyer of a credit default swap receives credit protection, whereas the seller of the swap guarantees the credit worthiness of the product. By doing this, the holder of the fixed income security transfers the risk of default to the seller of the swap.[35] It gives the buyer of the CDS insurance against the risk of default on any given debt instrument, whether it be a corporate bond, an auto loan, or, a subprime mortgage. Trade in credit default swaps is based on the likelihood that whatever it is they are insuring will default. The greater the chance investors believe that a default will occur, the higher the price of the CDS. Like so many other businesses on Wall Street, the CDS market made a great deal of sense before it spun out of control.[36]

In its simplest form, a CDS is an insurance policy, typically on a corporate bond with semi-annual premium payments and a fixed term. For example, an investor purchasing $100 million in General Electric bonds might worry that the company could default on its bonds. The investor decides it would be wise to purchase a type of insurance policy to insure that s/he doesn't lose the whole $100 million if the company defaults on its bonds. Therefore, the investor decides to pay $200,000 a year to buy a ten-year credit default swap on $100 million in General Electric bonds. In case the company, General Electric, does not default on its bonds, the most the investor could lose would be $2 million: $200,000 a year for ten years. In the case the company does default on its bonds, the insurer of the credit default swap would then have to pay the investor $100 million. The most the investor who bought a CDS could make would be $100 million if General Electric defaulted on its debt any time in the next ten years and the bondholders received nothing. But the CDS insurer knows that General Electric is a good company, and the risk of default is slim. Therefore, the CDS insurer feels pretty secure that s/he will make $200,000 of easy money each year with little risk of losing the whole $100 million.[37] So far, sounds easy enough.

Managing the risk of default is fundamental to the world of finance. Therefore, the market for CDSs grew at an explosive rate. In June 2008, it was estimated that the total nominal value of CDSs issued was $54 trillion (some estimates claim $60 trillion), close to the total GDP of the whole planet, and many times more valuable than the total number of all the stocks traded in the world.[38]

The CDS, which the financial industry had invented as a way of making lending safer, turned out to magnify and spread risks throughout the global financial system. As Lanchester claims, "It's as if people had used the invention of seat belts as an opportunity to take up drunk driving."[39] They spread risk throughout the financial system, not least because most of them trade "over the counter," between one institution and another, with no one to oversee the process, such as the stock exchange. This means there is no central register of CDSs and no one is responsible for assessing and managing market wide risks.[40] It is another unregulated market. Another way to think about a CDS wasn't insurance at all, but outright speculation.

5. Synthetic Collateralized Debt Obligations

By 2005, Wall Street firms were still trying to meet investor demands for all the mortgage-related products they had created. But they were running out of ways to do it. CDOs fueled demand for mortgage-backed securities. Mortgage backed securities fueled demand for mortgages. The problem was that there simply weren't enough new mortgages to meet the world wide demand Wall Street had created for the mortgage-backed CDOs. Since Wall Street had run out of real mortgages to package up and sell, financiers started to create hypothetical ones. By the mid-2000s, Wall Street's financial schemers had churned out even more products in the CDO family – products that would eventually help devour the balance sheets of the very banks that created them. In a flood of ingenuity, Wall Street invented synthetic products based on synthetic products. It was obvious that these products provided new chances for risk-taking and for earning hefty fees for financiers. In addition to the now staid CDO and CDS, there was a Wall Street creation known as a synthetic CDO and its renegade sister, a synthetic CDS.[41]

A **synthetic CDO** is a complex financial security used to speculate or manage the risk that an obligation will not be paid. Two or more counterparties, who have different viewpoints about what will ultimately happen with respect to the underlying reference securities, typically negotiate the terms of the contract. Financiers typically divide synthetic CDOs into credit tranches based on the level of credit risk assumed. They first created them in the late 1990s, but the CDOs were not widely used until the mid-2000s.[42] Wall Street had huge financial incentives to create ever more complex and non-transparent products such as synthetic CDOs.

Rather than sell these risky CDOs, the banks could also keep some of them and get the cash flows they generated. To protect themselves against default, banks insured themselves by purchasing credit default swaps (CDS) from insurance companies such as American International Group (AIG). In essence, they swapped the risk of default for a cash payment to the insurer. The CDS underwriting institution then aggregated the CDS income stream into pools, which they divided into tranches with different risk profiles. These were called **synthetic CDSs**, which is a form of collateralized debt obligation (CDO) that invests in credit default swaps (CDSs).

Synthetic CDOs get their cash flows from insurance premiums paid by the buyers to cover the risk of debt default. To make things even more complicated, institutions can even insure against the risk of default on securities they do not own. These synthetic CDOs effectively bet against subprime mortgages or risky corporate bonds, once again leveraging these bets with cheap credit. Any default could therefore result in claims to insurance underwriters many times as large as the supposed value of the underlying securities. The problem was that in many of the deals the banks, such as Merrill Lynch, would end up owning as much as 90 percent of the dollar amount. After all, they thought it had virtually no risk.[43]

It is hard to understate the insanity that seemed to have crept into the CDO market by 2006-2007. Young synthetic CDS inventers only a few years out of business school were working 14-hour days and making a million dollars a year to put together CDOs and synthetic CDOs to feed the demand their bosses had created for these products. It is clear that few of these people really understood the bigger picture. Their sole focus was on doing the math required of them to get the pieces in place to make a CDO and get it the necessary favorable credit rating.

What is even more insane is that practically all of these financial products had as their foundation borrowers with generally poor credit ratings, who were paying back their mortgage loans, student debt, automobile payments, and credit cards. When I mentioned above that debt piled upon debt piled upon more debt exacerbated the financial crisis, now you understand what that means. The only thing that stood in the way of this money-making engine was the shortage of borrowers willing to take on even more debt.[44]

Insights: Financial Products

An apt metaphor for the financial products sold leading up to the climax of the crisis in 2008 is a house of cards. This means that the cards are not really something of true value – like a bushel of wheat or barrel of oil, or a small business on Main Street – and when the reality sets in that the house of cards has no value, it collapses. Everyone who owns individual cards in the house of cards then tries to sell his/her cards, but alas since everyone knows that the cards are now worthless; no one will buy them. Those who made a profit bought the cards when the price was climbing and then sold their cards at a higher price before everyone knew they were worthless. The value of the cards was worthless, but the fortunate investor who sold at the right time made a profit. Wall Street's financial games added no value to the world economy, but they did create a profit – a profit Wall Street quickly devoured and hungered for more.

The government was perfectly capable of regulating the financial markets, but because the dominant neoliberal attitude prevailed, devising and implementing effective mechanisms with which to regulate the industry were only half-hearted at best. In the deregulatory frenzy of the 1980s onward, even attempts to restrict the worst lending practices – such as predatory lending in the subprime market – were beaten back by well-paid lobbyists of the financial sector in cahoots with sympathetic politicians of both political parties. One of the reasons for regulation is to ensure the stability of the financial system. America's subprime financial institutions created an array of subprime mortgages all designed to maximize the fees they generated. Good financial markets are supposed to reduce fees due to efficiency, supposedly what markets do best. But that is not what happened; bankers love fees and they strove to maximize, not minimize them.[45]

The financial wizards of Wall Street got carried away with themselves in the euphoria of enormous wealth; they deceived themselves, as well as those who bought their products. When the market crashed, they, like the buyers of their products, were left holding billions of dollars' worth of toxic products. Banks were holding more and more risky assets, their own foolish creations, with borrowed money at that. They couldn't tell, nor could their investors, what was the difference between triple A rated corporate bonds and triple A rated subprime loans. They didn't even know what was on their own balance sheets.[46]

When the house of cards finally collapsed, the crisis had drastic effects at home and abroad. It took some of the most venerable institutions along with it: Lehman Brothers, Bear Stearns, and Merrill Lynch. But the travails did not stop at the U.S. border. These securitized mortgages, many sold around the world, turned out to be toxic for banks and investment funds as far away as Norway, Bahrain, and China.[47]

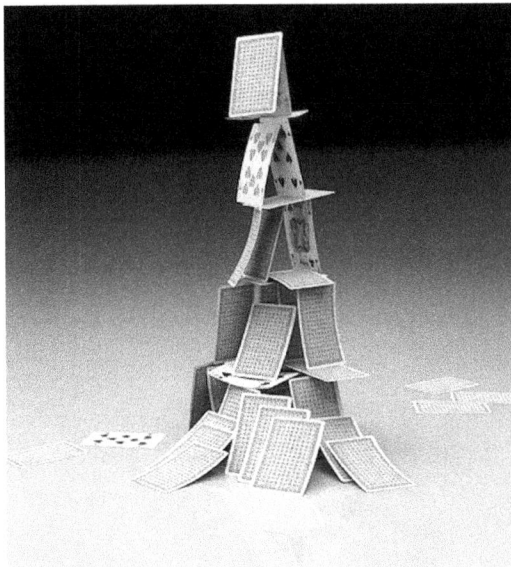

Advocates of the reckless subprime mortgages argued that these financial innovations would enable large numbers of Americans to become homeowners for the first time. They did become homeowners – but for a very short time and at a very high cost. The number of Americans who are homeowners at the end of this episode is lower than at the beginning. [48]

The lure of easy profits from transaction costs and fees distracted many big banks from their core functions of lending money and managing risk. They did not focus on lending to small and medium-sized businesses, which are the basis of job creation, but instead concentrated on promoting securitization, especially in the mortgage market. According to Stiglitz, the financial wizards on Wall Street were "not the least bit interested in innovations that might have helped people keep their homes or protect them from sudden rises in interest rates." The wizards were actually engaged in clear and simple gambling.[49]

Investor Warren Buffet aptly compared the new financial products to weapons of mass destruction – first, because they are lethal, and second, because no one knows how to track them down. The trouble with the securitization model was that it broke with the fundamental principle that a bank had to individually assess and monitor every loan. The new instruments made that impossible. The mathematics of valuation models – dreadfully complex equations – took the burden of assessing risk. The whole idea that a banker looks a borrower in the eye and makes a decision on whether he can trust him seemed to be very old fashioned.[50]

Questions to Consider

1. Why did I call these financial products that I explained above a house of cards? Do you think this is an apt metaphor? Why or why not?

FATAL FLAW #7: FINANCIAL SPECULATIVE MANIA

One of the results of the crisis of 2008 is that the economic differences between what has been cleverly labeled Wall Street vs. Main Street has affected more and more people. Although the label is framed as if it was an action thriller destined for the big screen, there is some truth to the media hype – it is a thriller and it should be played out on the political big screen. It would be a thriller which would truly horrify us! There has been an increasing disconnect between the productive economy of Main Street and the increasingly non-productive, speculative, yet profitable economy of Wall Street. Since the 1980s, there has been a political policy shift from supporting the productive economy to favoring the speculative financial sector of Wall Street. With more money concentrated in the financial sector, the financial class has been able to successfully lobby politicians for political policies that favor their industry.

The potential for problems in the banking sector should come as no surprise once it is recognized for what it is – making loans with other people's money. Future markets, options, derivatives, buying on margin, hedge funds, CDOs, CDSs, and a host of other financial inventions all do one of two things: they either increase the number of ways it is possible to speculate, or they increase the amount of leverage speculators can obtain by using less of their own money and more credit to buy something they hope to profit from. If credit provides funding for some productive activity, such as transportation or medical research, it can be beneficial. But, as in all too many cases in the past 30 plus years, the extension of credit has not increased the productive economy, but rather has been concentrated in disruptive speculative activity that ultimately crashes the whole credit system.[51]

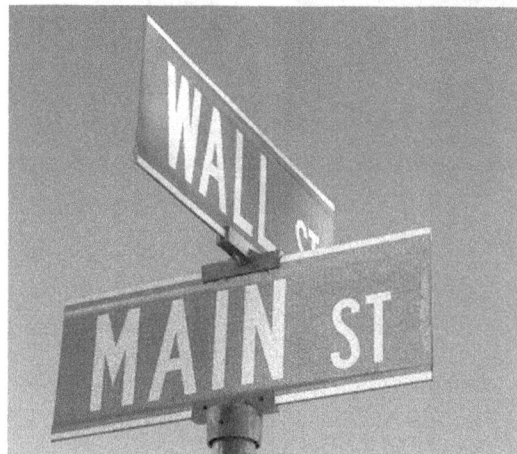

Now here is something to ponder. According to economist Nomi Prins, a person in the financial sector once commented to her "that finance is one of the few disciplines based on the creation of absolutely nothing. It is based on the principle of continuously pushing nothing for something throughout the system as long as someone else is around to pay for it." Other critics, such Walden Bello agree. He states "The problem with investing in financial sector operations is that it is equivalent to squeezing value out of already created value. It may create profit, yes, but it does not create new value – only industry, agricultural, trade, and services create new value."[52] In other words, creating financial products that we have talked about above is not really contributing anything to the real economy; hence, the disconnect between Wall Street and Main Street.

You may be wondering why Wall Street traders are so wealthy if they do not create value. It does seem strange that this can happen. But they generate huge fees on their wild investment schemes, and they create profit through speculation, not adding value. Wall Street does not necessarily base profit on value that industry creates. Investment operations become very volatile, and prices of stocks, bonds, and other forms of investment can depart very radically from their real value. For example, the stock of Internet startups in the 1990s kept on rising, driven mainly by upwardly spiraling financial valuations, then crashed. Profits depended on taking advantage of the upward price departures from the value of the commodities, and then selling before the reality enforced a correction in the market – that is, when the asset crashed back to real values. In order to make a profit one has to sell an inflated asset in a bubble economy before that bubble pops.

To be fair, the financial sector has done a good job in some areas and has played a key role in the country's economic growth. Financial innovations in centuries past, such as insurance and commodity options, have proven their value. One area of positive innovation was in the procedure for making home loans. Many potential homeowners in the pre-World War II era had to save a whopping 50 percent of the price of the home to purchase it. This deferred the dream of home ownership for all but a select few. But adjustments in the financial sector have now made it easier for homebuyers to purchase a home. More recently, the financial sector has provided funding for some of the start-up venture capital firms on the West coast. They have also provided capital to many new entrepreneurial companies and community banks, credit unions, and local banks that supply consumers and small to medium-sized enterprises with the finances they need. However, these examples distinguish between productive and speculative investments. Productive investments are financial resources which reinforce the manufacturing production in a particular nation, while speculative investments normally entail fast profits in the stock market – they do not provide a country with a sustainable basis for long term economic growth – and they are more volatile. Stiglitz points out, "In spite of the pride about 'financial sector innovations' in the bloated financial sector, it is not clear that most of the innovations actually contributed very much to increased productivity or to the success of the U.S. economy or the living standards of the vast majority of Americans."[53]

The number of speculative manias in the U.S. has had the function of absorbing investments that did not find profitable returns in the real economy. Investors made more money in speculative activity on Wall Street than they could in the real Main Street economy. Walden Bello states the reason for stagnation in the real economy is because of overcapacity. He goes on to reason that too much world-wide competitive production drove down the price of goods and profit margins. Therefore, the smart money on Wall Street sought out greater returns in the speculative economy. This atmosphere of a speculative economy on Wall Street filtered down to Main Street consumers, who were able to use the increased values of their home as an ATM. Thus, their consumer buying was not only artificially propping up the U.S. economy but also holding up the world economy owing to the stimulus to global production triggered by American consumer spending. The attractiveness of finance relative to other sectors of the economy, like trade and industry, was underlined by the fact that in the late 1990s, the volume of transactions per day in foreign exchange markets came to over $1.2 trillion, which was equal to the value of trade in goods and services in an entire quarter.[54]

Since the profitability of the financial sector is dependent on speculative coups, it is not surprising that the financial sector lurches from one bubble to another or from one speculative mania to another. Because speculation drives the financial sector, finance driven capitalism has experienced about 100 financial crises since neoliberals deregulated and liberalized capital markets in the 1980's.[55]

Robin Hahnel in his article "Capitalist Globalism in Crisis," excerpted in the textbox, explains how bubbles and speculation form a dynamic feedback loop in the financial sector.

Financial Products and Speculators: A Dynamic Duo[56]

New financial products add new markets where bubbles can form and burst. Increased leverage compounds the damage from any bubble that does burst. A bubble is simply a rising price that becomes a kind of self-fulfilling prophesy. If the price of something rises, people may look for less expensive substitutes and buy less of the goods whose price has risen. But if the price of something is rising, it is rational for speculators to buy more of it pulling the price even higher in anticipation of being able to sell it later for a profit. This is how speculative buying can build a bubble. A bubble can burst if a few notable speculators switch from buying to selling, and other speculators become convinced the price is headed down and also decide to switch from buying to selling. In general, the greater the percentage of market participants who are speculators, the more susceptible a market will be both to bubble formation and bursting. Recent changes in the global credit system have created more markets dominated by speculators operating with greater leverage.

In the crisis of 2008, financial speculators outsmarted themselves by creating more and more complex financial contracts – including exotic futures instruments, such as credit default swaps. This enabled investors to bet on the odds that the banks' own corporate borrowers would not be able to pay back their debt. However, Warren Buffet, a grand speculator himself, eliminated derivatives from his investment portfolio long before the recent crisis. He is the same Warren Buffet who called derivatives in 2003 "financial weapons of mass destruction" devised by "madmen" whom he defined as "geeks bearing formulas."[57]

LEGENDARY INVESTOR AND BILLIONAIRE WARREN BUFFET, KNOWN AS THE "WIZARD OF OMAHA." HE WARNED AGAINST THE DANGERS OF DERIVATIVES.

Insights: Financial Speculative Mania

A smooth-running global economy requires the trilogy of equality, efficiency, and risk management; global financial speculation flunks all three criteria. Economies have become more unequal, both within and between nations. Economies have become more inefficient with huge sums of money wasted in speculative manias in which speculation puts the entire system at greater risk of collapsing. However, a small number of traders get very rich. Economist Robert Kuttner notes, "Developing countries need capital. The damage is not done by long-term investment in actual enterprises, but by short-term loans and financial bets on currency movements, because that sort of money can fly out just as quickly as it rushes in."[58] With the liberalization of the global economy, a new challenge is the global regulation of finance to avoid the speculative manias that put the entire global economy at risk.

Questions to Consider

1. What does Walden Bello mean when he states "The problem with investing in financial sector operations is that it is equivalent to squeezing value out of already created value?" Do you agree with his statement?
2. If there is little value created in the financial sector, how do financiers make money?

FATAL FLAW #8:
MORAL HAZARD AND LACK OF TRANSPARENCY

Moral hazard and transparency are two similar concepts that I have included as flaw #8. The concept of moral hazard is simply someone's willingness to take risks – particularly excessive risks – that s/he would normally avoid, simply because s/he knows someone else will shoulder whatever negative consequences will follow. For example, someone who has auto theft insurance may be more willing to park his car in a place where it might be stolen or neglect to buy an anti-theft device than someone who lacks that insurance. The car owner knows the insurance company will cover the loss; the problem will fall on someone else's shoulders.[59]

Moral hazard played a significant role in the economic crisis. Roubini explains, "In the securitization food chain, a mortgage broker who knowingly brought a liar loan to a bank got compensated for his efforts but bore no responsibility for what would happen as the mortgage moved down the line. Likewise, the trader who placed enormous bets on a CDO would be rewarded handsomely if he succeeded but was rarely punished if he failed." Moral hazard was an especially acute problem because of the way that financial firms provided compensation.[60]

The market repeatedly mispriced and misjudged risk in the financial system. The market badly misjudged the risk of subprime mortgage defaults and made an even worse mistake trusting the rating agencies and the investment banks when they repackaged the subprime mortgages with a triple A rating. The banks also badly misjudged the risk associated with the high degree of leverage that they thought was reasonable. Yet, the banks went ahead despite all the warnings with their risky decisions because of moral hazard. They believed that if troubles arose, the Federal Reserve and the Treasury would bail them out, and they were right.[61]

The story of the multi-billion dollar insurance firm **American International Group (AIG)** exemplifies the concept of moral hazard, euphemistically called TBTF – too big to fail. AIG was the largest underwriter of commercial and industrial insurance in the U.S. The problem for AIG began in the early 2000s, when the formula that AIG analysts dreamed up to cope with corporate credit risk was applied to consumer credit risk. The banks that used AIG to insure loans to corporations now came to them to insure messier loans that included credit card debt, student loans, auto loans, prime mortgages, aircraft leases, and just about anything else that generated a cash flow. Since the loans were sufficiently diverse, AIG analysts assumed that it would be unlikely that they would all go bad at once.[62] They were wrong.

Problems started at the end of 2004, when U.S. subprime mortgage loans replaced many of the student and auto loans. The loan packages went from containing 2 percent subprime loans to 95 percent subprime loans. Yet, no alarm bells went off. AIG brass, by all accounts, simply rubber-stamped the deals. According to Lewis, "Everyone concerned, apparently assumed they were being paid insurance premiums to take basically the same sort of risk they had been taking for nearly a decade. They weren't."[63]

At the height of its credit-default-writing frenzy in 2005-2006, AIG sold credit protection on virtually anything. AIG reigned as the single biggest player in the CDS market. And why not? It had a stellar triple A credit rating and a very low cost of borrowing money. Because of its reputation, it barely needed to keep any money in reserve for the insurance it sold, which its computer models said it would never need to pay off.[64] In a financial system that was generating complicated risks, AIG's FP (Financial Products) division became a huge swallower of those risks. In the early days AIG must have thought that the insurers were paying them to insure events extremely unlikely to occur. Its success bred copycat companies, such as Zurich Reinsurance, Swiss Reinsurance, and Credit Suisee Financial Products. All of these companies were places to hide the new, risky financial products that Wall Street was creating far from the full view of bank regulators.[65]

AIG was worth $200 billion at its peak and definitely too big to fail. If the federal government had not stepped in with a bailout, the company would have gone the way of the investment bank Lehman Brothers: bankruptcy courts and financial ruin. But AIG was too big to fail. On September 17, 2008, the company announced a loss for the quarter – not the year, the quarter – of $62 billion, the worst corporate quarterly loss in history. To stabilize, AIG would need lots of government support. That's what too big to fail means. The U.S. govern-

AIG BUILDING, LOWER MANHATTAN, NEW YORK CITY, USA.

ment stepped in with a bailout worth $85 billion, in return for 80 percent of the company. They issued another $37.8 billion in credit on October 6, another $40 billion on November 10, and another $30 billion on March 1, 2009.

Cleverly, the equation read: AIG+CDS+CDO+TBTF=$173,000,000,000.[66]

At its low point, the capitalization of the company was worth no more than $2 billion. Saving the company had cost 85 times as much as buying it would have been. The U.S. Treasury with its massive infusion of bailout funds saved AIG. The lesson of AIG was crystal clear: the government would never again allow a financial institution of comparable size to collapse. The government bailed out AIG because it had the entire economic system over a barrel.[67]

Transparency

Financial markets lack transparency and are complex. **Transparency** is another word for information. Vast portions of global capital flow through secrecy havens like the Cayman Islands – a $2 trillion banking center in the Caribbean Sea. Many companies deliberately create these loopholes in the global regulatory system to facilitate money laundering, tax evasion, regulatory evasion, and other illegal activities.[68] Sheer complexity also played a significant role in the 2008 crisis. The financial products were so complex that no one could fully understand the risk implications. Computers running models that couldn't possibly include all of the pertinent information were determining the value of complex products. In fact, some very important information was not included in the models, such as the possibility that housing prices would fall. Computer models were used to maximize the amount of money that could be made by slicing and dicing mortgages into triple A tranches. Without such alchemy, the products would have gotten a straight F.[69]

The lack of transparency has cost society and the economy an enormous amount. The big banks don't like transparency. Stiglitz notes, "A fully transparent market would be highly competitive, and with intense competition, fees and profits would be driven down. The complexity thus allowed for higher fees, with the banks living off increased transaction costs."[70] With complexity and lack of transparency, banks have the power to exploit the uninformed, and they did so, ruthlessly.

TRANSPARENCY IS HIDDEN IN SUCH PLACES AS THE CAYMAN ISLANDS IN THE CARIBBEAN.

Questions to Consider
1. Why is moral hazard a problem in the financial sector?
2. Why do financial companies resist transparency?

FATAL FLAW # 9: DECEPTIVE RATING AGENCIES

There would have been no credit crisis and, therefore, no economic crisis if not for the involvement of the credit rating agencies. They were the oil that greased all the moving parts in the great machine Wall Street assembled to package and sell U.S. subprime mortgages around the world. Their supposed job was to protect investors when the machine went haywire. Instead, they protected the profits they were making.[71]

A **credit rating agency** (CRA) is a company that assigns credit ratings for issuers of certain types of debt. Debt issues with the highest credit ratings – triple A – from the agencies will have the lowest interest rates. The credit rating agencies' analyses highly influence the investors' confidence in the borrowers' ability to meet their debt payment obligations. The credit rating agencies perform work similar to consumer credit bureaus. The credit scores that the latter produce for individuals influence the rates of interest at which individuals may borrow. Perhaps some of you know your credit score. If it is high, then perhaps you can borrow money at a lower interest rate than if you had a low score.

The top three credit rating agencies dominate the business of deciding how safe or unsafe a particular piece of debt is. Those companies are Standard & Poor's (42.2% market share), Moody's Investors Service (36.9%), and to a lesser extent Fitch Ratings (17.9%). Standard & Poor's (S&P) is owned by the McGraw-Hill Company (they publish textbooks as well). France's Fimilac owns Fitch. Moody's is the only public company of the three and boasts having Warren Buffet among its largest investors.[72]

Until the early 1970s, the rating agencies relied on investors to furnish the bulk of their revenues. They derived their income from publishing rating manuals and offering investment advisory services. But this changed when the agencies realized they could make more money with the issuer-pays model. Rating so-called "structured products" remained a small business for many years; the industry paid little attention to the potential conflict of interest raised by the issuer-pays model. Payment by the issuer had become standard practice 30 years later, when structured products (such as CDOs) contributed to the bulk of profitability for the rating agencies.[73] Thus, it should have been to no one's surprise that the rating agencies gave high ratings to mortgage-backed security bonds. In a clear case of conflict of interest, they depended on doing business with and being paid by the same institutions whose bonds they rated.

Looking at the way the rating agencies structured incentives explains their failure to analyze the poor quality of the securities they were rating. The banks that originated the securities were paying the rating agencies to "objectively" rate their securities. Standard & Poor's and others might not have understood risk, but they did understand incentives. They had a clear incentive to satisfy those who were paying them. And cut-throat competition among the rating agencies just made matters worse: if one rating agency didn't give the grade that the investment bank wanted, they could turn to another.[74]

MCGRAW HILL BUILDING, KNOWN TO EDUCATORS FOR ITS TEXTBOOKS, OWNS STANDARD AND POOR'S. ON NOVEMBER 26, 2012, MCGRAW SOLD THEIR EDUCATIONAL DIVISION TO APOLLO GLOBAL FOR A REPORTED $2.5 BILLION

Increasingly, the ratings agencies had an interest in giving customers what they wanted – and if a customer wanted a triple A rating for a CDO made up of subprime mortgages, there was a good chance s/he got it. They also garnered income from other, equally problematic sources. Roubini explains, "A bank putting together a structured financial product would go to one of the ratings agencies and pay for advice on how to engineer that product to attract the best possible rating from the very agency the bank would ultimately pay to rate its securities. The rating agency described this service as "consulting" or "modeling." It was a bit like a professor's accepting a fee in exchange for telling students how to get an A on an exam."[75] They raked in fees as they told the investment houses how to get good ratings and then made still more money when they assigned the grades. Smart investment bankers soon figured out how to extract the highest mix of ratings from any set of securities.[76]

There is another reason why the rating agencies performed so miserably: they used the same bad models that the investment bankers used. For example, they assumed that houses would never decline in value, and certainly there could not be a price decline in many parts of the country at the same time. They ignored the warning signs of a classic housing bubble: low interest rates, lax regulations, and close to full employment. A change in any of these factors could and would affect markets throughout the country – and indeed throughout the world.[77]

A ratings downgrade from S&P or Moody's often requires that a company must post more collateral as a type of insurance policy against default. For example, because AIG had an excellent credit rating before the crisis, it held very little in reserve to pay claims on the mortgage-backed securities it was insuring. But when S&P and Moody's downgraded its credit rating, they forced AIG to increase its reserves because its payment on its insured products was more in doubt. AIG couldn't come up with the billions in collateral it needed to stash in reserve and, thus, turned to the government for a bailout. A credit rating downgrade can also result in a company's having to pay a higher interest rate when it borrows funds. That's why corporations fight to stay in the good graces of the rating agencies. The better or higher the credit rating, the cheaper it typically is for a corporation to borrow money. The lower the rating, the more it will cost that company to borrow money.[78]

Managers of pension funds, for example, have to be sure the securities they buy are safe, and the credit rating agencies play a vital role by certifying their safety. However, this was not the scenario that played out in the run-up to the financial crisis of 2008. Financial markets created an incentive structure which ensured that each of those in the chain of financial manipulation played a role in the grand deception with enthusiasm.[79] Moody's claimed that it "has no obligation to perform, and does not perform, due diligence." S&P claimed, "Any user of the information contained herein should not rely on any credit rating or other opinion contained herein in making any investment decision." With those disclaimers, what then was the purpose of a ratings agency? I would answer that question: the purpose of the rating agencies was profit. At Moody's, profits quadrupled between 2000 and 2007, and it boasted the highest profit margin of any company in the S&P 500 for five of those years. Moody's operating margins during these years hovered slightly above 50 percent.[80] The credit rating business was, indeed, very lucrative.

Questions to Consider

1. Would you change or not change the issuer-pay model for paying credit rating agencies?
2. How would you change the model? If you want to keep the existing model the same, why?

FATAL FLAW # 10: BLOATED COMPENSATION PLANS

The value of money is ephemeral. The financial world does not create anything beyond the temporary profits that it extracts, which makes bonuses on Wall Street as fleeting as they are excessive. Traders are as good as their last trade or whether they beat or missed analysts' expectations of their firm. According to Prins, "On Wall Street pay is based on the deals that closed that year, never mind whether the long-term effects of those deals are disastrous. The bonus system, as a form of compensation, is gluttonous in the short term and careless in the long-term."[81]

Wall Street doesn't produce anything of lasting value. Prins points out that the financial sector pays people for creating an illusion of value that they base on some ill-defined notion or demand for a particular product, on assumptions, on internal evaluations, and on sheer spin. The more competitive and complex the financial industry became, the more firms had to find ways to extract money from increasingly complex securities and transactions they created. Plain-vanilla securities, as financiers called them, didn't return as much to investors or make as much for Wall Street bankers at year's end. Transactions are fleeting and revenues are booked up front, regardless of how transactions turn out in the end. It doesn't matter if a merger fails or succeeds; investment banks collect their fees nonetheless. Complexity comes up as one of the most overused excuses for executives to collect the big bucks.[82]

Few people resent Bill Gates or the late Steve Jobs for making their wealth because they created it with concrete achievements, on products and services that a vast number of people actually use and have a need for. An actor or actress might get paid millions for a film, but at least the film has lasting life and entertainment value. The same goes for an overpaid football or baseball player. At least he might produce a great moment that becomes part of the national culture. But for the most part Wall Street simply does not provide any immediate benefit to most of the country. Pushing money around and extracting huge profits are not activities that make Americans better, safer, or even more entertained.[83]

Managers (the agents) run most modern corporations not the shareholders (principals). These two groups don't see eye to eye: the shareholders want to maximize their long-run returns from ownership of the company, but the managers want to maximize their short-term income, bonuses, and other forms of compensation. The complex problem clearly has no easy solutions, but a real issue is compensation. That is where many of the problems originate.[84]

Those in the financial sector had more opportunity and stronger incentives to do mischief at other peoples' expense than the average worker. Rather than simply paying employees a salary, the banks paid the traders and others who worked at investment banks, hedge funds, and other financial services firms for their performance based on a system of annual bonuses related to income (fees) they helped to generate. While financial firms have over the years paid bonuses as a form of compensation, in the 2000s, the major investment banks – Goldman Sachs, Morgan Stanley, Merrill Lynch, Lehman Brothers, and Bear Stearns – paid ever more staggering sums. In 2005, the big five firms paid $25 billion in bonuses; in 2006, $36 billion, and in 2007, $38 billion. The ratio of bonuses to base pay skyrocketed. In 2006, the average bonus accounted for 60 percent of total compensation at the two biggest investment banks. In some cases the figure was much higher: bonuses 10 or even 12 times the size of base salaries became commonplace in many firms at the center of the crisis. Even after the federal government bailed out these firms, they brazenly continued to pay bonuses.[85]

Supporters of the bonus compensation system argue that this system provides strong incentives for executives to work hard for the betterment of the company. This argument is disingenuous because the banks found ways to pay the executives well, even when the firm floundered. There is, it turns out, little relationship between pay and performance, a fact that the crisis highlighted when executives at companies with record losses got multimillion dollar bonuses. Some firms even went as far as to change the name of the pay for performance bonuses to retention bonuses. Nevertheless, pay is high when performance is good and when it is poor. And the bonus system, which focused on short-term profits made over the course of a year, encouraged risk taking and excessive leverage on a widespread scale.[86]

Another example of an incentive distortion is that many executives receive some of their pay from stock options. Those receiving stock options had an incentive to do everything they could to get their firms' stock price up – including creative or illegal accounting. The higher the share price, the better they did. They knew that the higher the reported profits were, the higher the share prices would be, and they knew that it was easy to deceive markets. One of the easiest ways to increase profits was to manipulate the balance sheet. Cleverly, accountants moved potential losses off balance sheets into shadowy accounts with one hand, while recording profitable fees with the other.[87]

Poor corporate governance provides a cover for executives to get away with these deceptions. The shareholders only technically run American corporations. In many cases, management runs the companies for their benefit. In many corporations where ownership is widely diversified among different shareholders, management appoints most of the board, and it appoints people who are likely to serve their best interests. The board decides on management pay, and the company, in turn, provides ample rewards for its board members. It's a cozy relationship.[88]

There are numerous problems with the compensation system on Wall Street. This system encourages risk taking that generates oversize returns in the short term, with little consideration of long-term consequences. One way to fix the system, according to Roubini, "is to create bonus pools that aren't calculated on short-term returns but are based on a longer time horizon – say 3 years or

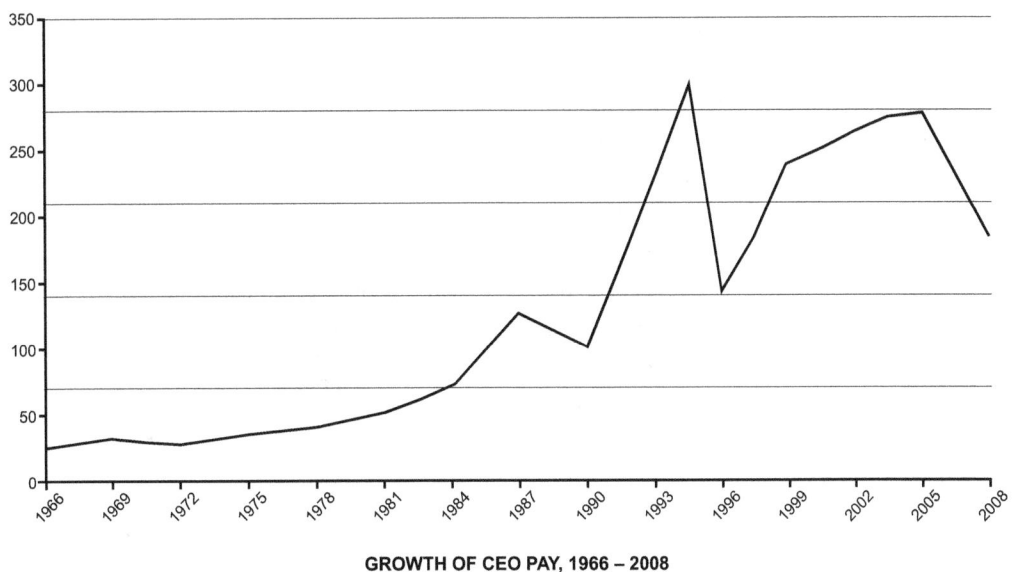

GROWTH OF CEO PAY, 1966 – 2008

so. Instead of rewarding its employees for making their particular canny bets, a firm averages their performance over the course of several years." Removing traders' incentives for taking on short-term risk will probably cause compensation to decline.[89] This is not a bad thing.

Hedge fund managers have come under increasing scrutiny because of their outrageous compensation. There were just 610 hedge funds with $39 billion in assets in 1990. By the end of 2006, there were 9,462 hedge funds with $1.5 trillion in assets under management. Until recently, no government regulations governed hedge funds. Plus, those hedge funds can borrow or leverage substantial amounts of money against their assets. In addition, hedge fund head honchos make 2 percent of all returns and charge 20 percent fees simply for taking investor money. In 2009, the 25 best-paid hedge fund managers together earned $25.3 billion, an average of $1 billion each.[90]

With Wall Street generating huge profits in the 2000s, the financial sector minted a new generation of wealthy individuals. Those who worked in the financial industry earned an astounding $53 billion in total compensation in 2007. Goldman Sachs ranked at the top of the five leading brokerages at the onset of the crisis in compensation paid. It accounted for $20 billion of that total, which worked out to more than $661,000 per employee. The company's chief executive, Lloyd Blankfein, alone took home $68 million.[91]

In recent years, the financial services industry – and compensation within it – has undergone exorbitant and utterly unwarranted growth, driven by financial liberalization, financial innovation, elimination of capital controls, and the globalization of finance. The financial crisis has not curbed these excesses. Compensation has continued to climb to all-time highs.

Questions to Consider

1. Would you recommend changing the compensation plans for Wall Street executives?
2. What plan would you recommend? Why. If you think the plan should remain the same, why?

CONCLUDING INSIGHTS:
THE 10 FATAL FLAWS IN THE FINANCIAL SECTOR

As we have seen from the ten fatal flaws in the financial sector, the industry has been able to create its own financial Wall Street economy separate from the Main Street economy of the vast majority of Americans. The two economies operate on separate planes. But the Wall Street economy feeds on the Main Street economy; it would not be able to exist without it. To be fair, there are still many valuable actions that Wall Street performs. But as we have seen in this and the previous chapters, the excesses have permeated the Wall Street economy so deeply that purging the glut will not be an easy chore. Wall Street will use its immense riches and political clout to resist every effort by politicians and the citizenry to pry open its treasure chest of financial tricks for full examination and reform. It will not be an easy task, but we need to do it.

Questions to Consider

1. How would you plan to solve the 10 fatal flaws in the financial sector?
2. If you think the financial sector works fine the way it is and has no flaws, explain your position?

CHAPTER FIVE

The Financial Crisis of 2007-2008

"We all knew the trigger had been poor subprime lending but I noted that this had been part of a much broader erosion of standards throughout corporate and consumer credit markets. Years of benign economic conditions and abundant liquidity had led investors to overreach; market participants and regulators had become complacent about all types of risks."[1]

Hank Paulson, Secretary of the Treasury (2006-2009)

THE FALL OF LEHMAN BROTHERS

Monday morning broke on this beginning-of-fall day, September 15, 2008, like any other day throughout the United States – it seemed uneventful. But it was far from uneventful in the tiny enclave known as Wall Street, located at the southern tip of the island of Manhattan in the financial center of the world: New York City. In fact, the reverberations from the day's events would ripple throughout the world. Some insiders refer to it as the 9/11 of the financial world – the fall of the venerable 158 year old financial mainstay, Lehman Brothers. The firm was at the epicenter of the financial crisis gripping the nation. It had lost billions of dollars in the sub-prime mortgage crisis, which had sparked the plummeting of the financial markets that cost investors trillions of dollars in lost value. Its fall was swift.

Lehman Brothers started small and inconsequentially. In 1844, 23-year-old Henry Lehman, the son of a cattle merchant, immigrated to the United States from Bavaria, Germany. He settled in Montgomery, Alabama, where he opened a dry-goods store. His two younger immigrant brothers, Emanuel and Mayer, joined him in the business. In 1850, the firm changed its name to "Lehman Brothers." Eventually the business started to trade in a lucrative commodity – cotton – and in 1858 opened a branch office in New York City. Soon after the end of the Civil War, the firm moved its headquarters to New York City, where it helped found the New York Cotton Exchange in 1870. Emmanuel Lehman became a member of the New York Coffee Exchange as early as 1883 and eventually the New York Stock Exchange in 1887. The financial establishment now considered Lehman Brothers to be an investment bank.

Emmanuel's son Philip expanded his father's business and became a partner in the family-owned firm in 1887. He was the firm's managing partner from 1901 until his retirement in 1925. He was also the first chairman of the board of the Lehman Corporation. Philip was notable as one of the first financiers to recognize the potential of issuing stock as a way for new companies to raise capital.

Management of the company passed on to Philip's son, Robert Lehman, upon his retirement. Robert was the first to invite non-family members to become partners in the essentially one-family firm. He understood that the right partners could expand the company's opportunities. Under Robert, the bank concentrated on rapidly developing consumer companies with financing deals arranged in retailing, airlines, and entertainment. He guided his company through the perils of the stock-market crash of 1929 and the ensuing Great Depression of the 1930s. After World War II he expanded the company's international operations. He was one of the wealthiest people in the United States. After 44 years as patriarch of the firm, he died in 1969, leaving no member of the Lehman family actively involved with the partnership.

With no clear successor, the firm floundered in the early 1970s. In 1973, the board of directors brought in Pete Peterson as the CEO

FORMER LEHMAN BROTHERS HEADQUARTERS, NOW OWNED BY BARCLAYS, IN THE TIMES SQUARE AREA OF NEW YORK CITY.

to save the firm. Under his leadership, the firm returned to profitability through the turbulent 1970s and became the fourth largest investment bank at the time. As a result of an inter-company power struggle, the board of directors promoted Lewis Gluckman to co-CEO in the early 1980s. The conflict created dysfunction in the company, prompting its sale to Shearson/American Express in 1984. In 1988, as a result of more mergers and reshuffling, the company incorporated as Shearson Lehman Hutton. During the 1980s and early 1990s, Shearson Lehman aggressively built its leveraged finance business along the lines of its rival Drexel Burnham Lambert, the leveraged buyout king. In 1994, amidst the merger mania of the time, management spun off Lehman Brothers Inc. in a successful initial public offering (IPO) on the stock exchange. Investors eagerly bought up shares of the new company.

In 1994, the Lehman board of directors appointed Richard S. Fuld as CEO of the company. Fuld began his career with Lehman Brothers in 1969, the year the firm's senior partner, Robert Lehman, died, and he remained at the company until its bankruptcy. He began as a commercial paper trader and rose rapidly through the ranks. By 2008, at the time of Lehman's bankruptcy, Fuld had been with the company for almost 40 years, and was the longest-tenured CEO on Wall Street. Lehman Brothers performed quite well under Fuld's leadership. On December 17, 2005, when *International Financing Review* announced its 2005 Annual Awards – one of the securities industry's most prestigious honors – it had this to say: "[Lehman Brothers] not only maintained its overall market presence, but also led the charge into the preferred space by ... developing new products and tailoring transactions to fit borrowers' needs…Lehman Brothers is the most innovative in the preferred space, just doing things you won't see elsewhere."[2] Fuld also took in numerous honors for his management of the firm. In 2006, *Institutional Investor* magazine named Fuld America's top chief executive in the private sector. In March 2008, Fuld appeared in *Barron's* list of the 30 best CEOs and it dubbed him "Mr. Wall Street." He received nearly half a billion dollars in total compensation from 1993 to 2007. By 2007, Fuld had turned a 1993 yearly loss of $102 million at Lehman's into a profit of $4.2 billion. But the good times would not last.

Almost overnight the successful investment bank and exemplary CEO turned from the darlings of Wall Street to the humiliation of filing the largest bankruptcy in U.S. history. There was another side to Fuld's personality. He was nicknamed the "Gorilla" on Wall Street for his competitiveness. *Condé Nast Portfolio* ranked Fuld number one on its Worst American CEOs of All Time list, stating he was "belligerent and unrepentant." Fuld's darker personality traits emerged for full public viewing as the drama of Lehman's fall unfolded.

Lehman borrowed significant amounts of money to fund its investing strategies, a process known as leveraging, in the years leading up to its bankruptcy in 2008. A significant portion of this investing was in housing-related assets, making it vulnerable to a downturn in that market. Lehman's leverage ratios reflected its risk-taking, which increased from approximately 24:1 in 2003 to 31:1 by 2007. The profits rolled in during the boom time, but this vulnerable position meant that just a 3 – 4 percent decline in the value of its assets would entirely eliminate its book value, or equity, a very precarious financial position. Since investment banks such as Lehman were not subject to the same regulations as depository banks, their risk-taking was more excessive. In 2008, Lehman faced an unprecedented loss due to the escalating subprime mortgage crisis. Lehman's losses were apparently a result of having held on to the dicey subprime and other lower-rated mortgage tranches. In the first half of 2008 alone, Lehman stock lost 73 percent of its value as the credit market continued to tighten. In August 2008, Lehman reported that it intended to release 6 percent of its work force, 1,500 people, just ahead of its third-quarter-reporting deadline in September. Because of its dire financial predicament, feelers went out for a buyer of the firm. The state-controlled Korea Development-ment Bank was one of its main suitors, but the bank never consummated the marriage. In September, investor confidence in the company continued to erode as Lehman's stock lost even-more of its falling value. Treasury Secretary Hank Paulson, former CEO of rival investment bank Goldman Sachs, did not indicate that the U.S. government would come to the rescue of the ailing giant.

On September 13, 2008, Timothy F. Geithner, then president of the Federal Reserve Bank of New York and future Treasury Secretary in the Obama administration, called a meeting to discuss the future of Lehman, which included the possibility of an emergency liquidation of its assets. The slim hope that Barclays of London would purchase all or part of the firm had vanished, leaving bankruptcy the only option. Leaders of major Wall Street banks and high-ranking government officials convened September 14 to try to prevent the bank's liquidation. They did not reach a solution. Lehman Brothers filed for Chapter 11 bankruptcy protection on September 15, 2008.

The fall of Lehman Brothers alone did not cause the financial crisis, nor did just the sub-prime mortgage market. There was a lot more to it than simply a few bad apple bankers making unwise loans to foolish homeowners, who bought houses they couldn't afford. As we can see from the previous chapters, there is a lot more to the financial system than meets the eye. The financial crisis of 2008 is no exception.

Questions to Consider

1. Lehman's as a company was 158 year old. What circumstances and actions took place that ended its long and storied history?
2. What is your reaction to its bankruptcy in September 2008?

FINANCE IS THE CIRCULATORY SYSTEM

Finance is like the circulatory system in the human body, and the banking system is the heart of the economy. Ideally, the banking system pumps the lifeblood of the economy – money – to the places where it needs it most. If the banking system is the heart of the financial sector, in 2008, it suffered a heart attack, a massive one. This heart attack could have caused the death of the TBTF banks the way they were structured, and hence, the death of the U.S. economy, but the U.S. government revived it on its deathbed. The government administered massive shocks to the dying heart, frantically trying to revive the comatose banking system. They put it on life supports, infused it with government loans and guarantees, paid for by the taxpayers. Slowly it began to revive. At the time of this writing, the government revival of the TBTF banks has perhaps saved the system from financial collapse. But the whole circulatory system – the financial sector – has many plugged arteries that need

CEO DICK FULD, FORMER CHAIR OF BANKRUPT LEHMAN BROTHERS, AFTER TESTIFYING BEFORE CONGRESS ON OCTOBER 6. 2008.

tending. Will the patient – the financial sector – return to its old ways of undisciplined living that caused its heart attack in the first place or has it changed its habits to a more sober and simple living style that will unclog the arteries and prevent another heart attack?

In this chapter, we will examine some of the highlights of what took place during the financial crisis of 2007-2008. We will look at not only the events but also a few of the prime players in the crisis as well. Keep in mind the questions: "What is the prognosis for the heart attack patient? And is there a chance for recovery?"

Countrywide Financial Corporation[3]

Countrywide, at first glance, was not the typical subprime lender. Founded in 1969 by David Loeb and Angelo Mozilo, it grew to become the nation's largest and most profitable mortgage lender. At its height Countrywide Financial Corporation became a $500 billion home loan machine with 62,000 employees, and 900 offices. Mozilo was famous for being an obsessively hands-on manager, as well as a terrifying boss. For many years the company had a reputation for conservative lending practices and excellent cost controls. In 2003, *Fortune* magazine lavished praise on it as one of the most successful American companies, with 23,000 percent stock appreciation since 1982.

ANGELO MOZILO, FORMER CEO OF COUNTRYWIDE FINANCIAL, ACQUIRED BY BANK OF AMERICA IN 2008.

Mozilo was ambivalent toward the subprime mortgage strategy, but in the end perhaps some combination of ego, greed, laziness, and perhaps fatigue (he underwent spinal surgery several times during the bubble) won out over both ethics and caution. In the midst of the bubble, as Mozilo approached retirement age, he announced an absurdly ambitious goal for Countrywide: a 30 percent share of the whole U.S. mortgage market. This required aggressive expansion into the whole spectrum of toxic loan products, which Mozilo pressured Fannie Mae to buy. The rest he sold to Wall Street, which Mozilo didn't have to pressure to buy.

Countrywide also lobbied the political establishment intensively and used techniques verging on bribery to get favorable treatment from lawmakers. Mozilo created a special "Friends of Angelo" VIP unit to provide vastly improved customer service and favorable mortgage terms to dozens of Fannie Mae executives, members of Congress, congressional staff members, and various prominent people. There were many notable recipients of Mozilo's largesse. One recipient was former *Tonight Show* host Ed McMahon, who eventually defaulted on his $4.8 million loan. In the political realm, recipients included the Democratic Speaker of the House Nancy Pelosi and Democratic Senator Christopher Dodd, chairman of the Senate Banking Committee, as well as three successive CEOs of Fannie Mae.

By 2006, Countrywide and its practices had become increasingly fraudulent. When the bubble peaked and everything at Countrywide started to go bad, Angelo Mozilo resorted to various forms of deception, both personal and corporate. First, he intensified efforts to quickly get rid of dubious loans, so that Countrywide wouldn't own them when they failed. Throughout the email trails Mozilo left, he crassly urged his subordinates to "comb the assets" and sell off the riskiest ones while there was still time. Secondly, Mozilo protected himself financially, as many executives did. As Countrywide started to falter, Mozilo borrowed $2 billion from Countrywide to repurchase its own stock, in order to prop up the stock price. At the same time that Countrywide was buying back its stock and Mozilo was telling the world that everything was fine, he was actually selling his own Countrywide stock – over $100 million in the year before the firm collapsed. Yet, Mozilo repeatedly declared that the company was on sound financial footings. All of these pronouncements were false.

Countrywide's fall was as spectacular as its rise. When its collapse was eminent, Countrywide sold itself to Bank of America in January 2008, at a fire sale price. This transaction would prove to be a very costly mistake on the part of Bank of America. Countrywide's toxic loans continue to poison Bank of America – and the national economy. Of the 14 million loans Bank of America managed in 2010, Countrywide originated 10 million of them. At the same time, of those who borrowed from Countrywide, 15 percent were behind on payments, compared with 6 percent for loans that Bank of America originated.[4]

The **Securities and Exchange Commission**, an arm of the federal government that regulates the financial industry, was beginning to uncover Countrywide's illegalities. In June 2009, the agency filed civil fraud and insider trading charges against Mozilo and his top lieutenant. In October of the same year, Mozilo agreed to repay $45 million in ill-gotten profits and $22.5 million in civil penalties as part of a settlement with the SEC, but he admitted no wrongdoing. In June 2010, Countrywide Home Loans as part of Bank of America, agreed to pay $108 million to settle federal charges that the company overcharged customers who were struggling to hang onto their homes. In December 2011, the Justice Department announced that Bank of America had agreed to pay $335 million to settle allegations that Countrywide discriminated against black and Hispanic borrowers during the housing boom. This was the largest residential fair-lending settlement in history. A department investigation concluded that Countrywide had charged higher fees and rates to more than 200,000 minority borrowers across the country than to white borrowers who posed the same credit risk. The Justice Department also said that Countrywide steered more than 10,000 minority borrowers into costly subprime mortgages when white borrowers with similar credit profiles obtained prime loans. By 2012, Countrywide's losses and legal liabilities were so severe as to threaten Bank of America's continued viability. Another TBTF bank was teetering on the verge of collapse.

Mozilo, however, is not on the verge of financial collapse. In fact, he is quite comfortable. His total compensation during the bubble was more than $450 million, and as a result of his stock sales over the years, he remains extremely wealthy, with a net worth estimated at $600 million in 2010.

Questions to Consider

1. What is your reaction to the story of Angelo Mozilo and Countrywide Financial Corporation?

SETTING THE STAGE OF THE FINANCIAL CRISIS

In a period of less than 18 months, Wall Street had gone from celebrating its most profitable age to finding itself on the brink of ruin. Just as Wall Street concocted trillions of dollars of wealth, that wealth swiftly vanished. The crisis reconfigured the financial landscape. The calamity would definitively shatter some of the most cherished principles of capitalism. The idea that financial wizards had conjured up a new era of low-risk profits and that American-style financial engineering was the global gold standard was officially dead – at least for the moment.[5]

In 2007, at the peak of the economic bubble, the financial services sector had become a money-producing machine, ballooning to more than 40 percent of total corporate profits. Financial products – too complex to understand – were driving the nation's economy. The mortgage industry provided the loans that served as the raw material for Wall Street's elaborate creations, repackaging and then reselling securities as many times as necessary to generate fees, and then selling them to an unsuspecting world.[6]

Financial titans were confident that they had invented a new financial model that they could successfully export around the globe. "The whole world is moving to the American model of free enterprise and capital markets," proclaimed Sandy Weill, the CEO of Citigroup in the summer of 2007. He lamented, "Not having American financial institutions that really are at the fulcrum of how these countries are converting to a free-enterprise system would really be a shame." But the big brokerage firms had constructed their empires on a shaky foundation; they built it on a pile of enormous debt. Many Wall Street firms had unsustainable debt to capital ratios of 32 to 1. To be clear, this strategy worked spectacularly well for awhile – it always does in a bubble – validating the industry's complex models and generating record earnings pocketed by the financial elite.[7] When it failed, however, the catastrophic results trickled down to the 99 percent who bore the burden of the financial excesses.

Cheap and plentiful money issued by the Federal Reserve contributed to the Wall Street juggernaut that emerged after the collapse of the dot-com bubble and the post-9/11 downturn. The surplus savings in Asia combined with unusually low U.S. interest rates began to flood the world with money. The subprime mortgage market, awash with liquidity, was a crowning example of cheap money run amok. At the height of the housing bubble, banks were eager to make home loans to nearly anyone who had a heart beat and signed on the dotted line. With no documentation, a prospective buyer could claim a six-figure salary and walk out of a bank with a $500,000 mortgage, topping it off a month later with a home equity line of credit. Home prices skyrocketed. In the hottest real estate market in memory, ordinary people turned into speculators, flipping homes and tapping home equity lines of credit to buy SUVs and power boats.[8]

At the time, Wall Street supposedly believed that its new financial products – securitized mortgages – had diluted, if not removed, risk. The financial "wizards" split the mortgages up into individual pieces and sold those pieces to investors, collecting gargantuan fees in the process. Thinking they were really the wizards the media called them, the bankers gobbled up mountains of mortgage-backed assets from one another. What ended up the biggest risk of all was the interconnectedness among the nation's financial institutions. As a result, if one fell, the rest felt the impact, like a series of falling dominoes.[9]

Of the pre-crisis Big Five Investment Banks – Bear Stearns, Lehman Brothers, Goldman Sachs, JP Morgan, and Morgan Stanley – Bear Stearns, the weakest and most highly leveraged, was the first to fall. But everyone knew that even the strongest banks could not withstand a full-blown investor panic, which meant that no one felt safe, and no one was sure who else could be next. This bubble actually created a risk to the entire financial system. Along with a systemic failure of the financial sector, this drama is also a human one, a tale about the fallibility of people who thought they themselves were too big to fail.[10]

The 2008 crisis bears so many eerie similarities to the lead-up to the Great Depression. The same forces were at work in the years leading up to the so-called Great Recession: the irrational euphoria, the pyramids of leverage, the financial "innovations," the asset price bubbles, the panic, and the runs on banks. Change a few

SANFORD "SANDY" WEILL, CEO OF CITIGROUP.

particulars of the storyline, and you could be reading about the legendary South Sea Bubble of 1720, the global financial crisis of 1825, the boom and bust of Japan's Lost Decade (1991-2000), the American savings and loan crisis in the 1980s, or the dozens of crises that hammered emerging markets in the 1980s and 1990s. Although not all origins are the same, they, nonetheless, share striking similarities.[11]

The following is a story about how one mortgage company, Ameriquest, turned the staid and conservative field of mortgage lending into one in which the money was as abundant as flies on a carcass and those involved were as predatory as vultures searching for a fresh kill.

Ameriquest

It was the 2004 holiday season, and a college student – let's call him Bob – was home in Sacramento, California. One night, out on the town, he met another young man Bob nicknamed Slickdaddy G. Slickdaddy G, who was 26, was a "larger-than-life personality type," Bob recalls. "He had perfectly highlighted blond hair, short and gelled, perfect white teeth, and perfectly bronzed skin."

AMERIQUEST®
MORTGAGE COMPANY

He also had his own limo driver and a seemingly endless supply of cash. Bob joined Slickdaddy G for a night of club hopping, picking up pretty girls and drinking Dom Perignon. The crew ended up at a penthouse apartment called "the P" – where an "insane party" was taking place. "A DJ, and more girls, booze, and drugs than you can imagine," says Bob. "It was one of the crazier experiences of my life to this point." The next morning, Bob asked Slickdaddy G, "What the hell do you do?" "Ameriquest" came the reply. "I'm in the mortgage business."[12]

The subprime bubble was as wild as anything ever seen in American business. Slickdaddy G told Bob that in one especially good month he took home $125,000. In some places, like Ameriquest's Sacramento offices, drug usage was an open secret, former loan officers say, especially coke and meth, so that the loan officers could sell 14 hours a day. And the money poured in.[13]

Ameriquest rose to be the U.S. leader in subprime lending in 2003, having driven its volume to $39 billion, up from just $4 billion in 2000. An assistant attorney general in Minnesota requested Ameriquest's files in 2003 and was amazed to see file after file list the applicant's occupation as "antiques dealer." Borrowers told of signing a loan application and finding at closing that lenders had fabricated an entire financial record for them, tax forms and everything. Americaquest landed on the "Worst Ten in the Worst Ten" list of unethical businesses in 2003.[14]

Clueless Citigroup senior management purchased Ameriquest in the summer of 2007, even as the subprime bubble was collapsing, an event that contributed to the firm's receiving billions of dollars in a taxpayer bailout. Ameriquest was the object of major lawsuits filed by more than 20 state attorneys general during the bubble, while federal regulators and law enforcement agencies did nothing. In 2005, President Bush appointed Ameriquest's CEO, a major Republican donor, as the ambassador to the Netherlands.

Ameriquest was just one of the leading unethical mortgage lenders, many of them in the largely unregulated shadow banking sector. These lenders were not traditional banks that took consumer deposits for savings and checking accounts, but existed solely to feed the securitization food chain. They got their funding from Wall Street – the same firms that bought their loans. Much like the investment banks, Ameriquest and other lenders relied on very short-term credit. And when it dried up, the whole industry unceremoniously collapsed.

Questions to Consider

1. Do you think the story about Ameriquest was an aberration or do you think it was fairly common in the mortgage lending business in the mid-2000s leading up to the 2008 crisis?
2. Why didn't federal regulators put a stop to its illegal and unethical practices?

EVENTS OF THE 2008 FINANCIAL CRISIS

By the spring of 2006, the financial system with its astonishing dependence on leverage – and its blind faith that asset prices would only continue to rise – was primed for a monumental collapse. Housing starts had leveled off, and home prices – which had doubled over the previous decade – stopped rising. Simply, the supply of new homes began to outstrip the demand, and a rise in interest rates made mortgages more expensive. The hundreds of unregulated nonbank mortgage lenders, who had been at the forefront of originating subprime mortgages, relied heavily on short-term financing from larger banks. Since subprime mortgage borrowers were defaulting at an accelerating rate, the larger banks refused to renew these lenders' lines of credit. Since there was no "lender of last resort," the nonbank lenders began to fail, just as in the bank runs of the 1930s.[15]

By the end of March 2007, the number of nonbank lenders that had collapsed soared to 50 or more. On April 2, the nation's second-largest subprime lender – New Century Financial – went bankrupt after its funding dried up. Prosecutors later charged it with a significant number of "improper and imprudent practices related to its loan originations, operations, accounting and financial reporting processes." At the same time, others who were in the business of originating mortgages – thousands of small-time mortgage brokers – went out of business. Most market commentators claimed that the problem was restricted to one small sector of the financial system. Roubini claims, "This too often happens as financial crises gather steam: the problem is widely seen as 'contained'."[16]

Hedge funds operate much as banks do, getting short-term investments from individuals and institutional investors, as well as short-term repurchase agreements, or "repos" from investment banks. Like conventional banks, hedge funds invest their short-term borrowings for the long term. For example, two hedge funds run by Bear Stearns sank billions of short-term loans into highly illiquid subprime CDO tranches. Headquartered in New York City with offices worldwide, Bear Stearns was an investment bank founded in 1923 and it survived the Great Depression. At its peak it employed 15,500 people around the world. The Bear Stearns' hedge funds had undergone explosive growth, based on overleveraging subprime and other risky securities, which they spun into supposedly high-quality assets and the various rating agencies rated triple A. Once demand dried up for these types of securities, their values plummeted. This meant that their value as collateral for borrowing also shrunk. To make up for this difference, creditors started to ask Bear Stearns to post more collateral. At the same time, investors were pulling out. The only way for the bank to come up with the money to post as collateral was to sell the assets at bargain-basement prices, which further decreased the value of the funds. The hedge funds needed money to put up for margin calls, which was money required to pay the borrowing costs. In the end, the funds ran out of cash completely.[17] In March 2008, the government orchestrated the sale of Bear

AS OF JANUARY 1, 2007, NEW CENTURY WAS THE 2ND BIGGEST U.S. SUBPRIME MORTGAGE LENDER. FOUNDED IN 1995, HEADQUARTERED IN IRVINE, CA

Stearns to JPMorgan Chase for $10 per share, a price far below its pre-crisis 52-week high of $133.20 per share, but not as low as the $2 per share originally agreed upon. In January 2010, JPMorgan ceased using the august Bear Stearns name. During that time, the remnants of the shadow banking system collapsed, and even the conventional banking system came under assault. The crisis was just beginning.

By late summer of 2007, the balance sheets of a range of financial institutions showed a distressing surprise: various hedge funds, banks, conduits, SIVs and others revealed that they held a puzzling array of toxic assets. Where might others lie? By the end of 2007, weighty uncertainty prevailed. Which banks had toxic assets buried off their balance sheets? The financial system lacked transparency, and much of its activity took place outside the gaze of regulated exchanges. As happens more often than not, crises wane before waxing anew; a period of calm may come before the storm of even the worse outbreaks of panic and disorder. This was that period of calm. But things were about to get worse.[18] The storm was gathering.

In the spring of 2008, the pressure for the government to do something about the crisis quickly mounted. By then the securitization pipeline had all but shut down, not only for ordinary mortgages but for credit card loans, auto loans, and other consumer credit products as well. The economy was grinding to a standstill.

The federal government-sponsored entities (GSE), Fannie Mae and Freddie Mac, also started to waver. Latecomers to the securitization club, they had leveraged themselves at the ratio of 40 to 1 by issuing debt that benefitted from the implicit backing of the U.S. Treasury Department. Their tried-and-true conservative lending principles were thrown out the window, as they had used part of their purportedly risk-free debt to procure risky mortgages and asset-backed securities. Fannie Mae and Freddie Mac stuffed their investment portfolios with toxic subprime mortgages and subprime securities.[19] Their troubles dated from 2004-2006, when the two GSEs purchased $434 billion in securities backed by subprime loans, further fueling the boom in subprime lending. In 2004 alone, they purchased $175 billion in subprime securities, accounting for 44 percent of the market and an increase of 116 percent from 2003, when they bought $81 billion. In 2005, Fannie Mae and Freddie Mac purchased $169 billion of subprime securities, accounting for 33 percent of the market, while in 2006, they scaled their purchases back to $90 billion. However, from 2007 onwards, as housing prices started to plummet, delinquencies and foreclosures began rising sharply. The GSEs recorded $14.9 billion in combined net losses in 2007, depleting their capital reserves and undermining their financial strength.[20] Concerns about their solvency grew.

On July 30, 2008, President George W. Bush signed a law that enabled the government to expand its regulatory authority over Fannie Mae and Freddie Mac and authorized the U.S. Treasury to advance funds for the purpose of stabilizing the two institutions. Stabilizing them didn't work.

On September 7, 2008, the government authorities dismissed the chief executive officers and board of directors of Fannie Mae and Freddie Mac, and authorities placed the companies into the conservatorship of the Federal Housing Finance Agency, with the government's commitment to keep the corporations solvent. Billions of dollars in mortgage losses in both companies had eroded their cash reserves; they needed to replenish their capital. A **conservatorship** is essentially the equivalent of a Chapter 11 bankruptcy, with new leadership appointed to the bankrupt company. A conservatorship implies a more temporary control than **nationalization**, through which the government would more completely take over the enterprise.

The intervention leading to the conservatorship of these two entities has become the largest in government history and was justified by the Treasury Department as a necessary step to prevent further damage to the financial sector. The Treasury committed itself to infuse as much as $100 billion into each GSE for a total of $200 billion to keep them both solvent and operating. In exchange, each GSE would issue to the government $1 billion of senior preferred stock in the companies. Together, the two GSEs had more than $5.2 trillion in outstanding mortgage-backed securities (MBS).[21] In 2009, they held almost half of the estimated $12 trillion U.S. mortgage market.[22]

Questions to Consider

1. Why did the federal government choose the conservatorship path to dealing with Fannie Mae and Freddie Mac rather than nationalization? Which approach would you choose? Why?

Update Fannie Mae and Freddie Mac

In December 2011, federal regulators from the Securities and Exchange Commission (SEC) charged six former executives – including former CEOs – at mortgage giants Fannie Mae and Freddie Mac with securities fraud, alleging they misled investors about their exposure to risky subprime mortgage debt. The SEC, which regulates the securities industry, said it sued three former executives at Fannie Mae and three at Freddie Mac. Among those charged were former Freddie Mac CEO Richard Syron and former Fannie Mae CEO Daniel Mudd. "Fannie Mae and Freddie Mac executives told the world that their subprime exposure was substantially smaller than it really was," said Robert Khuzami, Director of the SEC's Enforcement Division. Khuzami added that these misstatements "misled the market about the amount of risk on the company's books." The SEC said both firms have agreed to cooperate with the agency and have entered into non-prosecution agreements. About $169 billion in federal aid have propped up Freddie Mac and Fannie Mae since the government rescued them in 2008. Fannie and Freddie own or guarantee about half of U.S. mortgages, or nearly 31 million loans.[23]

By the end of the summer in 2008, as Lehman Brothers and Merrill Lynch slid inescapably toward bankruptcy, Secretary of the Treasury Hank Paulson called a meeting of the city's financial elite at the office of the Federal Reserve in Lower Manhattan on Saturday, September 13. Paulson told the assembled bankers that the duty of dealing with the panic would rest with all of them. He prodded them relentlessly to figure out a way of either buying Lehman or organizing its orderly liquidation. After an all-night session, they reassembled the following morning but came back with no deal; the government would let Lehman go bankrupt. At the government's beseeching, the old, venerable firm, Merrill Lynch, fearful of sharing Lehman's looming bankruptcy fate, hastily accepted a purchase deal from Bank of America.[24]

FANNIE MAE HEADQUARTERS AT 3900 WISCONSIN AVENUE, NW IN WASHINGTON, D.C.

Lehman's bankruptcy on September 15, 2008, sent shock waves through the financial markets. Lehman's collapse did not cause the financial crisis; it was the consequence of flawed lending practices and inadequate oversight by government regulators. Whether the government bailed out Lehman Brothers or not, difficulties lay ahead for the global economy.[25]

Lehman's bankruptcy shock waves first hit the insurance giant AIG. When Lehman declared bankruptcy, all the major ratings agencies downgraded AIG's credit rating. Its losses had been mounting for months, but the downgrade called into question the guarantees that the insurance company had conferred on half a trillion dollars' worth of triple A-rated CDO tranches. Unable to survive on its own, AIG became a ward of the state with a handover of most of the firm's com-

mon stock to the government in exchange for an infusion of cash. In effect, it was not so much a government bailout of the company as it was a bailout of all the banks that had purchased insurance from AIG. It would have been perfectly appropriate in a business sense if the government had requested that the banks take a "haircut" – a loss – on those tranches they had insured as a penalty for their unwise decision in trusting AIG to insure them against losses. But the government did not do so. Instead, the government paid 100 cents on the dollar – the full value – even though the market value of the tranches had fallen far below that price. By this time any talk of holding the line against moral hazard had evaporated. Like the sheriff restoring order in the Wild West, the government was stepping in to save the banks from collapse.[26]

HANK PAULSON, TREASURY SECRETARY

AIG and Hank Greenberg

American International Group (AIG) dates its history back to 1919, when Cornelius Vander Starr established an insurance agency in Shanghai, China. Starr was the first Westerner in Shanghai to sell insurance to the Chinese, which he continued to do until communism took hold in 1949 and communist leader Mao Zedong ousted AIG from the country. Starr then moved the company headquarters to its current location in Lower Manhattan in New York City. The company went on to expand, often through subsidiaries, into other markets, including parts of Asia, Latin America, Europe, and the Middle East.

In 1962, Starr gave management of the company's lagging U.S. holdings to Maurice R. "Hank" Greenberg, who shifted the focus of the company from personal insurance to high-margin corporate coverage. Greenberg focused on selling insurance through independent brokers rather than agents to eliminate the expense of agent salaries. Because of his success, in 1968, Starr named Greenberg his successor. He took the company public in 1969 and grew it into one of the largest insurance and financial services corporations in the world.

Beginning in 2005, AIG became embroiled in a series of fraud investigations conducted by the Securities and Exchange Commission (SEC), U.S. Justice Department, and New York State Attorney General's Office. In February 2005, amid a major accounting scandal, AIG ousted Greenberg from his long-held position at AIG. The New York Attorney General's investigation, headed by Eliot Spitzer, led to a $1.6 billion fine for AIG and criminal charges for some of its executives.

On September 16, 2008, AIG, a significant participant in the CDS market, suffered a liquidity crisis following the downgrade of its credit rating from triple A to double A. After AIG had shown that it could not find lenders willing to save it from insolvency, the Federal Reserve created a credit facility for up to $85 billion in exchange for an 80 percent equity interest in the company. A small branch of the company based in London with only 375 employees had managed to insure enough toxic CDOs to bring down countless other divisions that employed more than a 100,000 people.[27] By May 2009, the Federal Reserve Bank and the U.S. Treasury had increased the potential financial support to AIG, with an additional bailout of $70 billion, a $60 billion credit line and $52.5 billion to buy mortgage-based assets owned or guaranteed by AIG, increasing the total amount available to as much as $182.5 billion. AIG subsequently sold a number of its subsidiaries and other assets to pay down loans received from the government.

The question is where did the AIG money from the government go? By June 2009, the U.S. government began paying off AIG's credit bets and the corporate clients to whom it owed money for insurance claims. Interestingly, some of the biggest players in the financial crisis insured their exotic CDOs and CDSs with the now-insolvent AIG. The bailout channeled the money from the government through AIG and then awarded it to AIG's corporate customers clamoring for a pay-off to their insurance claims. The bailout awarded billions of taxpayer-funded dollars to some of the biggest names in the financial business: Societe Generale, $11.0 billion; Goldman Sachs, $12.9 billion; Merrill Lynch, $6.8 billion; Deutsche Bank, $11.8 billion; Barclays, $7 billion; and BNP Paribas, $4.0 billion. Nothing could better illustrate the way in which the financial crisis had become a systemic international crisis than the fact that the U.S. Treasury was transferring these gigantic sums to foreign banks.[28]

Probably the most egregious act, among the many committed by the firm, was in March 2009, when AIG announced that they were paying $165 million in executive bonuses. The company's financial unit alone handed out $450 million in total bonuses, and bonuses for the entire company reached $1.2 billion. President Obama responded to the planned payments by stating "[I]t's hard to understand how derivative traders at AIG warranted any bonuses, much less $165 million in extra pay. How do they justify this outrage to the taxpayers who are keeping the company afloat?"[29]

In a strange twist of events, the larger-than-life former CEO of AIG Hank Greenberg is striking back at the U.S. government for bailing out his former employer. He filed a lawsuit against the U.S. in 2011 claiming that its $182 billion bailout of the insurance giant during the 2008 financial crisis was unconstitutional. According to the lawsuit, which seeks at least $25 billion for Greenberg's new venture Starr International and other shareholders, the bailout, which gave the government a nearly 80 percent stake in the company, violated the fifth amendment because it took property from shareholders without just compensation. Upon bailing out AIG in 2008, the government became its majority owner, after its potential bankruptcy threatened to bring down the entire financial system. The bailout made the company one of the most contemptible public faces of the financial crisis, creating a public relations disaster for it. According to a recent Harris Interactive poll, AIG has the worst corporate reputation of any company, even surpassing the much-despised Goldman Sachs and British Petroleum (BP) to get the top spot. In another lawsuit, the company is also seeking potentially billions of dollars from firms such as Bank of America and Goldman Sachs, alleging that the insurance giant was victim to Wall Street's riskiest practices. Much of the $182 billion in rescue money went to pay AIG's insurance obligations to big banks.[30]

The good news in this otherwise sordid story is that AIG, through the sale of parts of its vast holdings, has apparently repaid the government its debt, with interest.[31]

Questions to Consider

1. How do you think the federal government should have handled the insolvency of AIG? Why.

Money Market Funds

The parts of the financial system that had so far escaped the crisis were now in trouble. Money market funds were one of the first to fall. Even though money markets are part of the shadow banking system, the public considers them a safe investment with a nominal interest rate paid. Even though the FDIC does not insure most money market funds, there is the implied assurance that they will not depreciate. A dollar will be worth a dollar no matter what. The no-matter-what day arrived on September 16, 2008, just after the collapse of Lehman Brothers, when one of the most prominent money market funds, Reserve Primary Fund, "broke the buck." Because of its exposure to Lehman's toxic debt securities, the net asset value of its money market fund dipped below $1, meaning that a dollar invested with the fund was no longer worth a dollar. This was almost unprecedented, and it sparked a run on the fund. Uncertainty surrounded the entire $4 trillion money market industry.[32] Since I had just resigned from my part-time position as a history instructor at the local community college to write books for the Center for Global Awareness, I had stashed my living expenses for two years in a money market fund. Along with millions of other people, I was worried. But the federal government stepped up to provide a blanket guarantee – the equivalent of deposit insurance – to all existing money market funds. They were safe, for the time being.

The Commercial Paper Market

Here is another financial term to mull over: the **commercial paper market**. It sounds like a high-quality greeting card company, but it isn't. Another part of shadow banking, this unnecessarily vague term describes what credit-worthy corporations do for their short-term borrowing needs, such as to meet regular operating expenses like payroll. Corporations can borrow billions of dollars for 30, 60, or 90 days, and when those debts come due, most corporations simply roll them over for another 30, 60, or 90 days term. The problem comes when no one wants to buy a corporation's commercial paper, and the company is unable to roll over the debt. Money market funds are generally large buyers of commercial paper, and they had completely retreated from the market during the crisis. AIG, for example, was unable to borrow on the commercial paper market, which contributed to its running out of cash. An overall lack of commercial paper resulted in the Federal Reserve's creation of the Commercial Paper Funding Facility (CPFF). Under this act, the Fed could finance approximately $1.8 trillion worth of commercial paper.[33] Now that would be an expensive greeting card!

As an investment bank, Lehman had no insured depositors; it borrowed short-term money through the commercial paper market. Although borrowing and lending is typically what banks do, this part of the financial system involving money markets and investment banks is part of the shadow banking system described in chapter 3. That's why these institutions arose, in part, to circumvent the regulations imposed on the real banking system. Lehman's collapse sparked a run on the shadow banking system, similar to the runs on the real banking system before deposit insurance (FDIC). To stop the run, the government provided insurance to the shadow banking system.[34]

Questions to Consider

1. During the 2008 crisis, do you think the federal government should have insured money market accounts that were not part of the FDIC program? Why.

2. What do you think would have been the ramifications if they did not insure the money market accounts?

The Federal Reserve: The Lender-of-Last-Resort

Before the crisis of 2008 and the subsequent bailout of Wall Street, the Federal Reserve maintained $770 billion of safe Treasury bonds on its books ready to step in as the national lender of last resort if need be. In an emergency, the Fed could loan financial institutions short-term money and, in return, these firms would post safe assets, such as Treasury bonds, as collateral. The better the collateral, the more favorable were the loan terms for the borrowing bank. It was a symbiotic relationship in which the Fed would receive interest payments on those Treasury bonds and hand a portion back to the Treasury Department. The financial crisis abruptly halted this low-risk practice. As the bailout unfolded, the complexity of the Fed's books increased along with its taking in toxic asset and mortgage-backed securities as collateral from banks wanting to get loans. The Fed's cloaked their new maneuvers in a veil of secrecy. Banks began to post all sorts of toxic, junk assets to the Fed just to get them off their books, and in return they received low-cost loans.[35] It was a strategy dreamed up in Wall Street heaven.

For a few weeks during the fall of 2008, a liquidity crisis occurred as corporate borrowing and lending effectively collapsed. The commercial paper market shut out perfectly solvent corporations as borrowing rates skyrocketed and blue-chip firms found themselves short of cash. In order to avoid further disaster, the Federal Reserve extended **lender-of-last resort** options to support nonfinancial corporations. Since other institutions were afraid to lend money, the Fed stepped in to do so as the only option available. These interventions had little or no precedent in the history of central banking. They amounted to a massive expansion of government support of the financial system. But they were only the beginning.[36]

After the initial credit crunch, money from the Fed freely flowed to the banks at very low interest rates, sometimes even 0 percent. But despite the generous extension of cash to the banks, they continued to refuse to make longer-term loans to many firms and businesses that needed credit to stay alive. Banks were getting no-interest loans from the Fed, but market rates for everyone else remained high. Financial institutions continued to stockpile cash in expectation of future losses on their toxic assets, or they sank it into the safest investments around: government debt, or the obligations of Fannie Mae and Freddie Mac. The banks could encounter very little risk and make a return. By borrowing money from the Fed at rates approaching zero, then taking that borrowed money to buy a ten-year or 30-year Treasury bond paying 3 to 4 percent made economic sense; it also allowed the banks to steer clear of all the risky borrowers who were clamoring for loans. While this strategy was disastrous for the Main Street economy, it made sense from the standpoint of self-preservation for Wall Street. [37] As of this writing, Wall Street is still following this strategy.

The Federal Reserve's Quantitative Easing

By the fall of 2008, the belief that financial institutions should fail outright without injections of government cash had evidently been pushed aside. The Fed was lending lots of money and allowing the use of low-grade assets as collateral. The Fed's supposed intent was to boost market liquidity in the face of a comatose credit market. Because lenders were holding on to their money, the Fed found ways to help increase the free flow of capital.[38]

The Fed would attack the problem of increasing the free flow of capital on multiple fronts; one of these fronts was an unconventional policy used by Central Banks called quantitative easing. When I heard the term quantitative easing I immediately thought of the times when I may overeat, and the waistband on my pants becomes too tight. If I had a really good elastic waistband on my pants, then the expanding elastic waistband could ease my overeating. End of my over-eating misery. In a way that is what the Fed did in the financial crisis. The overeating, though, was the wild gluttony exhibited by bankers, lenders, and home-buyers, which led to a situation where the Fed had to step in to ease the pain caused to the global economy. The Fed might not appreciate my waist band analogy, however, so a slightly more technical definition is in order. Central Banks (the Fed) use **quantitative easing** when interest rates are at or very near zero, and the government cannot lower them any further. In such a situation, the central bank may perform quantitative easing by purchasing a pre-determined number of bonds or other assets from financial institutions. In effect, the bonds pump more money into the economy. The goal of this policy is to increase the money supply rather than to decrease the interest rate, which is already around 0 percent. The government often considers this to be a "last resort" to stimulate the economy.[39]

Chairman of the Federal Reserve, Ben Bernanke, employed some highly unconventional measures in efforts to ease the crisis. The Fed started buying up long-term government debt: 10 and 30 year Treasury bonds. This act immediately injected massive amounts of liquidity into the markets because the Fed would pay for those bonds by creating money essentially out of thin air. As it purchased hundreds of billions of dollars' worth of bonds, cash would flow to the banks that sold them. As a result, the banks would have even more cash and would be more likely to lend it. By broadening the range of assets it held as collateral, the Fed sought to prop up financial markets.[40] An unintended consequence of this unorthodox remedy was that it sent a clear message to the financial markets that the Fed would try anything to prevent a financial crisis from spinning out of control. Although it was reassuring to the banks and general public, it created moral hazard on a grand scale. Sadly, the Fed's actions kept afloat both the insolvent and solvent banks; very few major banks and financial firms have declared chapter 11 bankruptcy. Disastrous financial institutions that no amount of liquidity can save remain in operation. According to Roubini, "Like the infamous zombie banks that became a symbol of Japan's Lost Decade (1990s), these firms must go bankrupt, and the sooner they do, the better."[41]

Another unintended consequence of the monetary policies pioneered by Chairman Bernanke is that the Fed has stepped into the financial system and effectively subsidized its operations, potentially incurring losses that could ultimately be the taxpayers' responsibility. The Fed's power to lend money turned into a means of spending money on the financial system. It basically granted many subsidies to the financial system in its time of need. When the time comes to sell the long-term debt the Fed has purchased from these zombie banks, they may end up having to unload these bonds at a substantial loss.[42]

The Fed used a sleight of hand trick to take on trillions of dollars in useless toxic assets from the banks, giving cheap loans in return to the very banks that had created the bad assets and the financial crisis in the first place. While the Fed was pumping trillions into the economy, the general public was largely distracted by the fray taking place in Congress over the much less expensive $700 billion Treasury bailout package that would be known as TARP.[43]

Questions to Consider

1. How would you assess the Federal Reserve's actions during the financial crisis? What group/s did their actions benefit the most?

The Troubled Asset Relief Program (TARP)

Let's review a moment – this can get confusing. In March 2008, the economic downturn put the huge investment bank Bear Stearns under significant financial duress and JP Morgan Chase acquired it for the bargain price of $1.2 billion. In September 2008, in the midst of the 2008 election, Lehman Brothers, the fourth largest investment bank, declared bankruptcy. The government placed Fannie Mae and Freddie Mac, the two mortgage giants, on federal life support. The federal government bailed out AIG, the country's largest insurer. At this point, Merrill Lynch, Morgan Stanley and Goldman Sachs, the three remaining independent investment banks, all faced financial runs that would quickly bankrupt them without government involvement. Bank of America quietly acquired Merrill Lynch, with some federal arm-twisting, for $50 billion. In the same month, JP Morgan Chase bought the failing Washington Mutual Bank (WaMu) for $1.9 billion. In October 2008, Wells Fargo purchased Wachovia in a $12.7 billion deal. Many other banks also faced insolvency, especially if they took big losses on their loans to other institutions that were about to go bankrupt.[44] The consolidations made the industry more concentrated than ever, the term TBTF was even more relevant than before the crisis. This was a very uncertain time.

An important secretive meeting took place in mid-September between leading Wall Street executives and government officials – Treasury secretary Henry Paulson, Federal Reserve Board chairman Ben Bernanke, and Timothy Geithner, then the head of the New York Federal Reserve Bank and later served as Treasury Secretary under President Obama, and Christopher Cox, head of the Securities and Exchange Commission (SEC). The Wall Street men had billions of dollars of toxic assets on their books with no buyers, and they thought it would be great if the U.S. Treasury would buy them. Paulson essentially agreed. Over the weekend, Paulson put together a short, three-page memo that he sent to the Senate Banking Committee on September 23, 2008, outlining his plans to have the

BERNANKE TESTIFYING BEFORE THE HOUSE FINANCIAL SERVICES COMMITTEE ON FEBRUARY 10, 2009.

Treasury purchase these toxic mortgage-backed assets right off the books of the banks that had made the bad bets in the first place.[45] The line coming out of the Treasury's office was that the economy would collapse if Congress did not immediately rescue the banks. They enlisted everyone that mattered in this massive public relations effort.[46]

The **Troubled Asset Relief Program (TARP)** was a government program to purchase assets and equity from financial institutions with the intended purpose to strengthen the financial sector. President George W. Bush signed the law on October 3, 2008. The $700 billion TARP blank check and the more valuable loans and loan guarantees from the Fed and Federal Deposit Insurance Corporation (FDIC), enabled the financial sector to survive the crisis they had created. The TARP $700 billion was the smallest part of the bailout. There was no Congressional furor about the trillions of dollars of Fed guarantees and loans. Wall Street was delighted with the government program to buy the bad assets. It was great for them to offload their junk to the government at inflated prices. The banks could have sold many of these assets on the open market at the time, but not at prices they would have liked.[47]

SPEAKER OF THE HOUSE, DEMOCRAT NANCY PELOSI (CENTER), TREASURY SECRETARY HANK PAULSON (RIGHT), SENATE MAJORITY LEADER HARRY REID (LEFT) DURING TARP NEGOTIATIONS IN FALL 2008.

Questions to Consider

1. Why was there such an uproar about the TARP program? Do you think this uproar was justified?

Bank Holding Companies

On September 22, 2008, under a provision in the Federal Reserve Act, the Fed granted bank holding status to two of the country's most powerful independent investment banks still left standing: Goldman Sachs and Morgan Stanley. A **bank holding company** (BHC) is a company that controls one or more banks, but does not necessarily engage in banking itself. The Fed has responsibility for regulating and supervising bank holding company activities, such as establishing capital standards, approving mergers and acquisitions and inspecting the operations of such companies. Becoming a bank holding company makes it easier for the firm to raise capital than as an investment bank. Goldman Sachs and Morgan Stanley were the only two remaining investment banks –JPMorgan acquired Bear Stearns in spring 2008 in a fire sale brokered by the federal government, Bank of America had agreed to buy Merrill Lynch for $50 billion, and Barclays of London agreed to buy the core capital-markets business of Lehman Brothers out of bankruptcy. Now Goldman and Morgan Stanley were able to compete directly with larger firms like Citigroup, JPMorgan Chase and Bank of America. These firms combined investment and commercial banking operations with the larger capital cushions that come with retail deposits. This federal action officially ended the last vestiges of the Glass-Steagall Act that had erected a fire wall separating commercial and investment banks.[48]

With the changeover to BHCs, the former investment banks had access to the Fed's discount lending window, effectively ensuring Morgan Stanley and Goldman Sachs easy access to massive lines of credit. They got guarantees and cheap loans from their BHC designation and essentially acted as they did before. By becoming BHCs, they got around disclosing how much their assets were worth, based on market values. Since many of their assets were toxic and worth far less than the market values, this move was advantageous to the investment banks. The BHCs could instead reclassify their assets as "held for investment" and not reveal their actual worth, just as the big banks did.[49] This meant that on the accounting balance sheet it looked as though they had far more in actual worth than they really did.

THE OBAMA ADMINISTRATION AND THE CRISIS: AN ANALYSIS

The important 2008 presidential and Congressional races took place amidst the financial turmoil. At the time of the crisis, the Democratic candidate, Senator Barack Obama from Illinois, was barely leading in the polls over the Republican candidate, Senator John McCain from Arizona. To avoid further instability, both candidates coordinated their campaign message to comply with that of the sitting president, George W. Bush. However, Obama appeared calm and deliberate in his dealing with the financial crisis compared to the often erratic and inconsistent message put forth by the McCain team. Voters took note. Obama captured 53 percent of the popular vote compared to McCain's 46 percent and won by a substantial margin in the deciding Electoral College vote. Obama quickly nominated Timothy Geithner as Treasury Secretary on November 24, 2008; the Senate confirmed him and the president swore him into office on January 26, 2009. Geithner largely continued the policies forged by his predecessor, Republican Hank Paulson. They both worked closely together during the financial crisis, when Geithner was Chair of the New York Federal Reserve, and after his nomination by President-elect Obama.

The Obama administration largely continued the Bush administration's financial policies that Paulson laid out. There would not be a radical departure in economic policies between the Republican and Democratic administrations. Stiglitz had strong words to say about the policies set out by President Obama, who maintained that the big banks are "not only too big to fail but also too big to be financially restructured, too big to play by the ordinary rules of capitalism. That means that if the bank is on the brink of failure, there is but one source of money: the taxpayer. He thinks all this talk of too big to fail was a ruse, a ploy that worked, based on fear mongering. Just as Bush used 9/11 and the fears of terrorism to justify so much of what he did."[50]

The Obama team had finally settled on a slight variation of Paulson's original idea of buying the toxic assets directly from the banks, aptly called "cash-for-trash." Stiglitz colorfully described Obama's strategy, "It was as if it had decided to use a private garbage-hauling service, which would buy the garbage in bulk, sort through it, pick out anything of value, and dump the remaining junk on the taxpayer. And the program was designed to give the garbage collectors hefty profits – only certain members of the Wall Street club would be allowed to 'compete,' after having been carefully selected by the Treasury. One could be sure that these financiers who had been so successful in squeezing money out of the economy would not be performing the duties out of civic-mindedness."[51]

TIMOTHY GEITHNER WAS SWORN IN AS TREASURY SECRETARY ON JANUARY 26, 2009.

The common element of the Paulson and Geithner plans was the insistence that the toxic assets on the banks' books were really worth more than anyone was willing to pay for them. As the reasoning went, if the market priced the assets properly, then the banks wouldn't be in trouble. So the plan was to use taxpayer funds to drive the prices of bad assets up to what the market supposedly considered to be their "fair" levels. Paulson proposed having the government buy the assets directly. Geithner instead proposed a complicated scheme by which the government would lend money to private inves-tors, who then would use the money to buy the toxic assets. The idea, says President Obama's top economic adviser, is to use "the expertise of the market" to set the value of the toxic assets. But the Geithner scheme offered a one-way bet: if asset values went up, the investors profited, but if they went down, the investors could walk away from their government-guaranteed debt. Economist Paul Krugman said about the plan, "So this isn't really about letting markets work. It's just an indirect, disguised way to subsidize purchases of bad assets." [52]

The Obama administration argued that it was necessary to do this to provide liquidity to the market. Lack of liquidity was depressing prices and artificially hurting banks' balance sheets. Ac-cording to Stiglitz, however, "The main problem was not a lack of liquidity. The real issue is that the banks made bad loans in a bubble and were highly leveraged. They had lost their capital, and this capital had to be replaced." [53]

The very expensive and politically-contrived TARP bailout failed to restart lending. One of the reasons for this was that the government was giving much of the money to the big banks, and to a large extent, these banks years ago had shifted much of their focus away from lending to small and medium-sized businesses to gimmicky financial products. If the goal of the bailout was to encourage job creation – or even job preservation – more credit needed to be available to the firms that were the source of most job creation. Small and medium-sized enterprises are the engines of job creation; therefore, the government needed to channel more money to small banks and community banks where they desperately needed it. [54]

Instead of channeling money to Main Street, the government lavished money on Wall Street. The government rewarded the biggest financial institutions that had made the biggest mistakes – some of whom didn't even do much or any lending. The AIG bailout was a particularly foolish exercise in propping up a company that had minimal impact on Main Street. Both the Bush and Obama administrations were using a variant of trickle-down economics – throw enough money at AIG, and some of it will trickle down to where it's needed. This approach was a very costly way of trying to stimulate the economy. The companies receiving AIG money (see above) made it very clear that little of it ended up in job-creation institutions – though that was the argument put forward in its defense. Some worried that the government needed to bail out all creditors, or otherwise some insurance and pension funds would experience significant losses. But, Stiglitz argues, "If we need to rescue pension funds and insurance companies, then we should do so directly, where every dollar of government money goes directly to the group that needs it. There is no justification for spending $20 to bail out investors so that $1 can go to a pension fund that might otherwise be in trouble." [55]

Stiglitz goes on to argue that instead of trying to save the incompetent, existing banks, the government could have given the $700 billion TARP money to the few healthy and well-managed banks or even used it to establish a new set of banks. At a modest leverage of 12 to 1, that would have generated $8.4 trillion of new credit – more than enough for the economy's needs. Even if the administrations had not done something as dramatic as establish a new set of banks, they might have used some of the money for creating new lending facilities and some to absorb some of the uncertainty of new loans by providing partial guarantees. [56]

While purporting to save free market economics, the government was creating a far cry from a truly free market. The bailouts did not enforce appropriate discipline on the banks, rewarding those that had been cautious and letting fail those that had taken on extraordinary risk. The banks that did the worst in risk management got the biggest handouts from the government. While the Obama administration had avoided the conservatorship route, what it did was far worse than nationalization: it was fake capitalism, the privatizing of gains and the socializing of losses. The perception and reality of the bailout was that it was unfairly generous to the bankers and unfairly costly to ordinary citizens. This has made dealing with the crisis all the more difficult.[57]

Questions to Consider
1. How do you think the Obama administration handled the financial crisis?
2. If you were his advisor at the time what advice would you have given him and his new administration?

THE FEDERAL RESERVE'S ROLE IN THE FINANCIAL CRISIS

The Federal Reserve was a partner in most of the bailouts. The Fed more than doubled its balance sheet (a measure of its lending) in the span of a few months, from $942 billion in early September 2008 to over $2.2 trillion in early December 2008. Banks just stuck the money they got from the government at near zero interest rates under their proverbial mattress. They needed the liquidity they got from the Fed, and the economy was in such a dire state it was no time to go out making loans. Large companies often get much of their funds in the form of commercial paper, not from banks. When that market also froze, respected giants like General Electric (GE) couldn't borrow any money. With lending at a standstill, the Fed took on a new role – it went from being a lender of the last resort to being a lender of first resort.[58]

During a time when banks couldn't unload their nonperforming, toxic assets at any price, the Fed inhaled trillions of dollars' worth of them and in return issued banks debt at very low interest rates. Because the Fed entered risky assets into their books as collateral for loans, they put themselves in the passive role of sitting and hoping the assets' value would turn around someday, or the banks that pawned them off would be able to retrieve them and pay back their loans. However, the Fed doesn't have to worry about positive returns: its supply of money is endless.[59]

Chair Ben Bernanke transformed monetary policy during and after the crisis, directing a stunning series of interventions into the financial system that even today few people understand. Some of these moves he had planned on making; others he put forth as the months passed and the danger of deflation and even a depression increased. They ranged from conventional monetary policy – reducing interest rates to zero, for example – to unparalleled measures heralding an expansion of the Federal Reserve's power over the economy. Also problematic is the fact that some of Bernanke's monetary policies breached the traditional fiscal powers of elected government – namely, the constitutional power to spend money that is reserved for Congress. In the recent crisis, the Fed pushed past its limits of powers: for example, swapping safe government bonds for toxic assets and the more radical move to purchase toxic assets and hold them on its balance sheet. Even if these measures prove effective, the acts amount to a subversion of the legislative process.[60]

CONCLUDING INSIGHTS: THE 2008 FINANCIAL CRISIS

The entire series of efforts to rescue the banking system were flawed. This was in part because those put in charge of the repair – Timothy Geithner and Hank Paulson – were advocates of deregulation. Stiglitz comments, "Perhaps not surprisingly, they all employed the same logic that had gotten the financial sector into trouble to get it out of it. The financial sector had engaged in highly leveraged, non-transparent transactions, many placed off the official balance sheet. They believed they could create value by merely moving assets around and repackaging them. The financial sector based the approach to getting the country out of the mess on the same principles. The banks shifted the toxic assets from their balance sheets to the government – but that didn't make them any less toxic. Off-balance-sheet and non-transparent guarantees became a regular feature of the Treasury, FDIC, and Fed."[61]

As a result of all the hoopla, the big banks are bigger and more profitable than ever. Did the bailouts save the American and world economy? Would we have been in a Great Depression instead of a Great Recession if government leadership had not acted quickly?

Economist Dean Baker argues "Now, the same crew that tapped our pockets [in 2008] is eagerly pitching the line that their bailout was good for us. It may be the case that the winners write the history books, but that doesn't prevent the rest of us from telling the truth. The specter of a second great depression was a fairy tale the bank lobby invented to make the rest of us feel good about having given them our money. We are also supposed to feel good that the banks repaid the vast majority of the TARP money. It is important to remember that the economy would be no less productive following the demise of these Wall Street giants. The only economic fact that would have been different is that the Wall Street crew would have lost claims to hundreds of billions of dollars of the economy's output each year and trillions of dollars of wealth. That money would, instead, be available for the rest of society."[62]

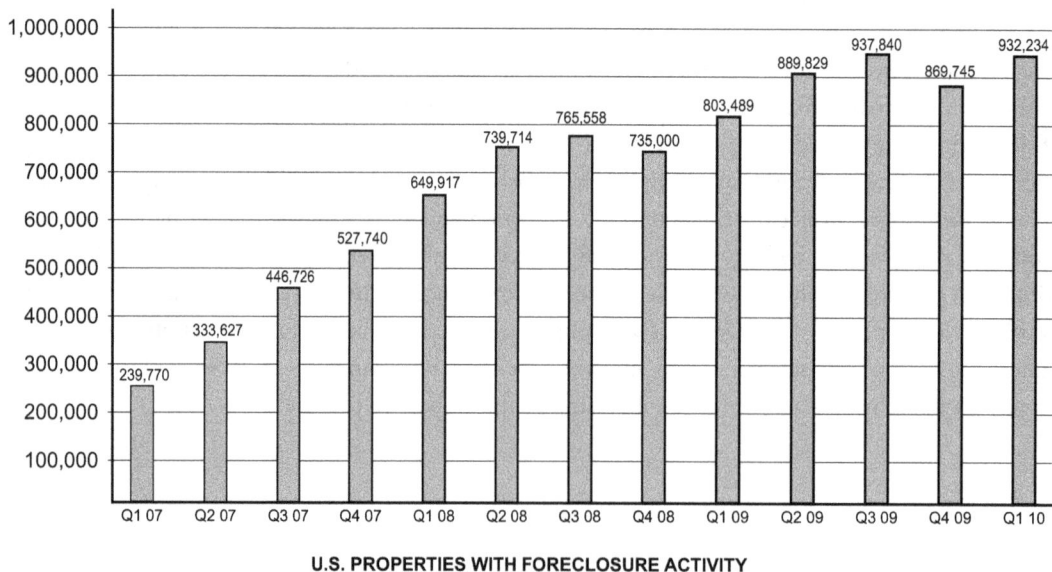

U.S. PROPERTIES WITH FORECLOSURE ACTIVITY

Pundits claimed that the subprime lending was necessary to extend the opportunity for home ownership to first-time home buyers. But the Center for Responsible Lending published numbers showing that between 1998 and 2006 only about 1.4 million first-time home buyers purchased their homes using subprime loans. That represented about 9 percent of all sub-prime lending. The rest were refinancing or purchasing second homes. The Center also estimated that more than 2.4 million borrowers who had gotten subprime loans would lose or already had lost their homes to foreclosure. By 2010, the homeownership rate had fallen to 66.9 percent, right where it had been before the housing bubble. In other words, subprime lending was a net drain on homeownership.[63]

The question the media often asks is, "Would the economy have collapsed if the federal government did not bail out the banks?" However, this question leaves out the distinction between the TBTF banks and smaller, national and community banks. The global economy with the TBTF banks as the cornerstone of the whole system would have collapsed without government intervention. The government injected the dying system of TBTF banks with a magic elixir of taxpayer money just in time to manage its revival. The TBTF banks have staged a remarkable recovery, now bigger and stronger than ever before. But if the whole system had collapsed, and the TBTF banks went bankrupt, perhaps the smaller banks would have stepped it to provide the needed banking services their dying big brothers had formerly performed. The decision to let the TBTF banks actually fail would have been a huge gamble for the new and inexperienced President Obama to have called. Instead, in keeping with his personality, he took a cautionary approach to reconstruct the system as it had been before. There would not be a different system of smaller, local, and community banks but instead a group of concentrated goliath banks that were now even more TBTF.

Questions to Consider

1. Do you think the economy would have collapsed if the federal government did not bail out the banks?

2. What do you think would have happened if the federal government did not bail out the banks?

CHAPTER SIX

The Aftermath of the 2008 Financial Crisis

The globalization of humanity is a natural, biological, evolutionary process. Yet we face an enormous crisis because the most central and important aspect of globalization – its economy – is currently being organized in a manner that so gravely violates the fundamental principles by which healthy living systems are organized that it threatens the demise of our whole civilization.

Elisabeth Sahtouris

THE NEW NORMAL: THE 5 Rs

We are still experiencing the aftermath of the financial crisis of 2008. It is difficult to write about the aftermath of the financial crisis because it is still in process. We are still experiencing the fallout from the excesses leading up to the crisis. What are the problems that have not been resolved? What leaders are providing sensible solutions to the turmoil? Should we return to the type of economy that brought about the financial crisis, reform it, or institute a more conservative version? Should we stage a revolution and overthrow the existing economy and let the pieces fall where they may? Should we send out more petitions and hold more rallies, or should we rebuild the economy in a more equitable and sustainable way? These are just a few of the many questions that I am thinking about as I write this final chapter.

The financial crisis of 2008 was such a monumental global event that it is difficult to wrap our minds around the enormity of the consequences. We are at a very critical juncture in our history. Our planet is in crisis. Pressing economic needs have eclipsed the environmental issue for the past several years. Yet, the issue has not gone away. Americans have built the U.S. economy upon the foundation of a system devised over 150 years ago. Its apparatus is no longer sufficient for a complex nation such as the U.S., nor is it appropriate for the global community bursting at the seams with 7 billion plus people and pressing environmental concerns. No wonder we as a collective people are confused, angry, and ready for real answers and solutions to the monumental problems we are facing. However, our political leaders, whom we turn to for guidance, are as stymied as the rest of us. They have no idea which way to turn and are floundering about for coherent solutions. In fact, many are merely clinging to the past, the system that got us into such trouble in the first place. How can we sort out the global economy amidst such turmoil, indecision, stalemate, and fear? The shrillness of the debate masks the uncertainty people feel.

In researching the topic of the global economy and the financial sector over the last couple of years, I have come to the conclusion that Americans and others in the global community have responded in different ways to our current economic quandary. These responses, or movements, each view the economic system very differently. Since the teacher in me is always trying to simplify complex ideas, I have called these responses listed in the textbox the 5 Rs. I am listing the 5 Rs in a logical order, not according to my preferences. The rest of this chapter is devoted to explaining each of the 5 Rs.

The 5 Rs: Responses to the Financial Crisis

1. **Revolt** – violently overthrow the whole system for a different system.

2. **Restore** – keep the same neoliberal system as before the crisis.

3. **React** – keep the same neoliberal system as before the crisis except make it more conservative.

4. **Reform** – keep basically the same capitalist system but reform or regulate its excesses.

5. **Rebuild** – gradually work to build a new economic paradigm.

REVOLT

There were lots of revolutions in the tumultuous 19th and 20th centuries. A **revolution** is an overthrow or repudiation and thorough replacement of an established government or political system by the people governed.[1] When we think of revolutions, we think of the biggies in our history books: the American, French, and Russian Revolutions and even the Chinese revolution in the 20th century. For example, change from one form of government to another marked the Russian Revolution. Headed by a tsar (czar), the land-owning class was the governing elite of pre-1917 Russia. Communist revolutionaries executed Tsar Nicolas II and his royal family before they took over the government, land, industry, and other institutions. Millions of deaths later, communists ruthlessly installed a new form of government.

BOLSHEVIK (COMMUNIST) FORCES MARCHING ON RED SQUARE IN MOSCOW, MARCH 1918, OVERTHROWING TSAR NICOLAS II AND ENDING THE RUSSIAN EMPIRE.

When the economic and political structures of a country break down, as is happening in some countries in Europe, Africa, and the Middle East, then the country is ripe for revolution. Greece has been in the news in the last serveral years for experiencing a breakdown in the rule of law. Greece is deeply in debt and struggling to avoid a debt default. No country is under more pressure to roll back spending than near-bankrupt Greece, a once booming nation now saddled with 35 percent youth unemployment and facing the prospect of years of depressed growth. Buckling under a culture of tax evasion by the elites and rampant overspending, Greece received a $170 billion bailout from the International Monetary Fund (IMF) and European Union in 2010.[2]

Greece is coping with protests that have extended well beyond ordinary civil disobedience. In reaction to a stagnant economy, corruption, and uninspired leadership, the Greek movement includes groups of urban guerillas, radical youths, and militant unionists, among others left behind in the global economy. Thousands of Greek rebels have joined an "I Won't Pay" movement, refusing to cover highway tolls, bus fares, even fees at public hospitals. The protests are an emblem of social discontent spreading across Europe in reaction to a new age of austerity and German power in the Euro zone.

Authorities say that anger against the government has now given rise to dozens of new revolutionary groups, whose tactics include planting gas canisters in mailboxes and destroying bank ATMs. Authorities have staged a series of raids, arresting dozens and yielding caches of machine guns, grenades and bomb-making materials. Unions and political movements have always used tough tactics in Europe. However, observers are noting a surge in militancy among a "lost generation" of young Europeans who have come of age in the aftermath of the global economic crisis. Also, fascist and far-right parties are strengthening, engaging in an increasing number of attacks against immigrants in many European countries. For most, protests have become a way to express genuine discontent. For others, they have become an invitation for more radical acts.[3]

The economic crisis has energized a radical minority that have positioned themselves as society's new avengers. Experts are increasingly concerned about growing militancy on the streets and the emergence of dozens of new revolutionary groups on the Internet. According to Bart Cammaerts, an expert on radical movements, "There is a sense of general injustice, that the government bailed out capitalism and the citizens are footing the bill while the capitalist system is running like nothing ever happened. And yet, things have happened. There are more taxes, less services, and anger is emerging from that tension."[4]

For some Greeks, like 20-year old Nikos Galanos, the revolutionary movement has become an outlet for anger. Over the past two years, he has become more involved in the Anti-Establishment Movement which heaves firebombs during protests. The movement's rallies draw small armies of 7,000 or more. "I don't support violence for violence's sake, but violence is a response to the violence the government is committing against society," Galanos said. He later added, "It is now hard for any of us to see a future here. I feel it's my duty to fight against the system."[5]

Revolutionaries are eager to overthrow the government that they blame for all their problems. But revolutionaries are often short-sighted and do not have a clear plan for what should follow once the government is toppled. Revolutions often result in more chaos, violence, and instability, rather than solving the issues leading to the revolution in the first place. It is not a sensible way to bring about change.

GREEKS PROTEST AUSTERITY MEASURES IN 2012.

Questions to Consider

1. What do you think would be the repercussions if a revolution broke out in your particular country?

RESTORE

The tumultuous events that occurred in 2008 have settled down we are no longer hearing the everyday headline news that another established financial firm has gone into bankruptcy courts, has merged with another conglomerate, or has been taken over by the federal government. There is a desire by many to return to what they perceive as "normal," whatever that means anymore. I used to live in Normal, Illinois, home of Illinois State University where I taught history. When people asked where I was from, I would reply Normal, Illinois, always bracing for the tittering giggles that would follow. Although normal was poked fun at in the past, today many people crave for a return to what they think is normal. As far as the financial sector is concerned, it looks as though the days of normal are long past.

The unknown future poses some real risks and uncertainties. When people are faced with an unknown future or the safety of restoring what they knew in the past, many choose the safer alternative. When I read or hear about women who remain in abusive relationships for years on end and never try to run away, I have difficulty understanding why they would endure such humiliation and threats to their safety and well-being, and often threats to their children as well. Yet, as I understand it, they feel that at least the present is a known quantity and they know what to expect, even if it is abusive, while the future is even more terrifying and uncertain. They choose to remain in the same situation.

Restoring the past is a powerful vision for many people at this point in time. Those in the political arena and in the financial sector are conducting their business as if the financial crisis was a mere blip on the financial radar screen, and by making a few tweaks and adjustments around the edges, business can basically go on as before. The financial sector is very profitable, and those involved have every reason to try and prevent the reining in of their speculative activity through the regulatory process.

In 2012, Republican presidential candidate Mitt Romney had as one of his campaign slogans, "restore America." Incumbent Democratic President Barack Obama no longer ran on his slogan of "change in America," as he successfully did in 2008. Instead, his campaign, too, had an element of restore America. But what does it mean: restore America? It is another vague campaign term that means many different things to different people. As in Romney's case, economically he wanted to restore the principles of neoliberalism, and in particular, the primacy of the financial sector from which he made his substantial fortune. For President Obama, he wanted to have some reforms of the financial sector, but not enough to significantly curb its economic dominance. Romney's running mate, Republican Congressman Paul Ryan of Wisconsin, had no desire to restore America as it was; his intention followed a more reactionary path, as explained later.

CAMPAIGN SLOGAN IN 2012 ELECTIONS

Restore: The Bailout

The bailouts were a clear way for the government to attempt to restore the economy to the way it was prior to the crisis. The bailouts included a number of different maneuvers attempted by the government. All citizens know that governments can spend money, but it can also make guarantees so that others will spend money with the risk of default transferred to the government, which can end up costing taxpayers money. A number of guarantees played an important role in taming the recent crisis, even as they opened the door to the problem of moral hazard. For example, it will be many years before the public knows the full cost of the rescue of Fannie Mae and Freddie Mac. The government guaranteed some $5 trillion worth of obligations insured by the two institutions, along with another $1.5 trillion worth of debt that they issued. Although the government won't lose this total amount, if housing prices continue to decline and many more mortgages go into foreclosure, the government could end up sustaining considerable losses.[6]

The Troubled Assets Relief Program (TARP) legislation passed by Congress allocated $700 billion to purchase toxic assets. The government used some of the money to prop up a host of failing companies, including the automakers GM and Chrysler and their financial arms, General Motors Acceptance Corporation and Chrysler Financial. All told these bailouts of the auto industry amounted to $80 billion. The government disbursed some of the money as loans; while they used the rest of it to pur-

CITIGROUP WAS A RECIPIENT OF TARP FUNDS IN 2008.

chase an ownership stake in the companies. The companies have since paid back the money lent to them. The government funneled a sizable portion of the TARP funds – some $340 billion – to nearly 700 different financial institutions, giants like Citigroup, Bank of America, and AIG, as well as a host of smaller banks. For the most part, the money spent on these ailing institutions consisted of the government purchasing preferred shares in the bank.[7]

By summer of 2009, the price tag for the federal government's bailout of the banks, including all federal loans, capital injections, and government loan guarantees, stood at approximately $13.3 trillion. This amount included $7.6 trillion from the Fed, $2.5 trillion from the Treasury, $1.5 trillion from the FDIC, $1.4 trillion from a joint effort, and $300 billion from a housing bill. This number is so huge it is almost meaningless. By comparison, $13.3 trillion is more money than the combined costs of every major U.S. war – American Revolution, War 1812, Civil War, Spanish-American War, World I and II, Korea, Vietnam, Iraq, and Afghanistan – whose total price tag adjusted for inflation is $7.2 trillion. (The government financed World War II mostly from the savings by the American people who patriotically bought war bonds.) Meanwhile, the financial crisis erased $50 trillion in global wealth between September 2007 and March 2009, including $7 trillion in the U.S. stock market and $6 trillion in the housing market, $7.5 trillion in pension plans and household portfolios, $2 trillion in lost income in 401Ks and individual retirement accounts, $1.9 trillion in traditional defined-benefit plans, and $3.6 trillion in non-pension assets.[8]

Since we have already discussed in this book the policies of neoliberalism and economic globalization, I will not add to the information. Suffice it to say that many of the restorers in America have largely morphed into a reactionary movement, in which the neoliberal policies are even more conservative.

Questions to Consider

1. What examples of the restore movement do you see in the political and economic arena?

REACT

Reaction is a movement that favors extreme conservatism or right wing political views. This movement opposes political, economic, or social change or reforms. Reactionaries are at one end of a political spectrum whose opposite pole is radicalism or revolution. I have included reaction as a third movement since many politicians and business leaders are moving even further to the right of the restore movement. They are advocating for more concentration of corporate power, smaller government, austerity programs to reduce the deficit, tax cuts including capital gains for the wealthy, vouchers for Medicare and schools, more deregulation, and increased privatization of public institutions such as schools, prisons, government services, the military, electricity, federal lands, and Social Security.

React: Austerity

One reactionary way to achieve this agenda is to institute austerity measures. The austerity camp sees the threat of government default on the debt as a bigger problem than stagnation and unemployment and refuses to consider any more stimulus spending. They want to cut government spending through **austerity** measures targeted at all social programs, especially education, Medicare, social security, infrastructure, and programs for the poor. For example, some, such as Paul Ryan, envision Medicare in the future to be a voucher system in which health care spending is restricted to a voucher amount supplemented by private insurance. However, reactionaries do not want to cut spending for the military.

Despite high rates of unemployment, the austerity and anti-deficit forces, at the time of this writing in 2012, have the initiative in three key Western countries: in Britain, where the conservatives won on a platform of reducing the government; in Germany, where the image of spendthrift Greeks and Spaniards financed with loans from hardworking Germans became the powerful horse Angela Merkel's party rode to maintain power; and in the United States, where Republicans have seized the austerity flag.[9]

The reduce-the-deficit slogan has gained ascendancy in the U.S. for a number of reasons. First of all, this call appeals to the anti-big government sentiments. Second, Wall Street has opportunistically embraced anti-deficit calls to divert governmental efforts to enforce regulations. It proclaims, "Big government is the problem, not big banks." Third, the reemergence of neoliberal believers, who the public temporarily discredited after the financial crisis, champion the idea that a deep economic slump would purge the excesses of a bloated government and lead to a healthier economy. Fourth, the anti-spending, austerity measures are supported by the vocal and popular Tea Party movement.[10]

React: The Banks

The financial crisis and bailout led to further concentration of the financial sector. The crisis gave stronger firms an opportunity to pick up weaker firms in a wave of mergers. And the Federal Reserve and Treasury Department orchestrated a large number of hastily arranged purchases of failing financial giants, such as Bear Stearns by Chase in March 2008 and the purchase of Wachovia by Wells Fargo in December 2008. Even some banks used the Fed's capital infusions for further

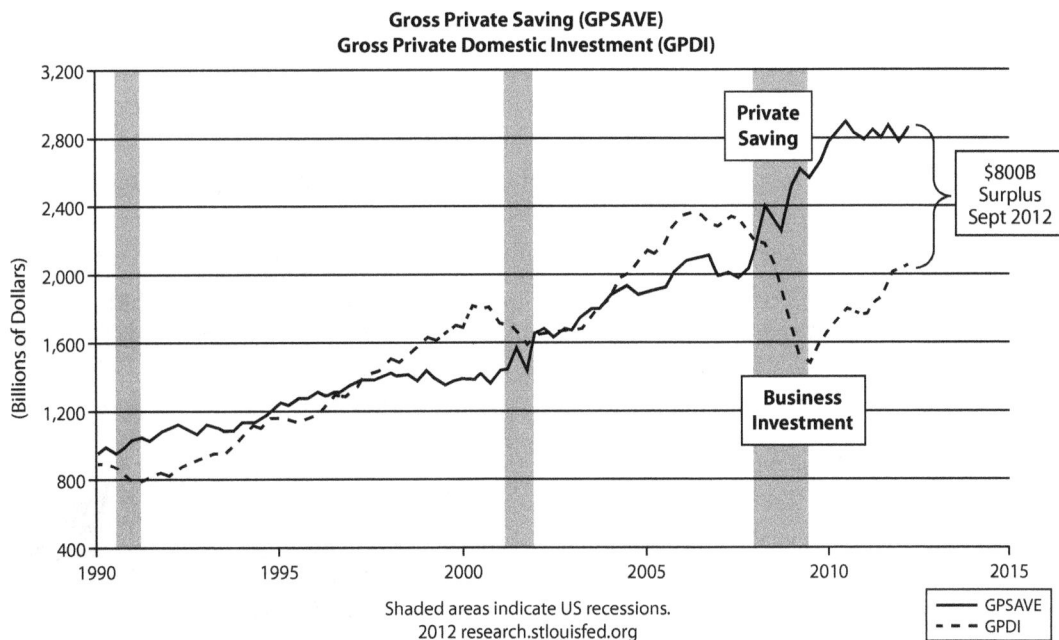

Gross Private Saving (GPSAVE)
Gross Private Domestic Investment (GPDI)

Shaded areas indicate US recessions.
2012 research.stlouisfed.org

EFFECTS OF AUSTERITY. U.S. SAVINGS AND INVESTMENT;
SAVINGS LESS INVESTMENT IS THE PRIVATE SECTOR FINANCIAL SURPLUS

mergers and acquisitions. The Treasury Department was "using the bailout bill to turn the banking system into the oligopoly of giant national institutions," as the New York Times reported.[11] The government bailout of the banking system has not merely restored it, but has made it bigger, stronger, more profitable and more politically influential.

Since the calamitous bank collapses of 2008 and the government bailout of Wall Street, the big six U.S. megabanks – Bank of America, Citigroup, J.P. Morgan Chase, Goldman Sachs Group, Wells Fargo, and Morgan Stanley – have staged a dramatic comeback. Profits, capital reserves, and stock prices are all up, while they have paid back government aid, and executive compensation is exploding. But, according to Rob Larson, "A closer look shows big-bank stability is just skin-deep, and opaque accounting rules hide a powder keg of bad debt and mounting funding issues." Smaller banks have experienced a different post-crisis environment. Despite some TARP bailout crumbs, they have gone under in record numbers – 140 failed in 2009, with a larger number in 2010.[12]

Banks have staged a staunch resistance to reform. The government gave banks money without agreeing to change their compensation structures or make other reforms; it simply allowed the banks to go on as before. At the moment when Wall Street was on its knees, politicians avoided passing serious reforms. Instead, the government helped re-establish Wall Street to its gargantuan status, thanks to taxpayer money and guarantees. About 50 very large banks and financial institutions push and pull financial markets. Bankers used bailout money to pay themselves $150 billion in bonuses – at a moment when the economic downturn forced over 29 million Americans into jobless or part-time jobs. Top hedge fund managers continued to walk off with over an astronomical $900,000 an hour in 2009. And they continued to pay an extra-low, 15 percent capital gains tax rate. Glass-Steagall was not brought back, nor were the "too big to fail" financial institutions broken up.[13] All of this has signaled a reactionary form of neoliberalism.

We are now in the worst of all worlds, where the government bailed out many TBTF institutions and they are now addicted to moral hazard; they expect the government to bail them out in the future. It is free money for capitalists, free markets for everyone else. The financial sector has not faced any real regulatory scrutiny, and no system is in place to put those institutions into insolvency should the need arise. Even worse, according to Roubini, "many of these institutions – starting with Goldman Sacs and JP Morgan Chase – are starting to engage once more in **proprietary trading**, which occurs when a firm trades various financial instruments with the firm's own money as opposed to its customers' money, so as to make a profit for itself." These strategies, which are compli-

cated bets on stocks, bonds, commodities, and derivatives driven by algorithms devised by the firm's traders, are more risky than other trading. Yet firms have resumed these practices.[14]

React: The Federal Reserve

Through its actions the Federal Reserve is helping to make the financial sector even more concentrated then before the crisis. By lending at practically 0 percent interest, it has provided cheap funding for financial firms. In a lot of ways, the Treasury Department's highly con-

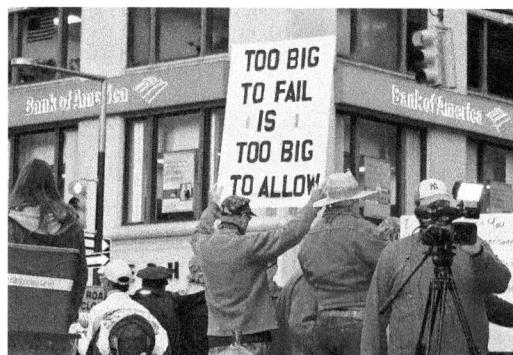

OCTOBER 25, 2011, A MAN AT OCCUPY WALL STREET PROTESTING INSTITUTIONS DEEMED TOO BIG TO FAIL

troversial $700 billion bailout gave cover to everything that was quietly going on at the Fed. Its accounting books became increasingly complex and risky. Its hasty maneuverings to transform investment banks into Bank Holding Companies and its speedy bank merger deals will most likely have lasting harmful repercussions. Big financial institutions drained trillions of dollars of public capital. Yet, they appear to be destined to remain financial behemoths. According to Prins, "[Chairman] Bernanke talks about the need for better regulation, yet skirts transparency with his own books. The Fed simply operates above any law and beyond reason. That is, always was, and will prove to be a developing disaster."[15]

The federal government doled out just over $13 trillion from the Federal Reserve, the Treasury department, and the FDIC, all going to the biggest players on Wall Street. If the government wanted to get bailout assistance to consumers who really needed it, they could have given it directly to them, or at least directed it to banks that were eager to give out or renegotiate loans. Yet, despite all the bailouts, there are still under-regulated financial institutions that operate across a more concentrated playing field than ever.[16]

React: Housing and Consumption

America now faces a social tragedy alongside an economic one. Millions of poor Americans have lost or are losing their homes – by one estimate, 2.3 million in 2008 alone. In 2007, foreclosure actions stood at almost 1.3 million, while almost 3 million homeowners received at least one foreclosure filing during 2009, setting a new record for the number of people falling behind on their mortgage payments.[17] Lenders filed a record 3.8 million foreclosures in 2010, up 2 percent from 2009 and an increase of 23 percent from 2008.[18] Millions more are expected to go into foreclosure from 2011 onward, although by 2012 the numbers have leveled off.

The bad mortgage debt on banks' books has ceased to be primarily a subprime phenomenon of low-income loan recipients; over a third of new foreclosures in early 2011 were prime fixed-rate loans, as job layoffs caused hardship for mortgage borrowers. The mortgage delinquency rate was hovering around 10 percent nationwide in late 2010, which included those behind on payments and those on the verge of eviction. However, the total number of loans that are 30 days or more past due, but not yet in foreclosure, declined in December 2011 to 8.15 percent. The number of properties that were either delinquent or in foreclosure in November 2011 totaled 6.167 million. Meanwhile, the banks have allowed extremely few mortgage borrowers to modify their mortgages or reduce their principal. Just 8 percent of delinquent borrowers received any modification, while only 3 percent have received reductions in the principal they owe. Remarkably, the banks still list the home mortgages on their balance sheets at inflated values, since they are for homes bought at the housing bubble peak, and government has not forced the banks to account for them at a reasonable value.[19] Hence, these toxic assets remain on the banks' books.

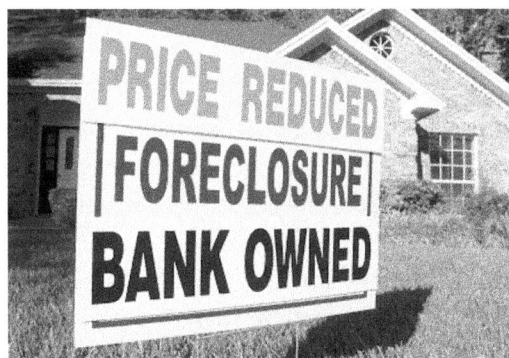

The housing bubble drove consumption prior to the recession. This bubble was the basis of the construction and consumption demand that drove the economic expansion through 2007. Now that the bubble has collapsed and trillions of dollars of wealth have disappeared, consumption levels, which are the driver of our economy, have significantly dipped. It will be difficult to restore the consumption levels of the 1990s and 2000s. The collapse of an $8 trillion housing bubble and the destruction of more than $6 trillion in stock wealth will subdue consumption for a number of years.[20]

There are looming problems in the financial markets posed by the collapse in commercial real estate and the lingering problems in residential real estate and credit card debt. Even if the economic situation restored the financial system to perfect health, there are still problems with the real economy. The deleveraging process – reducing, for instance, the abnormal level of household debt that was 1.3 times disposable income – requires higher-than-normal savings, which means lower levels of household spending.[21]

React: Labor and Social Inequality

In much of the non-financial sector, workers have increased their productivity, but the present system has largely transferred the gains from rising wages to greater corporate profits. This means that labor produces more goods and services for less personal income. An example is the factory that General Motors (GM) reopened in Orion Township, Michigan, where, under a deal negotiated with the beleaguered United Auto Workers (UAW) union, the company pays 40 percent of the workers crawling through cars on the assembly line $15 an hour. That's about half the traditional UAW wage.[22] The continuation of depressing the pay of labor is part of the reactionary movement. To return unemployment to levels prior to the financial crisis will require sustained growth in excess of 3 percent, and that's nowhere on the horizon.[23] The country has suffered unemployment rates hovering around the range of 7 to 10 percent since the beginning of the financial crisis, with more than 25 million people who are unemployed, underemployed or have given up looking for work altogether. The soaring unemployment caused tax revenues to tank, touching off fiscal crises in nearly every state. In reaction, governments dramatically cut spending and axed tens of thousands of teachers. Public school children all over the country were the ultimate losers, while the bankers who caused the crisis were the ultimate winners. For example, about 75 percent of the workforce, the average non-supervisory production worker in the U.S., has seen an 18 percent drop in real wages since the mid-1970s. Meanwhile, productivity has increased by more than 90 percent.[24] Yet, top hedge fund managers continue to pull in more than 26,000 times the pay of teachers. Are 25 hedge fund managers worth 658,000 teachers? Apparently they are, since that's what they netted in 2009. The government rescued many hedge funds and banks, but it left more than 30 million Americans scrambling for full-time work.[25] It is easy to trace where the money from higher productivity went: into the hands of the few.

Questions to Consider

1. In what ways has the reactionary movement gained traction in your particular country? Give examples.

Implementing the Restore/React Agenda

So far we have observed how those directing the political process have taken the initiative to implement either the restore or reactionary agenda. Yet, another part of the implementation process is to enlist popular, public support of the agenda through an energetic, visible mass movement. Movements of this type have emerged as grass roots efforts throughout U.S. history to advocate for their agenda on both sides of the political spectrum. One movement on the right is the Right to Life movement, which has tirelessly worked to outlaw or restrain abortion for women. A movement on the left was the anti-war movement in the 1960s to the early 1970s that publicly demonstrated to stop the war in Vietnam. We will first look at a movement on the right that seeks to implement the reactionary agenda – the Tea Party – and look at a reform movement at the end of the chapter.

A well-known and vocal reactionary movement is the Tea Party. They have gained force since the 2010 mid-term U.S. elections, when they elected numerous additional political representatives to support their already popular cause. Tea Party enthusiasts see government as the fundamental cause of all problems. To them, the governmental bureaucracy is restricting our freedoms and limiting our entrepreneurial spirit with a socialist system that redistributes wealth through high taxes to those who are too lazy to put in a good day's work. One way to restore America, they think, is to limit government authority, institute austerity measures, and follow the constitution in the way they think the Founding Fathers intended. I believe their motives are genuine, they see America adrift and they think they have targeted the problem. But the platform is disturbingly abstract, with solutions that are vague and hard to understand. However, the platform contains many words that resonate with Americans, such as liberty and freedom. If we dismantle government, as the Tea Partiers hope to do, then I worry about who will stand between the elites and the powerless. Governments throughout world history have on many occasions filled this role; otherwise, the elites are able to entrench their power and authority without any organized resistance.

The Tea Party has many different slick websites supporting its cause. One particular website – www.teapartypatriots.org/ – claimed to represent the official tea party organization. The website immediately took me to a pop-up that wanted me to sign a petition that stated, "The Supreme Court Ruled against the American People. It's Time for the People to Take Action." They want to repeal the Patient Protection and Affordable Care Act signed by President Obama on March 23, 2010, which they call Obamacare. They claim that a majority of people want to repeal the health care bill, although that figure is disputable. I visited another well-designed website, www.theteaparty.net, which has an easy way to access local meetings and events. Its mission is clearly stated "We the people preserving liberty and freedom in the United States of America."[26] The Tea Party is one of the many reactionary groups that are implementing their agenda through rallies, lobbyists, conferences, community meetings, creation of non-profit organizations, and petitions to sway political representatives. Often well-funded by wealthy individuals and corporations who would benefit from this agenda, the movement has enlisted a great deal of mass support and visibility.

TEA PARTY PROTESTERS ON THE WEST LAWN OF THE U.S. CAPITOL AND THE NATIONAL MALL AT THE TAXPAYER MARCH ON WASHINGTON ON SEPTEMBER 12, 2009.

Insights: Restore and React

I struggled with what terms to use to describe the restore and react categories of thought and action among many people today. At first, I observed that many of the actions of the government and the financial sector were to restore the systems to what it was before the crisis, but then I reasoned that actually the trend appeared to be a move even further to the right than what it was before the crisis. I then decided that we need a new category of thought and action to describe this trend; thus the term "react" seemed appropriate. The goal of many reactionaries is to continue the neoliberal principles that have been evolving over the last 30 plus years, yet entrench these principles into government policies and public thought with even more vigor. The deficit hawks were asleep when the Bush administration ran up huge deficits conducting two wars in the Middle East, massive tax cuts, and an expensive Medicare prescription plan. Now, when the country could benefit from stimulus spending, the deficit hawks are awake and keen on cutting spending to reduce the deficit. The banks are not just as big as before, but bigger. The mergers and acquisitions have led to monolithic financial structures that are indeed TBTF. The Federal Reserve has garnered more power than before the crisis. There is an increasing squeeze on labor and their wages, while social inequality is greater than before. Indeed, those supporting a reactionary movement appear to be moving forward with increased determination and zeal.

A debt-financed consumption binge supported by a housing bubble sustained the American economy – and to a large extent the global economy – before the crisis. People lived beyond their incomes because they believed house prices would rise forever. No one believes that now. The rest of the world is still striving to emulate the U.S., but if it does succeed, the world could not survive. The consumption style is not environmentally sustainable, yet in the 2000s Americans continued to buy bigger and bigger gas-guzzling cars – and the entire automobile industry's profitability rested on the assumption that Americans would do so forever. Much of the rest of the economy also rests on an unsustainable foundation. Energy is one of the most profitable sectors in the economy – coal, natural gas, and oil – but pours greenhouse gases into the atmosphere, even with incontrovertible evidence that it contributes to massive climate change.[27]

The model on which American growth is based has come to an end. The underlying debt-based consumption model of the American economy broke when the real estate bubble burst, and will not be so easily repaired. Even an arrest in the decline in real estate prices does not mean that they will return to where they had been. And that means that the economic downturn has greatly diminished the major source of wealth for most Americans – the equity in their homes.

Questions to Consider

1. Do you think the restore/react movement has viable solutions to our economic problems? Give examples.

REFORM

The fourth movement to galvanize in response to the financial crisis of 2008 is reform. **Reform** means to put or change into an improved form or condition. Reform is different from revolution. The latter means radical change, whereas reform may be no more than fine tuning, or at most re-dressing serious wrongs without altering the fundamentals of the system. Reform seeks to improve the system as it stands, never to overthrow it wholesale.[28] Thus, generally, reformers of the financial sector in the U.S. do not want to overthrow the whole capitalist economic system, but merely redress serious wrongs they see with the neoliberal model of capitalism and usher in a more regulated or managed form of capitalism.

The big question for reformers in the 21ˢᵗ century global economy is, "If there is a role for government in the global economy, what will that role be?" In the U.S. many in the neoliberal camp argue that the role of government is best when it governs least. Whenever the word reform surfaces, words like socialism, nationalization, communists, or do-gooders are hurdled like insults towards the would-be reformers. These words carry with them emotional baggage that makes clear thinking and sorting through solutions difficult. According to economic reformer Stiglitz, "The financial crisis showed that financial markets do not automatically work well, and that markets are not self-correcting. There is an important role for government."[29] If there is a reform effort to redo some of the undoings of the neoliberal policies that the government has enacted since the 1980s clearly, it will need to take the lead.

Even though some in the Obama administration and other reformers are putting forth a reform agenda, they are still promoting economic growth as the path to economic prosperity. They see it as the way to exit from economic stagnation and high unemployment. Instead of neoliberalism though, many reformers are endorsing a more managed or regulated form of capitalism, which supports an important role for government rather than relying on the "invisible hand" of the markets altogether. However, most of those who are critics of neoliberal policies, such as Joseph Stiglitz, Paul Krugman, Robert Reich, and others who I have cited in my sources, support economic growth as the way out of the current malaise with changes around the edges that they think will increase prosperity, such as a more equal tax system, targeted regulations, a stimulus to encourage consumer demand, and a curb on the excesses of neoliberalism.

In this section, I will highlight a few of the proposed reforms in the financial sector and some of the reforms that the government has already passed. However, there is much resistance to reform. In the early months of the Obama presidency, with general public support, his administration made timid attempts to initiate reform of the financial sector. However, those in the reactionary camp have waged a sizable backlash to stem the tide of reforms. In fact, the reforms that the government has passed have endured repeated efforts to chip away at their intent. Although Obama's health care bill survived a 5-4 vote by the Supreme Court in the summer of 2012, initiatives continue to dilute or overturn the bill. The same can be said about the Dodd-Frank Wall Street Reform Bill.

Reform: Stimulus

The reform camp thinks stagnation is a threat to the economy and suggests more **stimulus** (government spending) to counter it. They believe deflation is a big threat; therefore, the fear of too much government spending stoking inflation is misplaced. The burdening of future generations with debt is odd to them, since the best way to benefit tomorrow's citizens is to ensure that they inherit a healthy, growing economy. Moreover, reformers say government default is not a real threat for countries that borrow in currencies they control, like the U.S., since, as a last option it can simply repay debts by having its central bank print more money (quantitative easing).[30] Reformers believe that reactionaries

WHAT IS THE ROLE OF GOVERNMENT? THE U.S. CAPITOL BUILDING IN WASHINGTON D.C.

who want to impose austerity measures will not reduce the deficit but stymie growth and hurt the economy in the long run.

The question here is, "How much government spending is needed to stimulate the economy?" Economist Paul Krugman is a leading cheerleader in the stimulus camp but on these questions he betrays some unease, perhaps realizing that traditional Keynesian policy has its limits. Krugman states "Nobody can be sure how well these measures would work, but it's better to try something that might not work than to make excuses while workers suffer." The stark alternative to more aggressive deficit spending is "permanent stagnation and high unemployment."[31]

Government spending has what is called a **multiplier effect**. On average, the short-run multiplier effect of government spending for the U.S. economy is around 1.5. If the government spends a billion dollars now, GDP this year will go up by $1.5 billion. If the government invests stimulus money in assets that increase the country's long-term productivity, the country will be in better shape in the long run as a result of a stimulus. However, not all spending has the same multiplier effect: spending on foreign contractors working in Iraq has a low multiplier effect, because much of the consumption takes place outside the U.S.; so do tax cuts for the wealthy – who save much of what they receive from government rebates. Unemployment benefits have a high multiplier effect, because those who find themselves suddenly short of income spend almost every dollar they receive.[32]

Reform: Transfer Payments

Since the 1930s, a conventional way of dealing with economic downturns is **transfer payments**, whereby the federal government sends money to particular cash-strapped groups such as the poor, the unemployed or struggling state and local governments. Like tax cuts, they are part of the standard fiscal policy for dealing with economic crises and various recessions. Transfer payments come in many forms: unemployment benefits, food stamps, job retraining, and other special programs. Although these transfer payments helped arrest the current slide toward depression, some think the government also has to worry about deficits during a recession.[33] Economist Paul Krugman argues that the federal government should stimulate the economy through transfer payments to state and local governments, allowing the money to be used to rehire laid off teachers and police.[34] Krugman and others think that transfer payments are a better way to stimulate spending and revive the economy than tax cuts, which most conservatives support. An obstacle to tax cuts is that rather than going out and spending the money from special tax rebates or permanent reduction in tax rates, households often save it or use it to pay off their debts. As Roubini notes, "It has done nothing to stimulate demand. It also shifted debt from one part of the economy to another: private debt went down, but public debt went up."[35]

Reform: Break Up the TBTF Banks

America's major banks are too big to fail. The obvious solution is to break them up. Their competitive advantage arises from their monopolistic power and their hidden government subsidies and guarantees. This significantly distorts the financial sector, and the banks suspend the ordinary rules of capitalism to protect their bondholders and shareholders. Yet, when reforms are proposed to break up the banks or tax them or impose additional restrictions on them so that they would no longer be too big to fail, the financial sector lobbyists spring into action to prevent the government from enacting or implementing such reforms.[36]

Policies should force banks to recognize losses from their bad lending. Institutions like Citigroup became oversized, which employed more than 300,000 people and provided thousands of kinds of financial services at its peak. No one CEO, no matter how adept and visionary, can manage a global financial institution that enormous. In fact, Citigroup would not be in existence today if not for government recues and bailouts. Over the last 80 years, it has repeatedly overextended itself and teetered on the brink of insolvency. Citigroup is not the lone wolf in this category; many of the TBTF banks wouldn't even exist were it not for heavy helpings of government assistance. According to Roubini, "A global system of smaller, more specialized financial institutions can more than meet the needs of even the largest, most sophisticated firms."[37] But Wall Street lobbying has limited reforms by spending over $700 million in the years after the financial crisis, as estimated by the Center for Responsive Politics.[38]

Reform: The Financial Reform Bill

The **Dodd – Frank Wall Street Reform and Consumer Protection Act** is a federal statute instituting reform of the financial sector that President Barack Obama signed into law on July 21, 2010. Congress passed the Act in response to the late-2000s recession. At 2,300 pages, the Act represented a significant reform of the American financial regulatory environment and the nation's financial services industry. As with most reforms, there are arguments on both sides of the political spectrum: on the one hand critics contend the reforms were insufficient to prevent another financial crisis or future bail outs of financial institutions, and on the other hand, the financial sector argues that the reforms went too far and would unduly restrict the ability of banks and other financial institutions to make loans.

Those supporting financial reform see the act as putting an end to the potential abuses associated with having an oligopoly of banks controlling so much of the financial system. According to Roubini, "The reforms outlined go a long way toward increasing accountability and transparency in the financial system by reforming compensation, regulating securitization, bringing derivatives under public scrutiny, and putting the putative guardians of the system – rating agencies – on a very short leash." These reforms would also ensure that banks and other financial firms have enough capital to weather a major financial crisis.[39]

PRESIDENT BARACK OBAMA MEETING WITH REP. BARNEY FRANK, SEN. DICK DURBIN, AND SEN. CHRIS DODD, IN THE GREEN ROOM AT THE WHITE HOUSE PRIOR TO A FINANCIAL REGULATORY REFORM ANNOUNCEMENT ON JUNE 17, 2009.

But others question whether merely reimagining financial regulation is the way to prevent the next crisis. The bill arguably does nothing to slow the "financialization" of the U.S economy, which gobbles up more of the nation's economic activity than other economic sectors. Also, new regulations won't do anything to stop the financial sector from exerting its influence over Washington and the regulators themselves. During the 2000s, many of those who were supposed to be regulated overpowered the financial regulators. Another critic, Walden Bello, adds "The measure did not have the minimum conditions for a reform with real teeth: the banning of derivatives, a Glass-Steagall provision preventing commercial banks from doubling as investment banks; the imposition of a financial transactions tax or Tobin tax; and a strong lid on executive pay, bonuses, and stock options."[40]

Interestingly, even though Congress passed and the President signed the Dodd-Frank financial reform law, the government has had difficulty in instituting and implementing even the simplest and most obvious reforms, especially if those reforms happen to clash with powerful financial interests. The financial sector has called out its legions of lobbyists and lawyers to wage war against regulators over every line in the rulemaking process. You may be wondering how a financial lobby that represents a tiny minority of Americans, even one as large and powerful as the financial sector, could subvert a law passed by our duly-elected representatives. The manner in which they did so is instructive, since it is a blueprint followed by others who are out to obstruct the workings of government for their own self-serving agenda.

First, the financial sector made sure the law was not that sweeping in the first place. The main reason for the law was to make sure that the financial playground had some rules to play by, unlike the helter-skelter playground prior to the crisis. This meant moving swaps and other derivatives onto open exchanges and making sure that federally insured banks that dabbled in those risky markets retained more capital to back up their bets. The law aimed to prevent another disaster like the demise of AIG and Lehman Brothers. To restore the spirit of the Glass-Steagall Act, the so-called **Volcker Rule**, named after former Chair of the Federal Reserve Paul Volcker (1979-1987), would have prevented federally insured banks from engaging in dangerous speculation such as when the banks use customers' deposits to trade on the bank's own accounts to make a profit for itself. It also envisioned a powerful new **Consumer Financial Protection Bureau** to represent the interests of the consumers against Wall Street. And it would have cleaned up the mortgage markets by ending predatory home-lending.[41] To the average person the law seemed reasonable enough, but not to the Wall Street lobbyists. Even before Congress enacted the law, they immediately got to work, whittling the final bill down to its barely-recognizable final version. The lobbyists watered down all of the provisions. The best example of the water-down process was the most obvious and necessary reform of all – breaking up the TBTF banks. The bill did not include these reforms.[42]

Secondly, before the ink was even dry on the Dodd-Frank Bill, Wall Street started to lodge law suits against the bill. If they can tie up the law in court for a long period of time, it undermines the law. And, if a law suit doesn't

ELIZABETH WARREN SET UP THE CONSUMER PROTECTION ACT, STARTED JULY 2011, AS PART OF THE DODD–FRANK WALL STREET REFORM. SHE WAS PASSED OVER AS DIRECTOR BECAUSE OF WALL STREET OPPOSITION BUT WON ELECTION AS THE SENATOR FROM MASSACHUSETTS IN 2012.

succeed, there is always the appeals court. As is the plan by those opposing reform, the cases could drag on for months, if not years.

Third, if you can't win stall. Implementation is the key in any law passed; the Dodd-Frank Bill is no exception. However, the Securities and Exchange Commission has not got on board the implementation bandwagon. Delays by Congress in writing provisions of the law have turned into a stalling game that seems to know no limits. The deadline for implementation was July 21, 2012; two years after the bill signed into law had come and passed![43]

Fourth, don't fund the regulators. Congress controls the purse strings of the federal regulators who are charged with carrying out the Dodd-Frank law. Congress, doing the bidding of Wall Street, simply slashed the budget. Wall Street lobbied important lawmakers to rein in the regulators and Congress complied. Congress then forced the regulators to compromise on enforcement in order to stave off budget cuts.[44]

Fifth, pass lots of loopholes in the bill. Congress, with prodding from Wall Street, has embarked upon a campaign to write new laws designed to undercut the rules that the regulatory agencies had not even written yet. Are you confused yet? Well if you are, then Wall Street has succeeded in making the matter so complex and confusing that it has had its way. All of these loopholes are so oppressively dull and technical, that it is not worth the time to go through them (even if I could understand them all). But they are so important that they affect many of us in our daily lives.

Thus, two years after Congress passed the Dodd-Frank legislation, they have written only 108 of 398 required regulations, 148 deadlines have been missed (67 percent) and nearly two dozen Congressional bills scrapped parts of the proposed law. The writers of the draft measures implementing the Volcker Rule (which limits proprietary trading by banks) have riddled it with so many holes as to be almost meaningless. On the eve of the Great Depression in 1929, 250 banks controlled roughly half the nation's banking resources. Now, a mere six banks – Bank of America, J.P. Morgan Chase, Citigroup, Wells Fargo, Goldman Sachs Group, and Morgan Stanley[45] – control almost 74 percent of the nation's banking resources. As demonstrated time and again, corporations can undo the regulations affecting them.[46]

Implementing a Reform Agenda

Those wishing to implement the reform agenda have gone about it in a number of ways. Reformers have not been able to initiate a mass political movement, such as the Tea Party in the reaction camp; however, the approach many have used to initiate reforms is to respond. I am using respond in this case as an answer or reply in words or writing. After the 2008 financial earthquake rocked our whole economic system and threatened to pull the whole country – and thus the world – asunder, many people felt compelled to try and "do something" to remedy the economic instability. After all, it is a free country built on principles of public expression and participation; many thought it was their civic duty to voice their anxiety and concerns in a constructive way. However, not everyone responds to events and policies in the same way. Responders seem to boil down to two types: those on the political left and those on the political right. The two camps use some of the same tactics to get their messages out, and they both see government as a big part of the problem. But that is where the similarities stop. The right blames government and wants to limit government and its actions, while the left wants to reform government, make it accountable to the people, and channel its authority into cleaning up big corporations, such as banks, that they think have run amuck.

It is relatively easy to participate in initiating reforms and there are many opportunities to do so. Some responders sign letters or emails of protest and send them to public officials. Some responders go to local meetings to discuss the plight of the nation, some attend lectures and conferences to discuss with others outside their local community about what needs to be done, and some meet with public officials to voice their concerns. Some responders may attend rallies to collectively raise their voices of dissent or support for a particular cause. Some responders attend classes and workshops to educate themselves about particular issues. Some responders are non-partisan and work to do such things as register people to vote or aid disaster victims. Responding may be fairly easy to do, but it does take time and usually monetary contributions. Visit any non-profit website and there are pleas for much needed donations to support their worthy causes.

Many people voice their displeasure to what they see as perceived injustices via the internet. There are many opportunities to respond to different causes by different organizations that are sending messages to our elected representatives. I imagine thousands of well-meaning email petitions make their way every week into the email inboxes of political officials' office assistants. I know I have signed my share of email petitions supporting causes and issues that I feel are worthwhile. These efforts often make a difference in how our elected representatives vote on particular issues.

Even though responding does not fundamentally alter the existing paradigm, it does create a change in individual attitudes and behaviors. For example, I have participated in many change oriented study/discussion groups that have pledged to try to create the change we had been reading about. A big discussion about how to go about instituting change takes place, but in every case, initiatives fizzle out. Even though the initiatives may not take place, most participants have more fully educated themselves about a particular topic and they feel empowered with their new knowledge to spread the message to more and more people.

I was in a study group on globalization in 2003, where I first met Nancy Harmon, my partner at the Center for Global Awareness. We in the group thought that education was the key to spreading information about globalization to the general public, educators, and students. The group and its message so inspired me that I formed the Center for Global Awareness to carry out the mission of educating others about globalization and other global issues from an alternative perspective. Nancy, whom I reconnected with in 2009, decided to join with me in developing educational resources for our non-profit. And Nancy and her husband made a decision to share a house with a friend and her daughter, partly to share resources with more people and try to create a smaller ecological footprint. Responding worked for Nancy and me!

Questions to Consider

1. Do you think the reform movement has proposed viable solutions to our economic problems?
2. Are you engaged in any type of economic reform agenda? Do you think your reforms will help to create the change you envision?

REBUILD

The fifth response to the financial crisis is to rebuild the economy. By **rebuild** I mean developing an alternative economic structure that takes into consideration the environment and social and economic justice. It is not a revolution, where the whole existing economic structure is thrown out. As journalist Naomi Klein states, "It's largely about changing the mix in a mixed economy. Markets are a big part of the rebuild economy, but not the only part."[47] Because communism failed so miserably and collapsed so ignominiously, many say that the best available economic system is neoliberal capitalism. But in the estimation of many it is failing also. The public has not ushered out neoliberal capitalism on its deathbed, as was the case so dramatically with communism, but it is drawing its last breath on the hospital's gurney, only kept alive with intravenous feeding from the government.

So here is the rub. Some people are promoting a rebuilding of a different economy, a mixed economy. But what is the mix in a mixed economy? A **mixed economy** is a diverse economy in which a mix of different economic sectors prevents the concentration of wealth and power and cushions the downturn in one economic sector from paralyzing the whole economy. It entails enacting the trust-busting provisions of the Sherman (1890) and Clayton (1914) Anti-Trust Laws to break up large corporations, such as TBTF banks, into smaller entities. The government shores up its regulatory mechanisms to guarantee corporations are in compliance with existing laws. It means government policy targets small businesses and small agriculture as favored sectors of the economy, instead of mega agri-business firms. Public ownership of certain large utilities achieves efficiencies of scale and offers reasonable prices for consumers. Tax rates are more equitable and structured to encourage investment in companies and the creation of jobs rather than ostentatious consumption. And, most importantly, society upholds policies to protect and preserve the environment.

The traditional reform strategies – as explained in the section above – need help in bringing about solutions to ever more complex and pressing problems. Many possibilities for addressing problems have begun to take shape and move in a new direction. However, the rebuild strategy presents challenges to those advocating change. It is an evolutionary reconstructive strategy that is a form of change different not only from traditional reform, but different, too, from traditional theories of revolution. According to Gar Alperovitz, "The various efforts all also involve a sense of the importance of a long, evolutionary process that builds towards institutions and ideas that may offer ongoing ways to fundamentally alter economic and political relationships over time."[48]

SENATOR JOHN SHERMAN (R, OH), THE PRINCIPAL AUTHOR OF THE SHERMAN ANTITRUST ACT IN 1890.

I have organized this last section of the last chapter into five ways in which the rebuilding process can take place. I have tried to make the list positive, such as things that individuals can actually work on. Inspired individuals and groups can immediately implement some of these five actions. Although it takes more effort than changing light bulbs to energy-saving ones (an important action by the way), it doesn't

Rebuilding Actions

1. Emphasizing Small and Local
2. Challenging the Growth Model
3. Renewing Public Ownership
4. Healing our Planet
5. Creating Different Values

take monumental effort to start a community or school garden or buy fresh local produce at the farmer's market. This is not a definitive list but merely evolving suggestions on how we can build the road to a more sustainable, equitable, and life-affirming future.

Questions to Consider
1. Would you add or subtract from the list of rebuilding actions?

#1. Emphasizing Small and Local

When visionary writer E.F. Schumacher wrote *Small is Beautiful: Economics as if People Mattered* in 1973, he was expressing an idea that has relevance today. Over 40 years ago, he was able to describe what is happening today: our economy, society, institutions, and way of life have become so complex that they are overwhelming our capacity to deal with them. One way to deal with this over-powering complexity is to simplify – simplify everything! This means emphasizing local and small including business, electricity, health care, banking, housing, education, transportation, shopping and agriculture. Small, local, and diversified is the motto. There are different models for implementing this strategy; in this brief section I have highlighted two. Yet, there are many more possibilities emerging every day.

A **farmers market** is a collection of individual vendors – mostly farmers – who sell produce, fruits, meat products, and sometimes prepared foods and beverages. The local community benefits from farmers markets because farmers sell directly to consumers, keeping dollars circulating in the locality instead of being siphoned off to large corporate conglomerates. Consumers can buy direct from the farmer/producer and enjoy fresh, seasonal food grown within a drivable distance from their homes. In addition, local, fresh food is much healthier than heavily processed foods. And has a smaller carbon footprint than items shipped a long distance.

The Bank of North Dakota (BND) is a state-owned financial institution based in Bismarck, North Dakota. At the time of this writing, it is the only state-owned bank in the nation. Although state law requires state agencies to place their funds in the bank, local governments are not required to do so. Another fourteen states are considering creating state banks, following the long-established North Dakota model. Since 2010, legislators have introduced bills exploring or creating

A FARMERS' MARKET

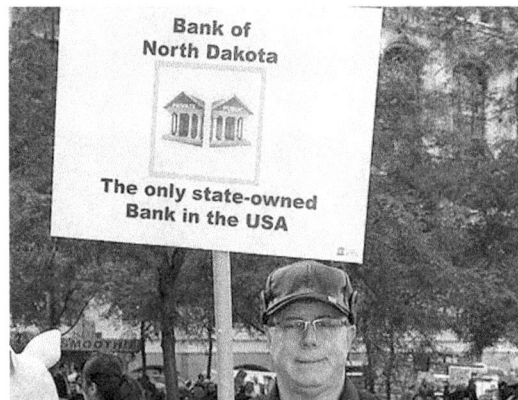

AN OCCUPY WALL STREET PROTESTER ON OCTOBER 2011 WITH A SIGN SUPPORTING THE BANK OF NORTH DAKOTA.

such banks in 17 states: Arizona, California, Connecticut, Hawaii, Idaho, Illinois, Louisiana, Maine, Maryland, Massachusetts, Montana, New Hampshire, New Mexico, New York, Oregon, Virginia and Washington.[49] This trend is likely to continue since money stays in the local and state economy instead of flowing to banking giants.

#2. Challenging the Consumer Growth Model

Our entire society is built on the consumer growth model, but challenges to this model are afoot. For example, challenging the consumer growth model are psychological studies showing that materialism doesn't lead to happiness and that more income and more possessions don't result in a lasting sense of well-being or satisfaction with life. Economist James Speth points out that "what makes people happy is warm personal relationships and giving rather than getting, things that are possible at a human scale."[50] More and more people sense a misdirection of life's energy. In one survey, 83 percent of Americans said society is not focused on the right priorities, 81 percent said America is too focused on shopping and spending, 88 percent said American society is too materialistic, and 84 percent want to spend more time with family and friends. These numbers suggest that rampant consumerism is not as widely embraced as the media portrays. Challenges to consumerism are emerging, such as practicing sufficiency, viewing overconsumption as silly, wasteful, and ostentatious, and establishing commercial-free zones. Instead of Gross Domestic Product (GDP), innovators are devising new measures to track social improvements.[51]

The economic concept of constant economic growth is so entrenched, yet we are living on a finite planet and continued, unlimited growth is impossible. After all, we are exploring the last frontier for precious resources, such as oil, in inhospitable climes such as the Arctic and dangerous deep water drilling. Even countries such as Saudi Arabia and China that cannot grow enough food for their people are snapping up valuable agricultural land in Africa.[52]

Can our environment survive in a system that requires exponential growth to continue? Naomi Klein asks, "Where is the imperative of growth coming from? What part of our economy is demanding growth year after year?" The dominant economic paradigm today is a particular brand of corporate capitalism in which shareholders who aren't involved in the business itself demand that their investments grow. Klein claims "That part of our economy has to shrink, and that's terrifying people who are deeply invested in it. We have a mixed economy, but it's one in which large corporations are controlled by outside investors, and we won't change that mix until that influence is reduced."[53] If you are a locally based business, you don't need continual growth year after year. Your business needs to provide enough revenue to pay salaries, expenses, and stash away enough for hard times in order to stay in business. The following is a sampling of different business models that don't necessarily rely on growth and are local; they also are models in which distant shareholders and corporate owners do not siphon off the revenues. These models are not

OIL DRILLING EQUIPMENT IN REMOTE NUIQSUT, ALASKA, NEXT TO THE NORTH SLOPE.

163

new they have a long history in the U.S. and Europe, but the fixation on neoliberalism over the last 30 plus years has overshadowed them.

Worker ownership is where the workers have an equal equity stake in the company they are working for; they share common goals, and they adhere to common principles and practices that broaden the definition of value beyond the "bottom line." Additionally, this model benefits from lower overhead costs, and offers benefit plans, such as healthcare and pensions.[54] Interestingly, the United Steel Workers Union advances this model, one they dismissed in the past. Now the union has become a strong advocate of worker ownership and is actively working to develop more businesses. They have based one successful model on the Mondragón Cooperative Corporation in the Basque country of Spain. Groups of worker-owned cooperatives employ 85,000 people in fields ranging from sophisticated medical technology and the production of appliances to large supermarkets and a credit union.[55]

In the United States, the most recent and advanced of these worker-owned initiatives is in the economically hard-hit city of Cleveland, Ohio. The "Cleveland Model" involves an integrated array of worker-owned cooperative enterprises targeted at the $3 billion purchasing power of such large scale "anchor institutions" as the Cleveland Clinic, University Hospital, and Case Western Reserve University. This association of enterprises also includes a revolving fund so that profits made by the businesses help establish new ventures. The first of the worker-owned companies, Evergreen Cooperative Laundry, is a state-of-the-art commercial laundry that provides clean linens for area hospitals, nursing homes, and hotels. It uses energy-saving design for its building and uses much less water per pound of laundry than its competitors. It includes 50 worker-owners, pays above-market wages, provides health insurance, and is still able to compete successfully against other commercial laundries. Another enterprise, Ohio Cooperative Solar (OCS), provides weatherization services and installs, owns, and maintains solar panels. Each year, the association plans to open two to four new worker-owned ventures. A 20-acre land trust will own the land of the worker-owned businesses. Like the Steelworkers, the Cleveland group has also drawn upon the experience of the Mondragón cooperative model. Exploratory efforts are currently underway to expand the Cleveland model in Atlanta, Pittsburgh, Washington, D.C., and several other communities.[56]

Worker-ownership or co-operatives (co-ops) are a practical alternative to a medieval pattern of ownership in which a mere one percent at the top owns roughly half of the nation's investment capital – more wealth than the entire bottom half of society taken together. But they are not the only way.

There are more than 4,500 not-for-profit community development corporations that operate affordable housing and other community-building programs in the U.S. In many cities new "community land trusts," increasingly use non-profit or municipal ownership to develop and maintain permanently affordable housing. Comprising an emerging "fourth sector" of the

A GREENHOUSE UNDER CONSTRUCTION IN 2012, PART OF THE GREEN CITY GROWERS COOPERATIVE IN CLEVELAND, OHIO. AN ENTIRELY WORKER-OWNED, YEAR-ROUND, HYDROPONIC FOOD PRODUCTION GREENHOUSE.

economy, and different from the government, business and non-profit sectors, "social enterprises" run businesses to support such missions as drug rehabilitation and training programs. Another 130 million Americans are members of urban food and housing co-ops, traditional agricultural cooperatives and credit unions. Additionally, our non-profit organization, the Center for Global Awareness, is one of approximately 1.5 million non-profits providing more than 10 percent of the nation's employment.[57]

These democratized ownership forms – including thousands of co-ops, land trusts, social enterprises, and worker-owned companies – are essentially anchored in, and supportive of, the local economy. Unlike private corporations, worker-owned companies rarely move to another city. As Aperovitz explains, "The fate of those who own the company is intimately tied to the fate and health of the locality in which they both live and work. Virtually all of the many other non-profit and related institutions based on de-mocratized ownership principles are similarly place-anchored."[58]

Questions to Consider

1. Do you think the consumer growth model needs to be challenged as the way your particular country's economy is organized? Explain.

#3. Renewing Public Ownership

I am making the case for renewing public ownership. But let me be clear, I am not calling for public ownership of small, medium-sized or even large businesses, nor the democratic enterprises described above. Even with this caveat, the first label that people would throw my way would be that I am a socialist, bent on destroying the fabric of America. If we look at things sanely, however, we would see that the U.S. has a mixed economy in which there already is public ownership. I don't think most of us would want to see the Grand Canyon turned over to private land developers or mining interests we want the government to preserve and protect this national treasure for ourselves and generations to come. We also have a post office from which everyone – I repeat everyone – gets mail service. The list goes on.

The first step toward renewing public ownership is recognizing that it is not a radical departure from the past. For example, the Tennessee Valley Authority (TVA), a public enterprise, established in 1933, is one of the largest energy companies in the nation. In fact, local public utilities and co-operatives supply more than 25 percent of electricity in the U.S. And, the government owns timber, mineral, oil and other resources on public land covering almost 30 percent of the nation's territory. The government runs two of the most cost-effective health providers in the United States: Medi-care and the Veterans Administration. The largest pension manager in the country is a public entity: the Social Security Administration. The US Postal Service, which employs 645,000 men and women, is another public enterprise that most experts generally regard as well-run.[59]

Public enterprises do not spend large amounts on advertising to sell their products, they do not add a profit margin to their prices, nor do they pay exorbitant executive salaries. The government-run Medicare administra-

PUMPING WATER FROM A WELL BEFORE THE CONSTRUCTION OF THE TVA.

tor made a base salary of approximately $170,000 in 2010 while Stephen Hemsley, CEO of the privately-held UnitedHealth Group, made a base salary of $1.3 million and received $101.96 million in compensation that same year. Thus, our private healthcare system costs the nation up to twice the share of GDP spent on equal or better care in many other countries – inefficiencies that waste perhaps a trillion dollars a year. Public enterprises do not force cities and states to pay millions in "incentives" to encourage businesses to locate in their locality, as private businesses often do. (Often these private businesses take these incentives, and then move on when they expire.) Public enterprises do not spend huge amounts of money lobbying public officials, as do corporate interests. And public corporations are open to public scrutiny, while private corporations keep most of their activities secret.

Many developed nations have found large-scale, publicly-regulated or controlled companies beneficial in such key areas of large scale operations as energy, transportation, and banking. In energy, for example, worldwide publicly controlled corporations produce roughly 75 percent of all oil. Saudi Aramco is the national oil company of Saudi Arabia and it was worth $781 billion in 2005, making it the world's most valuable company, almost twice as wealthy as ExxonMobil, the largest public company.[60] In transportation, the government runs high-speed rail systems in France, Spain, Belgium, Germany, Italy, the Netherlands, Turkey and South Korea. The public ownership of significant or controlling shares of airlines is common: France holds 16 percent of Air France-KLM; Sweden, Denmark and Norway hold a 50 percent stake in SAS; Israel owns 35 percent of El Al; Singapore has 56 percent of Singapore Airlines, which is ranked as one of the world's best. In banking, there are more than 200 public and semi-public banks and 81 funding agencies, accounting for one-fifth of all bank assets in the European Union. Japan's Post Bank is the world's biggest public bank and one of that nation's largest employers. Brazil has more than 100 state-owned or state-controlled enterprises, including Petrobras, an oil company known for its deep-water explorations. Other countries where public corporations exist side by side with private companies have better and faster Internet service than in the U.S.[61]

Another road to public enterprise would be to build on the government takeovers of auto companies in 2008-09. The government nationalized General Motors (GM) and Chrysler by using a joint ownership structure in which the union's health account owned 17.5 percent of GM and 63.5 percent of Chrysler. The public could benefit directly from its investment instead of seeing the taxpayers' stake sold off when post-bailout profits begin to flow. The Alaska Permanent Fund is also of interest as a model of public enterprise that transfers income from Alaska's public ownership of natural resources to its citizens.[62]

#4. Healing our Planet

The fate of our planet hangs in a precarious position. The earth's atmosphere, which cannot safely absorb the amount of carbon we are pumping into it, is only one of a number of significant enviromental crises facing all of us. We are also exploiting oceans, freshwater supplies, topsoil and biodiversity. Klein explains that much larger crises are "born of the central fiction on which our economic model is based: that nature is limitless, that we will always be able to find more of what we need, and that if something runs out it can be seamlessly replaced by another resource that we can endlessly extract." She continues, "The expansionist, extractive mindset, which has so long governed our relationship to nature, is what the climate crisis calls into question so fundamentally.

The abundance of scientific research showing we have pushed nature beyond its limits does not just demand green products and market-based solutions; it demands a new civilizational paradigm, one grounded not in dominance over nature but in respect for natural cycles of renewal – and acutely sensitive to natural limits."[63]

This is a tall order coming from a leading journalist and popular writer. Klein recognizes the essential logic of the neoliberal economic mode: unrelenting expansion of consumer markets, exploitation of the environment as resources for these markets, and bringing the world and its people into its economic web. It is simply and clearly unsustainable. Therefore, we must change it.

Some of the suggestions highlighted above can be helpful in bringing about a different civilizational paradigm, in Klein's words. There are far too many already underway to summarize in this brief section. However, the Civilian Conservation Corps (CCC) was one successful program from the past that worked in healing the planet and putting young men to work. The CCC was a public work relief program during the Depression. It operated under the Franklin Roosevelt administration from 1933 to 1942 for unemployed, unmarried men ages 17–23, whose family was on relief. It provided unskilled manual labor jobs related to the conservation and development of natural resources in rural lands owned by federal, state and local governments. The CCC employed my father in rural Wisconsin during the late 1930s, and he sent money home to his family, who were poor farmers barely eking out a living. Work varied from erosion control, planting trees, wildlife protection, and flood control to constructing foot trails and recreation facilities in parks. Today's Americorps is a similar model that is a viable alternative to help in healing the planet.

#5. Changing to Different Values

A society is shaped by the values and beliefs it extols; in turn, how the society is structured shapes its values and beliefs. In this interacting dance, a society forms such cultural traits as its economy, ways of living, technology, politics, religions, the way it treats the environment, and, thus, its worldview, or as Klein called it, a civilizational paradigm. Most of us were raised according to a modern worldview in which Enlightenment ideals of progress taught us that our ambitions could not be confined by nature's limits. This is true for the progressive left as well as the neoliberal right. Bringing about a different worldview means a reevaluation of the long cherished belief in rugged individualism and cut-throat competition to an ethic of more collective action and cooperation. Climate change is a message from the earth, screaming to us all that many of our culture's most cherished ideas and values are no longer working. It is a wake-up call that we must heed.[64]

CCC WORKERS CONSTRUCTING A ROAD, 1933.

Implementing a Rebuild Agenda: Resist

We have looked at different ways in which different movements have responded to the financial crisis: forming a mass political movement, responding to political representatives, and reforming existing laws and policies. When implementing a rebuild agenda, some people may take a more forceful step in their response to the financial crisis; they may engage in some

167

form of resistance. In this case, I am using the definition of a **resistance movement** as a group or collection of individual groups dedicated to opposing certain policies of a government or corporation. It may seek to achieve its objectives through the use of nonviolent resistance, sometimes called civil resistance or civil disobedience.[65] According to those waging resistance, they regard their movement as legitimate. In this fifth response category, resisters may organize or attend rallies and protests to seek a certain type of change in their government's policies. We often see or maybe attend particular rallies in Washington D.C. or elsewhere, where protesters carry clever signs and shout out their movement's slogans. Their aim is usually to make changes within the existing system, not change the entire system. McDonald's, for example, consumes vast quantities of eggs for its popular Egg McMuffin meal. Providing these eggs are large factory farms housing thousands of chickens in "battery cages," measuring about 72 inches square, about the size of a sheet of paper. Investigators have found these cages inhumane and unsanitary. Confronted with this information, McDonald's at first resisted improvements, but faced with a backlash of bad publicity it finally acquiesced in late 2011 to make improvements and ban the particular egg supplier charged with violations.[66] Although the protesters did not shut down McDonald's, they were successful in implementing successful changes around the margins.

An example of a resistance movement on the left side of the political spectrum is the Occupy Wall Street movement. It is essentially a leaderless movement with the slogan "we are the 99%." Supporters protest the way in which the 1percent is amassing wealth and power with the help of governmental policies and collaboration. It began as a protest on September 17, 2011, in Zuccotti Park, located in New York City's Wall Street financial district. Occupy protests and movements around the world have sprung up supporting the main issues of social and economic inequality, greed, corruption and the undue influence of corporations on government – particularly from the financial services sector. Although the Tea Party and Occupy Wall Street are both resistance movements, the Tea Party blames financial problems on too much government regulation while the Occupy movement targets the financial system and the government for not regulating it more.

Even though the slogan "we are the 99%" remains popular at the time of this writing, the movement has not produced tangible reforms. However, the movement has raised greater public awareness about widespread inequality because of its efforts. The Tea Party, on the other hand, has succeeded in getting like-minded candidates elected in the Republican Party, while the Occupy movement has not produced political candidates who have galvanized a significant voting bloc. In the months since it began, the Occupy Movement has been at risk of fading to the edges of political discourse. Many of the resisters of the movement have been arrested and forced to spend time defending themselves in court, deterring many from taking to the streets again and reducing their visibility.[67] The movement is essentially leaderless, making it difficult to engage in typical political organizing in support of state legislators and members of Congress, like the Tea Party has. Resisters at this point tend to be less united than the Tea Party movement and some activists do not see electoral politics as the best avenue for the movement to take. Because of heavy reliance on the social media, some claim this distorts the appeal to mainly the young, instead of appealing to a variety of people of different ages. All these factors have drained energy from the movement and have made it complicated to chart a direction. Occupy activists acknowledge that building and maintaining a populist movement is a daunting task.[68]

CONCLUDING INSIGHTS:
THE AFTERMATH OF THE 2008 FINANCIAL CRISIS

America will likely remain the world's largest economy for years to come. But it is not inevitable that the standard of living of most Americans will continue to increase as it did, for instance, in the years following World War II. Policies and wages in the U.S. are no longer operating within the confines of a national economy. Now the American standard of living and job opportunities compete with over 7 billion people on the planet. Many Americans have also been living in a fantasy world of easy credit, and that world is over. The country as a whole will face a drop in living standards. Not only was the country living beyond its means, but so were many families.[69] This is a stunning rebuke of what we thought life should be like in America. We thought each generation would have a better life than the previous generation, in a spiral of upward progression. These are intensely challenging revelations, shaking us to the very core.

We are deeply embedded in our current way of life. But we need to change. We must heed the call of the planet. Either we change the economy with planning and insight to a way of life of our choosing that is within nature's limits and more equitable for all, or we will have changes forced upon us by an angry planet ravaged by our excesses.

This brings us back to the rebuilding response described above. Rebuilding a more just, equitable and sustainable economy may be the most difficult and yet the most important challenge we face as a human species. It involves changing the way we think, work, act, what we prize, and what we believe in. This profound and deep examination of who we are as a people and what type of economy we want to leave for the next generations is not an easy shift and it seems an overwhelming task. But there are many signs of hope sprouting up amongst us. We need to ask ourselves what we can do individually and collectively to rebuild our economy.

On an individual level we can examine our daily decisions to make sure that each one of us has a positive impact on the way of life we want to help create. Are we conserving energy and water, recycling, eating healthy foods, buying fewer frivolous consumer items, composting, or supporting small local businesses? These small individual acts may seem insignificant but collectively they can have a domino effect that can bring about substantial change. We as individuals can collectively participate in building and supporting community banks, cooperatives, worker owned businesses, farmers markets, and land trusts mentioned above. We need to engage in both individual and collective actions to rebuild our economy.

Many people are becoming more aware that our economy needs fundamental change and they want to participate in bringing about long-lasting and life-enhancing changes. Many of us are joining with others to explore and take action in implementing options for a more just, sustainable, and peaceful world community. The choice is ours to make.

Questions to Consider

1. What do you think are the choices we need to make, if any, to rebuild our economy?
2. How has the increased dominance of the financial sector affected your life?

Endnotes

CHAPTER ONE

1. Mary Darby, "In Ponzi We Trust," *Smithsonian* magazine, (Dec. 1998). http://www.smithsonianmag.com/people-places/In-Ponzi-We-Trust.html?c=y&page=2

2. Matthew Bishop and Michael Green, *The Road from Ruin: How to Revive Capitalism and Put America Back on Top*, (New York: Crown Business, 2010) 32.

3. Darby, "In Ponzi", *Smithsonian Magazine.*

4. Bishop and Green, *Road from Ruin*, 32

5. Aidan Rankin, "Double Trouble: Capitalism and Communism," *Ecologist* (June, 2001).

6. Rankin, "Double Trouble," *Ecologist.*

7. "Neoliberalism," *World English Dictionary*, ret. 10/22/10. http://dictionary.reference.com/browse/neoliberalism

8. "Neoliberalism," World English Dictionary.

9. Richard H. Robbins, *Global Problems and the Culture of Capitalism*, (Boston: Allyn and Bacon, 1999) 11-12.

10. Jane Hiebert-White, "Health Affairs Blog," *Health Affairs* (June 2, 2009) ret. Oct. 2010. http://healthaffairs.org/blog/2009/06/02/52-million-uninsured-americans-by-2010

11. Ian Bremmer, *The End of the Free Market: Who Wins the War Between States and Corporations?* (New York: Portfolio, 2010) 33.

12. Bremmer, *Free Market*, 40.

13. Bremmer, *Free Market*, 21 and 42.

14. Bremmer, *Free Market*, 20-21.

15. Matt Rosenberg, "Sectors of the Economy," *About.com* ret. 10/28/11. http://geography.about.com/od/urbaneconomicgeography/a/sectorseconomy.htm

16. Rosenberg, "Sectors of the Economy," *About.com.*

17. Rosenberg, "Sectors of the Economy," *About.com.*

18. "Nonprofit Organization," *Wikipedia*, ret. 7/26/12. http://en.wikipedia.org/wiki/Non-profit_organization

19. Joseph E. Stiglitz, *Free Fall: America, Free Markets, and the Sinking of the World Economy*, (New York: W.W. Norton & Co., 2010) 65.

20. Walden Bello, "A Primer on the Wall Street Meltdown," *Focus on the Global South* (2008). http://www.waldenbello.org/index2.php?option=com_content&task=view&id=98&pop=1&page and Robert Reich, *Aftershock: the Next Economy and America's Future*, (New York: Alfred A. Knopf, 2010) 56.

21. John Perkins, *Hoodwinked: An Economic Hit Man Reveals Why the World Financial Markets Imploded—and What We Need to Do to Remake Them*, (New York: Broadway Books, 2009) 70.

22. Bello, "Primer," *Global South.*

23. Nouriel Roubini and Stephen Mihm, *Crisis Economics: A Crash Course in the Future of Finance*, (New York: Penguin Press, 2010) 190.

24. Stiglitz, *Free Fall*, 43.

25. Roubini, *Crisis Economics*, 191.

26. Roubini, *Crisis Economics*, 192.

27. Alejandro Reuss, "That 70s Crisis: What can the crisis of the U.S. capitalism in the 1970s teach us about the current crisis and its possible outcomes?" *Dollars&Sense*, (Nov./Dec., 2009).

28. Bello, Walden. "The Global Financial System in Crisis," Speech at *People's Development Forum*, (University of the Philippines, Mar. 25, 2008). http://www.waldenbello.org/index2.php?option=com_content&task=view&id=86&pop=1&page

29. Bello, "Global Financial System," *People's Development Forum*, 1.

30. Bello, "Primer," *Focus on the Global South.*

31. Roubini, Crisis Economics, 54.

32. Roubini, *Crisis Economics*, 55.

33. Roubini, *Crisis Economics*, 41 and Bishop and Green, *Road from Ruin*, 44.

34. Bishop and Green, *Road from Ruin*, 44.

35. Joseph E. Stiglitz, *The Roaring Nineties: A New History of the World's Most Prosperous Decade*, (New York: W.W. Norton & Co., 2003) 275.

36. Stiglitz, *Roaring 90s*, 276-277.

37. Stiglitz, *Roaring 90s*, 272-273.

38. Stiglitz, *Free Fall*, 185

39. Stiglitz, *Roaring 90s*, 276.

40. Stiglitz, *Roaring 90s*, 278.

41. Stiglitz, *Free Fall*, 13.

CHAPTER TWO

1. Nassin Taleb, *The Black Swan: The Impact of the Highly Improbable*, (New York: Random House, 2007).

2. Carmen M. Reinhart and Kenneth S. Rogoff, *This Time is Different: Eight Centuries of Financial Folly*, (Princeton: Princeton University Press, 2009).

3. Nouriel Roubini and Stephen Mihm, *Crisis Economics: A Crash Course in the Future of Finance*, (New York: Penguin Press, 2010) 17.

4. Roubini, *Crisis Economics*, 18.

5. Roubini, *Crisis Economics*, 18.

6. Roubini, *Crisis Economics*, 18-19.

7. Roubini, *Crisis Economics*, 19.

8. Andrew Beattie, "Market Crashes: What are Market Crashes and Bubbles," *Investopedia*, ret. 10/28/11. http://www.investopedia.com/features/crashes/crashes1.asp#axzz1c7HaHxUo

9. Beattie, "Market Crashes," Investopedia.

10. Beattie, "Market Crashes," Investopedia.

11. Mike Dash, *Tulipomania: The Story of the World's Most Coveted Flower & the Extraordinary Passions It Aroused*, (New York: Crown Publishing, 2010).

12. Dash, *Tulipomania*.

13. Dash, *Tulipomania*.

14. Beattie, "Market Crashes," *Investopedia*.

15. Andrew Beattie, "Market Crashes: The South Sea Bubble," *Investopedia*, ret. 10/28/11. http://www.answers.com/topic/the-south-sea-company

16. Beattie, "The South Sea Bubble," Investopedia.

17. Roubini, *Crisis Economics*, 62.

18. Roubini, *Crisis Economics*, 21-22.

19. Edward Chase Kirkland, *Industry Comes of Age: Business, Labor, and Public Policy 1860–189, Panic of 1873, in Wikipedia* (1967). http://en.wikipedia.org/wiki/Panic_of_1873

20. Charles Hoffman, *The Depression of the Nineties: An Economic History*, (Westport, CT: Greenwood Publishing, 1970) 109. http://akorra.com/2010/03/03/top-10-worst-financial-crisis-in-u-s-history/

21. Roubini, *Crisis Economics*, 23.

22. Andrew Beattie, "Market Crashes: The Florida Real Estate Craze," *Investopedia*, ret. 10/29/11. http://www.investopedia.com/features/crashes/crashes4.asp#ixzz1cBJYnx00

23. Beattie, "Florida Real Estate Craze," *Investopedia*.

24. James G. Smith, "Facing the Facts: An Economic Diagnosis," *Google*, ret. 10/31/11. http://books.google.com/books?id=v3-1r1gHcb4C&pg=PA14&lpg=PA14&dq=volume+of+dollars+in+circulation+in+1929#v=onepage&q=volume%20of%20dollars%20in%20circulation%20in%201929&f=false

25. Robert Shiller, *Irrational Exuberance*, (Princeton: Princeton University Press, 2005).

26. "The Crash of 1929: A Timeline," selected Wall Street chronology *PBS*, ret.10/31/29. http://www.pbs.org/wgbh/americanexperience/features/introduction/crash-introduction/

27. Andrew Beattie, "Market Crashes: The Great Depression 1929," Investopedia, ret. 10/31/11. http://www.investopedia.com/features/crashes/crashes5.asp#ixzz1cNfAFocP

28. William Goetzmann and Frank Newmanhttp,"Securitization in the 1920s," *National Bureau of Economic Research*, NBER Working Paper No. 15650, ret. 10/31/11. www.nber.org/digest/may10/w15650.html

29. Beattie, "The Great Depression 1929," Investopedia.

30. Roubini, *Crisis Economics*, 23-24.

31. Roubini, *Crisis Economics*, 47.

32. Roubini, *Crisis Economics*, 25.

33. Roubini, *Crisis Economics*, 48.

34. Bello, Walden, "A Primer on the Wall Street Meltdown," *Focus on the Global South*, (2008). http://www.waldenbello.org/index2.php?option=com_content&task=view&id=98&pop=1&page

35. Matthew Bishop and Michael Green, *The Road from Ruin: How to Revive Capitalism and Put America Back on Top*, (New York: Crown Business, 2010) 116-117 and Roubini, *Crisis Economics*, 25.

36. Les Leopold, "Is there a Global War Between Financial Theocracy and Democracy?" *Huffington Post*, in *CommonDreams.org*, (June 13, 2010). http://www.commondreams.org/print/57213

37. Joseph E. Stiglitz, *Free Fall: America, Free Markets, and the Sinking of the World Economy*, (New York: W.W. Norton & Co., 2010) xiv.

38. Reinhart, *This Time is Different*, 206-207.

39. Walden Bello, "The Global Financial System in Crisis," Speech at *People's Development Forum*, (University of the Philippines, March 25, 2008). http://www.waldenbello.org/index2.php?option=com_content&task=view&id=86&pop=1&page

40. Bello, Global Financial System," *People's Development Forum*.

41. Roubini, *Crisis Economics*, 63.

42. Bishop and Green, *Road from Ruin*, 136.

43. Bishop and Green, *Road from Ruin*, 137.

44. Bishop and Green, *Road from Ruin*, 137.

45. Bishop and Green, *Road from Ruin*, 137-138.

46. Bishop and Green, *Road from Ruin*, 138.

47. Bishop and Green, *Road from Ruin*, 138 and Roubini, *Crisis Economics*, 27.

48. Bishop and Green, *Road from Ruin*, 138.

49. Bishop and Green, *Road from Ruin*, 139.

50. Bishop and Green, *Road from Ruin*, 139.

51. Bishop and Green, *Road from Ruin*, 139.

52. Bishop and Green, *Road from Ruin*, 140.

53. Joseph Stiglitz, *The Roaring Nineties: A New History of the World's Most Prosperous Decade*, (New York: W.W. Norton & Co., 2003) 220-221.

54. "East Asian Financial Crisis," *AbsoluteAstronomy Encyclopedia*, ret. 11/16/11. http://www.absoluteastronomy.com/topics/East_Asian_financial_crisis

55. Robin Hahnel, "Capitalist Globalism in Crisis: Part II Understanding the Global Economic Crisis." *Z Magazine,* (Jan. 1, 1996) 7. http://www.zmag.org/ZMag/articles/jan99hahnel.htm

56. Bishop and Green, *Road from Ruin*, 122.

57. Hahnel, "Capitalist Globalism, Pt. II" *Z Magazine*, 7.

58. Hahnel, "Capitalist Globalism, Pt. II" *Z Magazine*, 8-9.

59. Dean Baker, "East Asia's Economic Revenge," *The Guardian/UK*, (Mar. 9, 2010), in *CommonDreams.org.* http://www.commondreams.org/print/39270

60. Hahnel, "Capitalist Globalism, Pt. II" *Z Magazine*, 7.

61. Bishop and Green, *Road from Ruin*, 123.

62. Bishop and Green, *Road from Ruin*, 124.

63. Bishop and Green, *Road from Ruin*, 117.

64. Baker, "East Asia," *The Guardian/UK.*

65. Walden Bello, "U-20: Will the Global Economy Resurface?" *Foreign Policy in Focus*, (2009). http://www.waldenbello.org/index2.php?option=com_content&task=view&id=108&pop=1&page

66. Baker, "East Asia," *The Guardian/UK.*

67. Bishop and Green, *Road from Ruin*, 124.

68. Bello, "Global Financial System in Crisis," *People's Development Forum.*

69. Bello, "U-20," *Foreign Policy.*

70. Bello, Walden. "Defy the Creditors and Get Away with It" Foreign Policy In Focus, (Washington, DC: November 3, 2010). http://www.fpif.org/articles/defy_the_creditors_and_get_away_with_it

71. Bello, "Defy," *Foreign Policy.*

72. Bello, "Defy," *Foreign Policy.*

73. James O'Toole, "Greek debt crisis: Shades of Argentina," *CNN Money.com*, (Nov 8, 2011). http://money.cnn.com/2011/11/08/news/international/greece_euro_argentina/index.htm

74. Bello," Defy," *Foreign Policy.*

75. Bello, "Defy," *Foreign Policy.*

76. Benjamin Dangl, "Occupy, Resist, Produce: Worker Cooperatives in Argentina" *Upside Down World*, (Mar. 6, 2005). http://upsidedownworld.org/coops_arg.htm and Bello, "Defy," *Foreign Policy.*

77. Bello, "Defy," *Foreign Policy*

CHAPTER THREE

1. Joseph E. Stiglitz, *Free Fall: America, Free Markets, and the Sinking of the World Economy*, (New York: W.W. Norton & Co., 2010) xx.

2. Stiglitz, *Free Fall*, 1 and 6.

3. Lanchester, John. *IOU: Why Everyone Owes Everyone and No Once Can Pay*, (New York: Simon & Schuster, 2010) 74.

4. Craig Hovey with Greg Rehmke, *Global Economics: The Complete Idiot's Guide,* (New York: Alpha, 2008) 136.

5. Joseph E. Stiglitz, *The Roaring Nineties: A New History of the World's Most Prosperous Decade,* (New York: W.W. Norton & Co., 2003) 141 and 161 and Lancaster, *IOU*, 65.

6. Stiglitz, *Roaring 90s*, 140.

7. Robert Kuttner, *The Squandering of America: How the Failure of Our Politics Undermines our Prosperity*, (New York: Alfred A. Knopf, 2007) 249.

8. Rob Larson, "Not Too Big Enough," *Dollars&Sense*, (July/Aug., 2010). http://www.dollarsandsense.org/archives/2010/0710larson.html

9. Larson, "Not Too Big," *Dollars&Sense.*

10. Stiglitz, *Free Fall*, 163 and Nomi Prins, *It Takes a Pillage: Behind the Bailouts, Bonuses, and Backroom Deals from Washington to Wall Street*, (Hoboken, New Jersey: John Wiley & Sons, 2009) 179.

11. Thom Hartman, "Is the Fix in on Derivatives?," *Thom's Blog*, (May 17, 2010), ret. 1/12/12.

12. James Kwak, "Shadow Banking for Beginners," *The Baseline Scenario*, (June 6, 2009), ret. 1/12/12. http://baselinescenario.com/2009/06/20/shadow-banking-system/

13. Nouriel Roubini, and Stephen Mihm, *Crisis Economics: A Crash Course in the Future of Finance*, (New York: Penguin Press, 2010) 80.

14. "Shadow Banking," *Wikipedia*, ret. 1/12/12. http://en.wikipedia.org/wiki/Shadow_banking_system#cite_note-Secret_Liens-0

15. Prins, *Takes a Pillage*, 180.

16. Robert Weissman, "12 Deregulatory Steps to Financial Meltdown," *CommonDreams.org*, (Mar. 7, 2008). http://www.commondreams.org/print/39177

17. Larson, Not Too Big, *Dollars&Sense.*

18. Larson, Not Too Big, *Dollars&Sense.*

19. Stiglitz, *Roaring 90s*, 222-223.

20. Stiglitz, *Free Fall*, 163 and Prins, *Takes a Pillage*, 179.

21. Matt Taibbi, *Griftopia: Bubble Machines, Vampire Squids, and the Long Con That Is Breaking America*, (New York: Spigel & Grau 2010), 65.

22. Weissman, "12 Deregulatory Steps," *CommonDreams.*

23. David Faber, *And Then the Roof Caved In: How Wall Street's Greed and Stupidity Brought Capitalism to its Knees*, (Hoboken, NJ: John Wiley and Sons, 2009), 103.

24. Weissman, "12 Deregulatory Steps," *CommonDreams.*

25. Taibbi, *Griftopia*, 67.

26. Patrice Hill, "McCain adviser talks of 'mental recession,'" *Washington Times*, (July 9, 2008). http://www.washingtontimes.com/news/2008/jul/09/mccain-adviser-addresses-mental-recession/

27. Weissman, "12 Deregulatory Steps," *CommonDreams.*

28. Weissman, "12 Deregulatory Steps," *CommonDreams.*

29. Bello, Walden, "A Primer on the Wall Street Meltdown," *Focus on the Global South*, (2008). http://www.waldenbello.org/index2.php?option=com_content&task=view&id=98&pop=1&page

30. Kuttner, *Squandering of America,* 157.

31. Hovey, *Global Economics*, 131.

32. Hovey, *Global Economics*, 130.

33. Hovey, *Global Economics*, 132-133.

34. Hovey, *Global Economics*, 131.

35. Hovey, *Global Economics*, 131-132

36. Prins, *Takes a Pillage,* 113-114.

37. Roubini, *Crisis Economics,* 144.

38. Roubini, *Crisis Economics,* 143.

39. Roubini, *Crisis Economics,* 73.

40. Roubini, *Crisis Economics,* 73.

41. Kuttner, *Squandering of America,* 156.

42. Kuttner, *Squandering of America,* 157.

43. Stiglitz, *Free Fall,* 4

44. Stiglitz, *Free Fall,* 80.

45. Kuttner, *Squandering of America,* 152.

46. Roubini, *Crisis Economics,* 63.

47. David Faber, *And Then the Roof Caved In: How Wall Street's Greed and Stupidity Brought Capitalism to its Knees*, (Hoboken, NJ: John Wiley and Sons, 2009) 61.

48. Roubini, *Crisis Economics,* 64.

49. Roubini, *Crisis Economics,* 64-65.

50. Roubini, *Crisis Economics,* 65.

51. Lanchester, *IOU*, 113 and Prins, *Takes a Pillage*, 53.

52. Stiglitz, *Free Fall,* 85.

53. Stiglitz, *Free Fall,* 86 and Roubini, *Crisis Economics,* 65.

54. Prins, *Takes a Pillage,* 52.

55. Faber, *Roof Caved In,* 18.

56. Stiglitz, *Free Fall,* 2.

57. Lanchester, *IOU,* 110.

58. Dean Baker in Bello, "Global Financial System," *Focus on the Global South.*

59. Stiglitz, *Free Fall,* 86.

60. Stiglitz, *Free Fall,* 2.

61. Bello, "Primer," *Focus on the Global South.*

62. Kuttner, *Squandering of America,* 156.

63. Stiglitz, *Free Fall,* 86.

64. Matthew Bishop and Michael Green, *The Road from Ruin: How to Revive Capitalism and Put America Back on Top*, (New York: Crown Business, 2010) 93.

65. Carmen M. Reinhart and Kenneth S. Rogoff, *This Time is Different: Eight Centuries of Financial Folly*, (Princeton: Princeton University Press, 2009) preface.

66. The U.S. National Debt Clock, ret. 4/15/13. http://usadebtclock.com/

67. Bishop and Green, *Road from Ruin*, 96.

68. Fact Check.org, ret. 1/14/12. http://factcheck.org/2008/02/the-budget-and-deficit-under-clinton/

69. Roubini, *Crisis Economics,* 81.

70. Stiglitz, *Roaring 90s*, 225.

71. Stiglitz, *Roaring 90s*, 232-234.

72. Justin Lahart, "In Time of Tumult, Obscure Economist Gains Currency," *Wall Street Journal*, (Aug. 18, 2007). http://online.wsj.com/article/SB118736585456901047.html

73. Minsky quote in Roubini, *Crisis Economics*, 50-51.

74. Lahart, "Time of Tumult," *Wall Street Journal.*

75. Roubini, Crisis Economics, 51.

76. Roubini, *Crisis Economics*, 82-83.

77. Prins, *Takes a Pillage,* 177.

78. Prins, *Takes a Pillage,* 146.

79. Clyde Prestowitz, *Betrayal of American Prosperity*, (New York: New Press, 2010) 2.

80. Stiglitz, *Free Fall,* 2.

81. Robert Reich, *Aftershock: the Next Economy and America's Future*, (New York: Alfred A. Knopf, 2010) 61-62.

82. Reich, *Aftershock*, 63 and Lancaster, *IOU*, 108.

83. Reich, *Aftershock*, 63 and 98.

84. Reich, *Aftershock*, 84.

85. John Quiggin, *Zombie Economics: How Dead Ideas Still Walk Among Us*, (Collingswood, Australia: Black Inc, 2012) 26-27.

86. Reich, *Aftershock*, 75.

CHAPTER FOUR

1. Walden Bello, "The Global Financial System in Crisis," Speech at *People's Development Forum*, (University of the Philippines, March 25, 2008). http://www.waldenbello.org/index2.php?option=com_content&task=view&id=86&pop=1&page

2. Joseph E. Stiglitz, *Free Fall: America, Free Markets, and the Sinking of the World Economy*, (New York: W.W. Norton & Co., 2010) 1.

3. Michael Lewis, *The Big Short: Inside the Doomsday Machine*, (New York: W.W. Norton, 2010) 172.

4. Stiglitz, *Free Fall*, 91.

5. Nouriel Roubini and Stephen Mihm, *Crisis Economics: A Crash Course in the Future of Finance,* (New York: Penguin Press, 2010) 65.

6. John Lanchester, *IOU: Why Everyone Owes Everyone and No Once Can Pay*, (New York: Simon & Schuster, 2010) 61.

7. Stiglitz, *Free Fall*, 78.

8. Stiglitz, *Free Fall*, 14.

9. Lanchester, *IOU*, 122.

10. Stiglitz, *Free Fall*, 14.

11. Matt Taibbi, *Griftopia: Bubble Machines, Vampire Squids, and the Long Con That Is Breaking America*, (New York: Spigel & Grau, 2010) 123.

12. Christine Williamson, "Institutional share growing for hedge funds," *Pension & Investments*, (Feb. 10, 2011), ret. 12/5/11. http://www.pionline.com/article/20110919/PRINTSUB/309199978

13. "Hedge fund industry assets swell to $ 1.92 trillion," *Daily Financial Services*, (Jan. 24, 2011), ret. 12/5/11. http://www.ft.lk/2011/01/24/hedge-fund-industry-assets-swell-to-1-92-trillion/

14. "Hedge Funds," *Answers.com*, ret. 12/5/11. http://www.answers.com/topic/hedge-fund#ixzz1fgSybhow

15. Nomi Prins, *It Takes a Pillage: Behind the Bailouts, Bonuses, and Backroom Deals from Washington to Wall Street*, (Hoboken, New Jersey: John Wiley & Sons, 2009) 102.

16. "Derivatives," *Investopedia*, ret. 12/5/11. http://www.investopedia.com/terms/d/derivative.asp#ixzz1fgiK05FS

17. Lanchester, *IOU*, 46-47.

18. Lanchester, *IOU*, 46.

19. Lanchester, *IOU*, p. 48.

20. "Notional Value," *Investopedia*, ret. 12/5/11. http://www.investopedia.com/terms/n/notionalvalue.asp#ixzz1fgxKdB9X

21. Lanchester, *IOU*, 49.

22. Stiglitz, *Free Fall*, 169.

23. Roubini, *Crisis Economics*, 199 and 203.

24. Lanchester, *IOU*, 52.

25. Warren Buffet in Lanchester, *IOU*, 56-57.

26. Lanchester, *IOU*, 112.

27. Matthew Bishop, and Michael Green, *The Road from Ruin: How to Revive Capitalism and Put America Back on Top*, (New York: Crown Business, 2010) 171.

28. Prins, *Takes a Pillage*, 11.

29. Lewis, *Big Short*, 258.

30. Lanchester, *IOU*, 119.

31. Roubini, *Crisis Economics*, 194.

32. "Tranche," Investopedia, ret. 12/7/11. http://www.investopedia.com/terms/t/tranches.asp#ixzz1fnfLBHQB

33. Lanchester, *IOU*, 118.

34. Lewis, *Big Short*, 73 and 141.

35. "Credit Default Swaps," *Investopedia*, ret. 12/7/11. http://www.investopedia.com/terms/c/creditdefaultswap.asp#ixzz1fhrmaPm7

36. David Faber, *And Then the Roof Caved In: How Wall Street's Greed and Stupidity Brought Capitalism to its Knees*, (Hoboken, NJ: John Wiley and Sons, 2009) 5.

37. Lewis, *Big Short*, 29.

38. Bishop, *Road from Ruin*, 174 and Lanchester, *IOU*, 80.

39. Lanchester, *IOU*, 80.

40. Lanchester, *IOU*, 79.

41. Faber, *Roof Caved In*, 104 and 107.

42. "Credit Default Swaps," *Investopedia*.

43. Bishop, *Road from Ruin*, 174 and Faber, *Roof Caved In*, 109.

44. Lanchester, *IOU*, 121.

45. Stiglitz, *Free Fall*, 80.

46. Lewis, *Big Short*, 172 and Stiglitz, *Free Fall*, 14.

47. Stiglitz, *Free Fall*, 77.

48. Stiglitz, *Free Fall*, 104.

49. Stiglitz, *Free Fall*, 6 and 13.

50. Lanchester, *IOU*, 74.

51. Robin Hahnel, "Capitalist Globalism in Crisis: Part II Understanding the Global Economic Crisis." *Z Magazine* (Jan. 1, 1996) p. 2. http://www.zmag.org/ZMag/articles/jan99hahnel.htm

52. Walden Bello, "A Primer on the Wall Street Meltdown," *Focus on the Global South*, (2008). http://www.waldenbello.org/index2.php?option=com_content&task=view&id=98&pop=1&page

53. Stiglitz, *Free Fall*, 77.

54. Bello, "Primer," *Global South*.

55. Bello, "Primer," *Global South*.

56. Hahnel, "Capitalist Globalism: Part II," *Z Magazine*, 2.

57. Bello, "Primer," *Global South*.

58. Robert Kuttner, *The Squandering of America: How the Failure of Our Politics Undermines our Prosperity*, (New York: Alfred A. Knopf , 2007) 248.

59. Roubini, *Crisis Economics*, 68.

60. Roubini, *Crisis Economics*, 68.

61. Stiglitz, *Free Fall*, 7.

62. Lewis, *Big Short*, 71.

63. Lewis, *Big Short*, 71.

64. Faber, *Roof Caved In*, 104.

65. Lewis, *Big Short*, 70.

66. Lanchester, *IOU*, 76.

67. Lanchester, *IOU*, 78.

68. Stiglitz, *Free Fall,* 160.

69. Stiglitz, *Free Fall,* 160-161.

70. Stiglitz, *Free Fall,* 161.

71. Faber, *Roof Caved In,* 81.

72. Faber, *Roof Caved In,* 81 and Mark Kolakowski, "Market Share %," *About.com*, ret. 12/10/11. http://financecareers.about.com/od/ratingagencies/a/ratingagencies.htm

73. Faber, *Roof Caved In,* 87.

74. Stiglitz, *Free Fall,* 92.

75. Roubini, *Crisis Economics,* 196.

76. Stiglitz, *Free Fall,* 93.

77. Stiglitz, *Free Fall,* 93.

78. Faber, *Roof Caved In,* 83.

79. Stiglitz, *Free Fall,* 91.

80. Faber, *Roof Caved In,* 85.

81. Prins, *Takes a Pillage,* 151.

82. Prins, *Takes a Pillage,* 152 and 157.

83. Prins, *Takes a Pillage,* 152-153.

84. Roubini, *Crisis Economics,* 184-185.

85. Roubini, *Crisis Economics,* 69.

86. Stiglitz, *Free Fall,* 151-152 and Roubini, *Crisis Economics,* 69.

87. Stiglitz, *Free Fall,* 152.

88. Stiglitz, *Free Fall,* 154.

89. Roubini, *Crisis Economics,* 188-189.

90. Prins, *Takes a Pillage,* 13 and Robert Reich, *Aftershock: the Next Economy and America's Future*, (New York: Alfred A. Knopf, 2010) 57.

91. Andrew Ross Sorkin, *Too big to Fail: The Inside Story of How Wall Street and Washington Fought to Save the Financial System from Crisis--and Themselves*, (London: Allen Lane, 2009) 4.

CHAPTER FIVE

1. Henry M. Paulson, *Inside the Race to Stop the Collapse of the Global Financial System,* (New York: Business Plus, 2010) 93.

2. Walden Bello, "A Primer on the Wall Street Meltdown," *Focus on the Global South*, (2008). http://www.waldenbello.org/index2.php?option=com_content&task=view&id=98&pop=1&page

3. Charles Ferguson, *Predator Nation: Corporate Criminals, Political Corruption, and the Hijacking of America*, (New York: Crown Business, 2012) 67-71 (a summary of these pages) and "Countrywide Financial Corporation," *New York Times, Business Section*, (updated Dec. 11, 2010). http://topics.nytimes.com/top/news/business/companies/countrywide_financial_corporation/index.html

4. Sarah Anderson, "For a new generation of Angelo Mozilo wannabes, the sky is still the limit," *CommonDreams.org*, (Dec. 13, 2010). http://www.commondreams.org/print/63399

5. Andrew Ross Sorkin, *Too big to Fail: The Inside Story of How Wall Street and Washington Fought to Save the Financial System from Crisis-and Themselves*, (London: Allen Lane, 2009) 3.

6. Sorkin, *Too big to Fail,* 4.

7. Sorkin, *Too big to Fail,* 4.

8. Sorkin, *Too big to Fail,* 5.

9. Sorkin, *Too big to Fail,* 5.

10. Sorkin, *Too big to Fail,* 7.

11. Nouriel Roubini, and Stephen Mihm, *Crisis Economics: A Crash Course in the Future of Finance*, (New York: Penguin Press, 2010) 15.

12. Bethany McLean and Joe Nocera, *All the Devils are Here: The Hidden History of the Financial Crisis*, (New York: Portfolio/Penguin, 2010) 125.

13. McLean and Nocera, *All the Devils,* 125.

14. Ferguson, *Predator Nation,* 60 and 72.

15. Roubini, *Crisis Economics,* 88-89.

16. Roubini, *Crisis Economics,* 90.

17. Roubini, *Crisis Economics,* 91 and Nomi Prins, *It Takes a Pillage: Behind the Bailouts, Bonuses, and Backroom Deals from Washington to Wall Street*, (Hoboken, New Jersey: John Wiley & Sons, 2009) 12.

18. Roubini, *Crisis Economics,* 95, 97, and 100.

19. Roubini, *Crisis Economics,* 103 and 108.

20. Investopedia Staff, "How Fannie Mae And Freddie Mac Were Saved," *Investopedia*, (Apr. 17, 2009), ret. 12/15/11. http://www.investopedia.com/articles/economics/09/fannie-mae-and-freddie-mac-saved.asp#ixzz1gd4FihIt

21. Dawn Kopecki, "U.S. Considers Bringing Fannie, Freddie on to Budget," *Bloomberg*, (Sept. 11, 2008), ret. 12/15/11. http://www.bloomberg.com/apps/news?pid=newsarchive&sid=adr.czwVm3ws&refer=home

22. "Fannie Mae and Freddie Mac," *Investopedia*. http://www.investopedia.com/articles/economics/09/fannie-mae-and-freddie-mac-saved.asp#ixzz1gd3ES36B

23. MSNBC.com staff and wire, "SEC charges ex-Fannie, Freddie CEOs with fraud," *MSNBC*, (Dec. 16, 2022), ret. 12/16/11. http://bottomline.msnbc.msn.com/_news/2011/12/16/9494796-sec-charges-ex-fannie-freddie-ceos-with-fraud

24. Roubini, *Crisis Economics,* 110.

25. Joseph E. Stiglitz, *Free Fall: America, Free Markets, and the Sinking of the World Economy*, (New York: W.W. Norton & Co., 2010) 119.

26. Roubini, *Crisis Economics*, 111.

27. Roubini, *Crisis Economics*, 208.

28. John Lanchester, *IOU: Why Everyone Owes Everyone and No Once Can Pay*, (New York: Simon & Schuster, 2010) 77.

29. "Obama's Statement on A.I.G," *The New York Times*, (Mar. 16, 2009). http://www.nytimes.com/video/2009/03/16/business/1194838676626/obama-on-a-i-g-bonuses.html

30. "Maurice 'Hank' Greenberg, "Ex-AIG CEO, Sues U.S. Over Constitutionality of Bailout," *Huffington Post*, (Nov. 11, 2011). http://www.huffingtonpost.com/2011/11/21/maurice-hank-greenberg-former-aig-ceo_n_1106092.html

31. Chris Rovnar, "AIG Announces Final Plan to Pay Back Government," *New York Magazine*, (Sept. 30, 2010). http://nymag.com/daily/intel/2010/09/aig_announces_final_plan_to_pa.html

32. Roubini, *Crisis Economics*, 111.

33. David Faber, *And Then the Roof Caved In: How Wall Street's Greed and Stupidity Brought Capitalism to its Knees*, Hoboken, (NJ: John Wiley and Sons, 2009) 5, 10 and 109.

34. Stiglitz, *Free Fall*, 119-120.

35. Prins, *Takes a Pillage*, 101.

36. Roubini, *Crisis Economics*, 112 and 148.

37. Roubini, *Crisis Economics*, 151.

38. Prins, *Takes a Pillage*, 101.

39. James Bullard, "Quantitative Easing—Uncharted Waters for Monetary Policy," *The Federal Reserve Bank of St. Louis*, (Jan., 2010), ret. 12/14/11. http://stlouisfed.org/publications/re/articles/?id=1862

40. Roubini, *Crisis Economics*, 152.

41. Roubini, *Crisis Economics*, 152 and 156.

42. Roubini, *Crisis Economics*, 156.

43. Prins, *Takes a Pillage*, 112.

44. Dean Baker, "Wall Street's Greatest Heist: The TARP," *The Guardian/UK*, (Sept., 21, 2010), in *CommonDreams.org*, http://www.commondreams.org/print/60544 and Prins, *Takes a Pillage*, 180.

45. Prins, *Takes a Pillage*, 27.

46. Baker, "The Tarp," *The Guardian*.

47. Stiglitz, *Free Fall*, 123.

48. Michael J. de la Merced, Vikas Bajaj and Andrew Ross Sorkin, "As Goldman and Morgan Shift, a Wall St. Era Ends," *Dealbook, New York Times*, (Sept., 21, 2008), ret. 12/14/11.

http://dealbook.nytimes.com/2008/09/21/goldman-morgan-to-become-bank-holding-companies/?hp

49. Prins, *Takes a Pillage*, 66-67

50. Stiglitz, *Free Fall*, 118.

51. Stiglitz, *Free Fall*, 128.

52. Paul Krugman, "Financial Policy Despair," *New York Times*, (Mar. 22, 2009), ret. 12/14/2011. http://www.nytimes.com/2009/03/23/opinion/23krugman.html?_r=1&ref=opinion

53. Stiglitz, *Free Fall*, 28.

54. Stiglitz, Free Fall, 133.

55. Stiglitz, *Free Fall*, 134.

56. Stiglitz, *Free Fall*, 133.

57. Stiglitz, *Free Fall*, 135.

58. Stiglitz, *Free Fall*, 136 – 137.

59. Prins, *Takes a Pillage*, 103.

60. Roubini, *Crisis Economics*, 136 – 137.

61. Stiglitz, *Free Fall*, 144.

62. Baker, "The Tarp," *The Guardian*.

63. McLean and Nocera, *Devils are Here*, 362.

CHAPTER SIX

1. "Revolution," *Dictionary*.com *Unabridged*, ret. 12/16/11.

2. Anthony Faiola, "In Greece, austerity kindles deep discontent," *Washington Post*, (May 13, 2011), ret. 12/16/11. http://www.washingtonpost.com/world/in-greece-austerity-kindles-deep-discontent/2011/05/05/AFUQGy2G_story.html

3. Faiola, "In Greece," *Washington Post*.

4. Faiola, "In Greece," *Washington Post*.

5. Faiola, "In Greece," *Washington Post*.

6. Nouriel Roubini and Stephen Mihm, *Crisis Economics: A Crash Course in the Future of Finance*, (New York: Penguin Press, 2010) 164 – 165 and 168.

7. Roubini, *Crisis Economics*, 168 - 169.

8. Nomi Prins, *It Takes a Pillage: Behind the Bailouts, Bonuses, and Backroom Deals from Washington to Wall Street*, (Hoboken, NJ: John Wiley & Sons, 2009) 14 – 15.

9. Walden Bello, "The Political Consequences of Stagnation," *Foreign Policy in Focus*, (Sept. 1, 2010). http://www.fpif.org/articles/the_political_consequences_of_stagnation

10. Bello, "Political Consequences," *Foreign Policy in Focus*.

11. Rob Larson, "Not Too Big Enough," *Dollars&Sense*, (July/August, 2010). http://www.dollarsandsense.org/archives/2010/0710larson.html

12. Rob Larson, Rob, "Underwater: Profits and pay are sky-high, even as bad loans are sinking the megabanks," *Dollars&Sense*, (Nov. 2010). http://www.dollarsandsense.org/archives/2010/1110larson.html

13. Joseph E. Stiglitz, *Free Fall: America, Free Markets, and the Sinking of the World Economy*, (New York: W.W. Norton & Co., 2010) 44 and Les Leopold, "Is there a Global War Between Financial Theocracy and Democracy?" *Huffington Post*, in *CommonDreams.org*, (June 13, 2010). http://www.commondreams.org/print/5721

14. Roubini, *Crisis Economics*, 224.

15. Prins, *It Takes a Pillage*, 124.

16. Prins, *It Takes a Pillage*, 5.

17. Les Christie, "Foreclosures," *CNN Money*, (Jan. 14, 2010). http://money.cnn.com/2010/01/14/real_estate/record_foreclosure_year/

18. Jon Prior, "Foreclosures," *Housing Wire*, (Jan. 13, 2011). http://www.housingwire.com/news/foreclosures-2011-break-last-years-record-realtytrac

19. Larson, "Underwater,"*Dollars&Sense* and Shirley Allen, 2011 statistics from "Mortgage Delinquencies Hold Steady, Foreclosure Inventory Shrinks, Low Rate Update," *Loan Rate Update*, (Jan. 20, 2012), ret. 1/20/12. http://loanrateupdate.com/mortgages/mortgage-delinquencies-hold-steady-foreclosure-inventory-shrinks

20. Dean Baker, "Surprises in Store for Economists," *The Guardian/UK*, in *Common Dreams.org*, (June 15, 2010). http://www.commondreams.org/print/57262

21. Stiglitz, *Free Fall*, 54-55.

22. Sheer, Robert. "Fail and Grow Rich on Wall Street," *TruthDig.com* in *CommonDreams.org*, (Nov. 24, 2010). http://www.commondreams.org/print/62801

23. Stiglitz, *Free Fall*, 53.

24. Les Leopold, "Help! What's the Cure for Financial Insanity?" *Huffington Post*, in *CommonDreams.org*, (May 14, 2010). http://www.commondreams.org/print/56090

25. Leopold, "Help!" *Huffington Post*.

26. The Tea Party, ret. 7/11/12, www.teapartypatriots.org/ and The Tea Party, ret. 7/8/12. http://www.theteaparty.net/index.php

27. Stiglitz, *Free Fall*, 187.

28. "Reform," *Wikipedia*, ret. 7/11/12. http://en.wikipedia.org/wiki/Reform

29. Stiglitz, *Free Fall*, 185 and 197.

30. Bello, "Political," *Foreign Policy in Focus*.

31. Paul Krugman, "Financial Policy Despair," *New York Times*, (Mar. 22, 2009), ret. 12/14/2011. http://www.nytimes.com/2009/03/23/opinion/23krugman.html?_r=1&ref=opinion

32. Stiglitz, *Free Fall*, 60-61.

33. Roubini, *Crisis Economics*, 160 and 163.

34. Krugman, "Financial Policy," *New York Times*.

35. Roubini, *Crisis Economics*, 164 – 165.

36. Stiglitz, *Free Fall*, 49-50 and 165.

37. Roubini, *Crisis Economics*, 227.

38. Larson, "Underwater," *Dollars&Sense*.

39. Roubini, *Crisis Economics*, 209.

40. Walden Bello, "Lessons of the Obama Debacle," *Foreign Policy In Focus*, (Oct. 10, 2010). http://www.fpif.org/articles/lessons_of_the_obama_debacle

41. Matt Taibbi, "How Wall Street Killed Financial Reform," *Rolling Stone Magazine*, (May 10, 2012). http://www.rollingstone.com/politics/news/how-wall-street-killed-financial-reform-20120510?print=true

42. Taibbi, "Wall Street," *Rolling Stone*.

43. Taibbi, "Wall Street," *Rolling Stone*.

44. Taibbi, "Wall Street," *Rolling Stone*.

45. "United States Largest Banks," *Info Please*, (2012) ret. 7/24/12. http://www.infoplease.com/ipa/A0763206.html

46. Gar Alperovitz and Thomas Hanna, "Beyond Corporate Capitalism: Not So Wild a Dream," *The Nation*, (May 26, 2012). http://www.commondreams.org/view/2012/05/26-0?print

47. Naomi Klein, "If You Take Climate Change Seriously, You Have to Throw Out the Free-Market Playbook," *Common Dreams*, (Feb.29, 2012). http://www.commondreams.org/headline/2012/02/29-4?print

48. Gar Alperovitz, "America Beyond Capitalism," *Dollars&Sense*, (Nov. 11, 2011). http://www.dollarsandsense.org/archives/2011/1111alperovitz.html

49. Alperovitz, "America Beyond Capitalism," *Dollars&Sense*.

50. Gus Speth, "Towards a New Economy and a New Politics," *The Solutions Journal*, (Volume 1, Issue 5, May 28, 2010) 27-29. http://www.thesolutionsjournal.com/print/619

51. Speth, "Towards," *Solutions Journal*.

52. Michael T. Klare, *The Race for What's Left: The Global Scramble for the World's Last Resources*, (New York: Metropolitan Books, 2012).

53. Klein, "Climate Change Seriously," *Common Dreams*.

54. United Steel Workers, "Worker Ownership for the 99%," *United Steel Workers*, (March 26, 2012). http://www.usw.org/media_center/news_articles?id=1038

55. Alperovitz, "America Beyond Capitalism," *Dollars&Sense*.

56. Alperovitz, "America Beyond Capitalism," *Dollars&Sense*.

57. Alperovitz, "America Beyond Capitalism," *Dollars&Sense*.

58. Alperovitz, "America Beyond Capitalism,"
    Dollars&Sense.

59. Alperovitz, "America Beyond Capitalism,"
    Dollars&Sense.

60. "Saudi Aramco," *Wikipedia*, ret. 7/20/12. http://
    en.wikipedia.org/wiki/Saudi_Aramco

61. Alperovitz and Hanna, "Beyond Corporate Capitalism,"
    The Nation.

62. Alperovitz and Hanna, "Beyond Corporate Capitalism,"
    The Nation.

63. Naomi Klein, "Capitalism vs. the Climate, *The Nation*,
    (Nov. 9, 2011). http://www.thenation.com/print/
    article/164497/capitalism-vs-climate

64. Klein, "Capitalism vs. Climate, *The Nation.*

65. "Resistance Movement," Some information from
    Wikipedia, ret. 8/2/12. http://en.wikipedia.org/wiki/
    Resistance_movement

66. Cynthia Galli, Angela Hill and Rym Momtaz,
    "McDonald's Target Dump Egg Supplier After
    Investigation." *ABC Investigative Unit: 20/20*, (Nov.
    18, 2011). http://abcnews.go.com/Blotter/mcdonalds-
    dumps-mcmuffin-egg-factory-health-concerns/
    story?id=14976054

67. Robert Stolarik, "Occupy Movement (Occupy Wall
    Street)," *New York Times*, (Aug. 6, 2012). http://
    topics.nytimes.com/top/reference/timestopics/
    organizations/o/occupy_wall_street/index.html

68. Stolarik, "Occupy Movement," *New York Times.*

69. Stiglitz, *Free, Fall*, 186.

Glossary

American International Group (AIG) exemplifies the concept of moral hazard, euphemistically called TBTF – too big to fail. AIG was the largest underwriter of commercial and industrial insurance in the U.S. (4)

Ames, Denise R. author of the Global Awareness Program series (GAPs) which includes this book, *The Global Economy: Connecting the Roots of a Holistic System*, *Waves of Global Change: A Holistic World History*, and *Waves of Global Change: An Educator's Handbook for Teaching a Holistic World History*.

Argentine economic crisis was a financial situation that affected Argentina's economy during the late 1990s and early 2000s. (2)

asset price inflation means that instead of stock or bond prices going up, other categories of assets go up in price. (3)

austerity to cut government spending through austerity measures, mainly target social programs, especially education, Medicare, social security, infrastructure, and programs for the poor. (6)

bank holding company (BHC) is a company that controls one or more banks, but does not necessarily engage in banking itself. The Fed has responsibility for regulating and supervising bank holding company activities, such as establishing capital standards, approving mergers and acquisitions and inspecting the operations of such companies. (5)

bond a debt security, the issuer owes the holders a debt and is obliged to pay interest and to repay the principal at a later date. (4)

Bretton Woods in July 1944 nearly 1,000 delegates from more than 40 countries gathered at the Mount Washington Hotel in the New Hampshire resort of Bretton Woods to finalize plans for a capitalist postwar monetary and financial order. (4)

bubble the radical rise of prices of an asset far beyond real values. (2)

capitalism an economic system in which private parties make their goods and services available on a free market and seek to make a profit on their activities. Private parties, either individuals or companies, own the means of production -- land, machinery, tools, equipment, buildings, workshops, and raw materials. Private parties decide what to produce. The free market is where businesses compete, and the forces of supply and demand determine the prices received for goods and services. Businesses may realize profits from their endeavors, reinvest profits gained, or suffer losses. (1)

central bank another name for the Federal Reserve in the U.S., the bank that governs the national or regional economy. (3)

classical economic order the system of capitalism, from the mid-19th century to 1914, relied on flexible wages, laying off workers or lowering their wages during bust cycles. Supporters also advocated for minimal government involvement in the economy. Based on the gold standard. The business sector influenced political policy. (4)

collateralized debt obligation CDO is a pool of debt that is added together and then sold as a set of bonds paying a range of interest rates. Those who issue the bonds pay interest and principal to the investors of the bonds. (4)

collateral a guarantee for a loan that is posted by a borrower with a bank or other financial institution. (2)

commercial banks lend out the money deposited in them. Called the piggy banks. (3)

commercial paper market part of shadow banking, it is what credit-worthy corporations do for short-term borrowing, such as to meet expenses like payroll. Corporations can borrow billions of dollars for 30, 60, or 90 days, and when those debts come due, they simply roll over the debt for another 30, 60, or 90 day term. (5)

commodification comes from the word commodity, used here as the process of turning something with little or no economic value into a product or service that has a specific value or a higher monetary value.

Commodities Futures Modernization Act of 2000 officially marked the deregulation of financial products known as over-the-counter derivatives, spearheaded by Senator Phil Gramm of Texas. (3)

Community Reinvestment Act in 1977, designed to encourage banks and savings associations to help meet the needs of all borrowers, including those in low-and moderate-income neighborhoods. (3)

comparative advantage countries should specialize in goods they can produce efficiently rather than trying to be self-sufficient. In a free market economy, a country's comparative advantage is traded internationally.

conforming loans mortgages which conformed to the rules of Fannie Mae and Freddie Mac. (3)

conservatorship similar to a Chapter 11 bankruptcy, new leadership is appointed to the bankrupt company. It implies a more temporary control than nationalization, in which the government more completely takes over the bankrupt enterprise. (5)

Consumer Financial Protection Bureau represents the interests of the consumers against Wall Street, it cleans up the mortgage markets by ending predatory home-lending. (6)

contagion fear that spreads across the entire financial sector and can contribute to the collapse of many financial companies. (2)

corporate raiders during the 1980s, they bought up a company's stock when it was undervalued, thus, the company's assets were worth more than their stock. The raiders would then sell off the assets of the company to make a profit, but then the companies taken over were no longer operational.

corporation is a formal business association with a publicly registered charter recognizing it as a separate legal entity having its own privileges, and liabilities distinct from those of its members.

correction is supposedly the market's way of showing, through price adjustments, the actual value of an asset. (2)

crash is a significant drop in the total value of a market, it almost always happens when a bubble pops, creating a situation where the majority of investors are trying to flee the market at the same time and consequently incurring massive losses. (2)

credit default swap (CDS), a form of insurance, the buyer of a credit default swap receives credit protection, whereas the seller of the swap guarantees the credit worthiness of the product. By doing this, the risk of default is transferred from the holder of the fixed income security to the seller of the swap. (4)

credit rating agency (CRA) assigns credit ratings for issuers of certain types of debt. Debt issues with the highest credit ratings – triple A – from the agencies will have the lowest interest rates. The analysis of the CRA influences the investors' confidence in the borrowers' ability to meet their debt payment obligations. (4)

credit risk – the possibility that a person or a company might default on payments of their debt. (4)

crony capitalism is based on shadowy political connections between government and business. (2)

debt simply is something that is owed or that one is bound to pay to or perform for another. (3)

deficit an excess of expenditure over revenue.

demand means goods and services are wanted or needed by consumers, inadequate demand could lead to prolonged periods of high unemployment.

deregulation removal or simplification of government rules that regulate the operation of market forces by eliminating or reducing government control of business, thereby moving toward a more free market. (3)

derivative is a security whose price is dependent upon or derived from one or more underlying asset. Fluctuations in the underlying asset determine the derivative's value. (4)

devalue used in this book to mean **to** make currencies worth less on the global market.

Dodd – Frank Wall Street Reform and Consumer Protection Act passed in 2010, it is a federal statute instituting reform of the financial sector. Passed in response to the recession after the financial crisis in 2008. (6)

dot-com bubble speculative bubble based on a new technology, the internet, covering the years 1995–2000. (2)

East Asian financial crisis beginning in 1997, financial institutions lost a large percentage of their asset values. The crisis raised fears of a worldwide economic meltdown due to financial contagion. (2)

economic globalization refers to the increasing integration and expansion of the capitalist economy around the world. Trade, investment, business, capital, financial flows, production, management, markets, movement of labor (although somewhat restricted), information, competition, and technology are carried out across local and national boundaries on a world stage, subsuming many national and local economies into one integrated economic system. There is also a growing concentration of wealth and influence of multi-national corporations, huge financial institutions, and state-run enterprises. (1,5)

Efficient Market Theory a set of assumptions or a philosophy that the market knows best and that if government interferes in the economy it will always cause problems. (1)

equity the difference between the market value and unpaid mortgage balance on a home.

fallacy of composition export-oriented economies in East Asia competed with high-cost Western producers. They under priced their competition but made a profit. As more export-oriented countries entered the export game, increased competition meant a slice into high profit margins. As competition increased, they competed more against each other than with Western producers. Exports slowed and investments were less profitable. (2)

Fannie Mae (Federal National Mortgage Association) authorized in 1938 by Congress, the GSE bought mortgages from lenders, thereby freeing up capital in order that those lenders could extend more mortgages. (3)

farmers market individual vendors who sell produce, fruits, meat products, and sometimes prepared foods and beverages. The local community benefits because farmers sell directly to consumers, keeping dollars circulating in the locality instead of being siphoned off to large corporate conglomerates. (6)

Federal Deposit Insurance Corporation (FDIC), part of the 1933 Glass Steagall Act, it insures deposits in certain commercial banks. (2)

Federal Reserve (sometime called the Fed or central bank) central banking system of the U.S.. Created in 1913 under President Woodrow Wilson Its conducts the nation's monetary policy, supervises and regulates banking institutions, maintains the stability of the financial system and provides financial services. (3)

Financial Services Modernization Act or **Gramm-Leach-Bliley Act** of 1999, rescinded the Glass-Steagall Act of 1933, signed by President Bill Clinton. Allowed commercial banks, investment banks, securities firms, and insurance companies to consolidate, which was prohibited by the Glass-Steagall Act. (3)

financialization a sector of the economy specializing in commodifying financial products that have a certain value and can be traded in the market place, such as insurance, loans, real estate sales, stocks, bonds, derivatives, etc. (1)

fine-tuning the economy, the Fed's actions in raising or lowering interest rates. (3)

fire sale prices are well below previous selling prices, takes place when panic selling ensues after a crash. (2)

"fire wall" slang term used to describe the separation between investment banks and commercial banks. (3)

fiscal policy governmental decisions on spending and taxes. (3)

float when a nation's currency value is allowed to fluctuate according to the foreign exchange market.

Freddie Mac (Federal Home Loan Mortgage Corp.) 1970, expanded the secondary mortgage market. (3)

futures trading for example, where a farmer will agree to a price for his/her next harvest months in advance. The future price of the harvest is thus a derivative, which can itself be sold. (4)

Ginnie Mae (Government National Mortgage Association), another GSE, they put together the first mortgage-backed securities. It pooled the mortgages it had originated, issued them as bonds, and then sold these pools of bonds as a mortgage-backed security to investors on the open market. (3)

Glass-Steagall Act of 1933, part of the New Deal regulatory reforms in the U.S. that prohibited a single company from offering investment banking, commercial banking, and insurance services. (2)

globalization complex, dominant, multi-dimensional phenomenon that interconnects worldwide economic, political, cultural, social, environmental, and technological forces that transcended national boundaries. Greatly intensifying since the 1980s, it reflects the many ways in which people are being drawn together not only by their own movements but also through the flow of goods, services, capital, labor, technology, ideas, and information. Globalization refers to the worldwide compression of space and time and reduction of the state in importance. In globalization the world becomes a single place that serves as a frame of reference for everyone, and it influences the way billions of people around the world conduct their everyday lives. (1)

Gramm-Leach-Bliley Act   see **Financial Services Modernization Act** (3)

Gross Domestic Product (GDP) a measure of a country's overall, official economic output. It is the market value of all goods and services officially made within the borders of a country in a year.

haircut a slightly reduced price. (2)

hedge fund a private pool of capital managed by an investment adviser. Open only to a limited number of investors who typically invest a minimum range from about $250,000 to $10 million. (4)

home equity loans homeowners refinanced their mortgages and withdraw their excess equity in their homes. (2)

Home Ownership and Equity Protection Act passed by Congress in 1994 in order to crack down on predatory lending practices. (3)

hostile takeovers corporate raiders buy up a company's undervalued stock, when a company's assets are worth more than their stock. Raiders sell off the company's assets for a profit. Company are then out of business.

illiquid assets not easily or quickly converted into money, like mortgages. (3)

inflation when price levels rise and the value of money drops. More money is needed than before to buy the same amount of goods and services. (3)

International Monetary Fund (IMF) part of the Bretton Woods agreement in 1944. It regulates an international monetary system based on convertible currencies, lends to countries experiencing temporary balance of payment problems, and facilitates global trade, while leaving sovereign governments in charge of their own monetary, fiscal, and international investment policies. (2)

investment banks issue bonds and shares of stock, and other complex financial instruments; trade on capital markets, and put together mergers and acquisitions, called casino banks. (3)

junk bonds a bond rated 'BB' or lower because of its high default risk. These bonds allowed companies that bankers would not previously have considered sufficiently credit worthy to issue debt. (4)

Keynes, John Maynard (1883-1946) British economist who shaped the transition from laissez faire capitalism to the era of social democracy in the 1930s. His policies are referred to as Keynesian Economics. (1)

laissez faire capitalism a French term that describes free trade, deregulated, unfettered capitalism. (1)

lender of last resort options were extended by the Federal Reserve to support nonfinancial corporations. Since other institutions were afraid to lend money, the Fed stepped in to do so as the only option available. (5)

leverage the use of debt to supplement investment. (2)

leveraged buyouts companies "go private" by buying up their own stock with borrowed funds to avoid the acquisitions of their corporation by another rival firm. (4)

liberalizing the international financial sector from all kinds of national regulations. (3)

liquid assets easily and quickly converted into money that are tradable on the open market. (3)

liquidity money. (3)

liquidity crisis when corporate borrowing and lending collapses, as it did during the financial crisis of 2008. Solvent corporations were shut out of the commercial paper market and found themselves short of cash. The Fed extended lender-of-last resort options to support nonfinancial corporations. (5)

Main Street considered the real economy, the part of the economy that produces real wealth, as opposed to the phantom wealth of the Wall Street economy. (1)

managed capitalism the government closely regulates the financial sector to prevent wild financial speculation and insures transparency of the system. Tariffs protect manufacturing jobs in the home country; therefore, wages and prices are set according to supply and demand at the national level rather than the global level. Services such as education, health care, the military, and prisons are government run and paid for through taxes. State sometimes owns large service providers such as utilities, airlines and transportation networks or regulates them. Government carefully regulates private enterprise, with high tax brackets for the wealthiest individuals. Corporations pay a larger share of their profits in taxes than in the neoliberal model. Labor unions have a say in wages and other benefits, as long as their wages keep up with productivity. There is a more equal circulation of wealth than with neoliberalism, hence a vital middle and working class and less of a concentration of wealth in the hands of the elite and corporations. (1)

margin calls banks or other financial institutions request that borrowers put up more cash or collateral to compensate for falling asset prices. (2)

market liberalization opening up internal markets to the inflow of money from other countries for investment, and the deregulation of their banks. (2)

Marx, Karl (1818-1883), who, along with co-author Frederich Engels, proposed a socialist/communist alternative to capitalism in their short book, the *Communist Manifesto* in 1848. They advocated for collective or governmental ownership and administration of the means of production and distribution of goods and services. (1)

mixed economy a diverse economy in which a mix of different economic sectors prevents the concentration of wealth and power and cushions the downturn in one economic sector from paralyzing the whole economy. (6)

monetary policy, the Federal Reserve influences the flow or availability of money and credit. (3)

moral hazard someone's willingness to take risks – particularly excessive risks – that s/he would normally avoid, simply because s/he knows someone else will shoulder whatever negative consequences will follow. (2)

mortgage a loan secured by real property through the use of a mortgage note.

mortgage-backed securities the collateral backing the securities were home mortgages. (3)

multinational corporations (MNCs) corporations that have services in at least two countries.

multiplier effect of a government stimulus infusion. On average, the short-run multiplier for the U.S. economy is around 1.5. If the government spends a billion dollars now, GDP this year will go up by $1.5 billion. (6)

nationalization the government completely takes over a private enterprise. (5)

neoliberalism modern politico-economic theory favoring free trade, privatization, minimal government intervention in business, and reduced public expenditure on social services, etc. (1)

nonprofit sector (quinary) an organization that uses surplus revenues to achieve its goals rather than distributing them as profit or dividends. (1)

notional value total value of a leveraged position's assets. (4)

option gives a trader the right, but not the obligation, to either buy or sell something at a specified future date for a specified price. (4)

originate and distribute investment banks and others gobbled up profitable pools of home mortgage bonds. (3)

originate and hold the bank would lend money to a homeowner, then collect payments on the principal and interest. The bank that originated the mortgage held the mortgage. (3)

panic selling investors during a crash engage in this, they hope to unload their declining stocks or other assets onto other investors at fire sale prices. Panic selling contributes to the declining market, which eventually crashes and affects everyone. (2)

Plaza Accord in 1985, the U.S. directed Japan to raise the value of the yen against the dollar to offset its huge trade imbalance with the Japanese. (2)

predatory lending mortgage lenders were doing everything they could to sign up borrowers for subprime mortgages. (4)

primary sector wealth creation that includes mining, agriculture, forestry, trapping animals, and fishing – changed natural resources into primary products. (1)

proprietary trading when a firm trades various financial instruments with the firm's own money as opposed to its customers' money, so as to make a profit for itself. (6)

quantitative easing used by Central Banks (the Fed) when interest rates are at or very near zero, and cannot be lowered any further, the Fed may purchase a number of bonds or other assets from financial institutions, therefore money is pumped into the economy. The goal is to increase the money supply rather than to decrease the interest rate, which is already around 0 percent, of-ten considered a "last resort" to stimulate the economy. (5)

quaternary sector of the economy is informational and intellectual activities, which include government, libraries, culture, scientific research and development, education, consultation, and information technology. (1)

reaction a movement that favors extreme conservatism or right wing political views. They oppose political, economic, or social change or reforms and are at one end of a political spectrum. (5)

rebuild developing an alternative economic structure that takes into consideration the environment, social and economic justice, and human well-being. (6)

reform change into an improved form or condition. Not radical change, reform may be no more than redressing serious wrongs without altering the fundamentals of the system. (6)

resistance movement a group or collection of individual groups dedicated to opposing certain policies of a government or corporation. (6)

revolution an overthrow or repudiation and thorough replacement of an established government or political system by the people governed. (6)

Riegle-Neal Interstate Banking and Branching Efficiency Act of 1994 overturned the Bank Holding Act of 1956 and allowed interstate mergers between adequately capitalized and managed banks. (3)

secondary sector manufacturing and construction – process raw materials into manufactured goods. (1)

Securities and Exchange Commission an arm of the federal government that regulates the financial industry. (5)

securitization illiquid assets – not easily or quickly converted into money, like mortgages – can be pooled and made into liquid assets – easily and quickly converted into money – that are tradable on the open market. (3)

service industries commodification of services, serving the customer rather than transforming physical goods. Includes retail, police, government, insurance, tourism, banking, education, public utilities, entertainment, legal, medical, accounting, finance, etc. (1)

services intangible goods which entrepreneurs transform into commodities. (1)

shadow banks money for lending to businesses comes from investors, they are not regulated by the government. (3)

socialism collective or governmental ownership and administration of the means of production and distribution of goods and services. (1)

sovereign wealth funds – a state-owned investment fund composed of financial assets such as stocks, bonds, property, precious metals or other financial instruments – that invest globally using pools of excess capital. (1)

spread difference in what interest is paid depositors and the interest that banks charge borrowers for loans. (2)

stagflation combination of low economic growth and high unemployment ("stagnation") with high rates of high inflation, occurred in the 1970s. (2)

state capitalism the state plays the role of leading economic actor and uses markets primarily for political gain. Public wealth, public investment and public enterprise offer the surest path toward economic development. (1)

stimulus government spending to counter economic stagnation and/or recession. (6)

structural unemployment a mismatch between workers' skills and the skills employers are seeking.

subprime mortgage a new market of riskier but more profitable home loans to less creditworthy borrowers. (3)

subsidy form of financial assistance paid to a business or particular economic sector.

supply and demand relation between these two factors determines the price of a commodity, thought to be the driving force in a free market. As demand for an item increases, prices rise.

synthetic CDO complex financial security used to speculate that an obligation will not be paid. Negotiated between counterparties that have different viewpoints about what will happen to the underlying security. (4)

synthetic CDS collateralized debt obligation (CDO), invests in credit default swaps (CDSs) or other assets. (4)

tertiary sector the service industry. (1)

trade deficit when a country imports more than it exports, it accumulates a trade deficit.

tranche a French word meaning slice or portion. In the world of investing, it describes a security that financers can split up into smaller pieces and then sold to investors. (4)

transfer payments a conventional way of dealing with economic downturns, whereby the government sends money to particular cash-strapped groups such as the poor, the unemployed or struggling state and local governments. (6)

transparency another word for information. (4)

Troubled Asset Relief Program (**TARP**) a $700 billion government program to purchase assets and equity from financial institutions in the fall of 2008 with the intended purpose to strengthen the financial sector. (5)

trust companies lightly regulated commercial banks bound together by complicated chains of ownership. (2)

tulip mania first financial crisis or speculative bubble in modern history, occurred in 17th century Netherlands. (2)

underwater the value of homes has fallen so much it is below the value of their original mortgage. (3)

Volcker Rule named after former Fed chair Paul Volcker, it would prevent federally insured banks from engaging in speculation such as when customers' deposits are used to trade on the bank's own accounts to make a profit for itself. (6)

Wall Street located in the financial district of lower Manhattan in New York City. A collective phrase to refer to the financial sector of the economy, the phantom economy, opposite of Main Street considered to be the real economy. (1)

worker ownership where workers have an equal equity stake in the company they are working for; they share common goals and adhere to common principles. (6)

Index

About the Author

Dr. Denise R. Ames is an educator with over 30 years teaching experience at secondary schools, universities, a community college, adult educational programs, and professional development workshops. She took her bachelor's degree in history education from Southern Illinois University, and master's degree and doctorate in history education with a focus in world history from Illinois State University. Her teaching topics range from academic subjects such as world history, global issues, United States history, Western Civilization, world humanities, cultural studies, and global business issues, to secondary social studies classes, pedagogy, and current topics such as global issues, the global economy, and global education.

Dr. Ames is currently the founder and President of the Center for Global Awareness, a non-profit organization developing globally-focused books and educational resources for students and educators in grades 9 through college. She is dedicated to working with teachers, students, and the general public to foster a better understanding of the myriad of global issues we face, a teaching model for world history, and the effects of the global economy on ourselves, the global community, and the environment. She has presented numerous classes, workshops, and lectures on her holistic world history and the global economy locally, nationally, and internationally. She is the author of *Waves of Global Change: A Holistic World History* and its accompanying book for educators: *Waves of Global Change: An Educator's Handbook for Teaching a Holistic World History*. Along with this book, *Financial Literacy: Wall Street and How it Works*, is her book *The Global Economy: Connecting the Roots of a Holistic System*. She is finishing her partially completed book for students and educators on human rights and a brief edition of *The Global Economy*.

World cultures and history have been Dr. Ames' life-long interest and study. Her extensive travels, personal experiences, reflections, and scholarly research have all contributed to her common sense approach to the often overwhelming subjects she teaches. Her extensive travels have taken her throughout Europe, and she has visited several countries in the Middle East/Southwest Asia region, including Iran, Syria, Palestine, Israel, Turkey, and Lebanon. She has also traveled to Mexico, Brazil, Paraguay, and Argentina. She visited the former Soviet Union in 1989 and taught word history at the Vladimir Pedagogical Institute in 1998. She found in her two trips to China, in 1991 and 2011 that the country had changed dramatically.

Along with her professional interests and work in history, global issues, and education, Dr. Ames has owned her own small business for eight years, constructed and remodeled eight houses, and exhibited and trained Arabian horses. She has two adult children and their spouses, and one granddaughter. She particularly enjoys traveling, hiking, yoga, reading, biking, gardening, and visiting with family and friends. She and her husband Jim currently reside near the campus of the University of New Mexico in sunny Albuquerque, New Mexico.

www.ingramcontent.com/pod-product-compliance
Lightning Source LLC
Chambersburg PA
CBHW062025210326
41519CB00060B/7107